The Commodity Culture of Victorian England

What does it mean to create a stable
system ~~As~~ for commodities?

Why does he begin w/ the Great
  Exhibition?

How does Richards define advertisement?
How does he define spectacle?

Explain Mx's notion of commodity fetishism

6 elements of new commodity
                      spectacle
        (1) Icon
        (2) commemmoration
        (3) utopia = democracy
        (4) language
        (5) figuration of consuming subject
        (6) abundance

Role of commodities in the Empire

Stanford
University
Press

Stanford,
California

The Commodity Culture of Victorian England

Advertising and Spectacle, 1851–1914

Thomas Richards

Stanford University Press,
Stanford, California
©1990 by the Board of Trustees of the
Leland Stanford Junior University
Printed in the United States of America
Original printing 1990
Last figure below indicates year of this printing:
00   99   98   97   96   95   94   93   92   91

CIP data appear at the end of the book

Published with the assistance of a special grant from
the Stanford University Faculty Publication Fund to
help support nonfaculty work originating at Stanford.

For Nan Goodman

Acknowledgments

This book has been many books. Trace elements of the book I began to write five years ago—a literary history of English advertising—survive here and there in this book, a cultural history of the semiotic consolidation of capitalism in the nineteenth and twentieth centuries. In great part I owe the restructuring of this project to the imagination of many friends, who projected possibilities beyond the horizon of what I had thought possible. Behind much of what I have written I hear the inflection of their voices, engaged, encouraging, extending, revising. Jointly and severally I thank them all: Rob Polhemus for telling me that Gerty MacDowell was a seaside girl; Mary Pratt for saying that the book I was writing must have lots and lots of pictures; Lucio Ruotolo for seeing advertising in places where I had not noticed it before; Deborah Nord and Steve Austad for reading my manuscript when it lay scattered between drafts; Jeff Knapp for helping me sort out the semiotics of the exemplary center; Walter Jackson Bate for imparting to me a keen awareness of the pleasures and pitfalls of narrating history; Robert Kiely for a sense of the book as a whole; Patrick Brantlinger and Richard Ohmann for pointing out final obstacles in the path of my narrative; Amanda Scanlan, Patrick Robbins, and Debbie Cohen for mining the labyrinth of Widener Library at Harvard; and Debbie again for preparing the index. Thanks to Helen Tartar, the best of all possible editors, and to Ellen Smith, my copy editor. Thanks to my parents and brother, who will see in this book a genealogy of America's first enclosed shopping mall, which opened in my

Minnesota hometown the year I was born. Thanks to Herbie Lindenberger for making history radically new and to Gary Harrison for making history newly radical. To Will Stone, who devoted to my text what Buddhism calls bare attention, I owe the debt of a thousand conversations that pivoted on this text but also touched everything under the sun. The English departments at Stanford and Harvard provided vital logistical support through a variety of funds, a Mabelle McLeod Lewis Memorial Fellowship at Stanford, a Clark Fund and a Hyder Rollins grant at Harvard. A grant from the American Council of Learned Societies enabled me to complete the manuscript. Elizabeth Gibb at the Stanford Slide Library took many of the photographs. Early versions of Chapters 2 and 5 appeared in *Victorian Studies* and *ELH*.

Contents

Figures

The Commodity Culture of Victorian England

Merchandise is the opium of the people.

—Situationist graffiti,
May 1968

Introduction

This is a book about how capitalism produced and sustained a culture of its own in the nineteenth and early twentieth centuries. It explains how the fundamental imperatives of the capitalist system became tangled up with certain kinds of cultural forms, which after a time became indistinguishable from economic forms. It shows how a small group of advertisers saw what was happening, placed themselves at the exact juncture of commerce and culture, and so became the minstrels of capitalism. And it shows how the new commodity culture dominated by advertising drew on and ultimately supplanted any alternatives to it. In the first half of the nineteenth century the commodity was a trivial thing, like one of Adam Smith's pins. In the second half it had a world-historical role to play in a global industrial economy. In the short space of time between the Great Exhibition of 1851 and the First World War, the commodity became and has remained the one subject of mass culture, the centerpiece of everyday life, the focal point of all representation, the dead center of the modern world.

The idea that there could be a specifically capitalist form of representation would have struck someone at the beginning of the nineteenth century as ludicrous. All over Europe there had once been a culture of open-air marketplaces, full of market songs like the "Moritat" of Brecht's *Threepenny Opera* and the cries of London echoed in Henry Mayhew, but it was dying out. The nation of shopkeepers had pushed shopping indoors, protecting it, regulating it, fixing its prices, but also silencing its most traditional representations. The getting of things was becoming a bland business conducted by the middle class. In the utilitarian political economy of the period, time spent distributing things was time lost; distribution was simply the shortest distance between the points of production and consumption. The structure of distribution, the commodity form of exchange, tended to be taken for granted. Early-nineteenth-century capitalists had been tutored by the assumptions set out in the previous century by Adam Smith, who regarded the commodity form as a platonic sort of form, an underlying master pattern that informs and pervades all exchanges, regardless of where they happen to take place. Smith thought of commodity exchange essentially as a conduit for money, and he describes it in essentially neutral terms; it is a given, which he sometimes likens to gravity, sometimes to the circulation of the blood. Commodities neither attract nor repel representation. They are simply there, stockpiled, ready and waiting to enter the long process of circulation to which he devotes the bulk of *The Wealth of Nations*.[1] Commodities are dead letters, supplies animated and actuated by the spirit of demand.

In the mid-nineteenth century the commodity became the living letter of the law of supply and demand. It literally came alive. In Dickens's novels furniture, textiles, watches, handkerchiefs seem to live and breathe. In painting the still life popular in the eighteenth century disappeared and was replaced by canvases depicting machinery in motion. In theaters stage machinery became the leading attraction. In music brass bands punched out staccato notes using metal instruments. In interior decoration fashion meant cramming the largest number of baubles into the smallest possible space. Victorian cities built vast auditoriums, banks, stock exchanges, and corporation headquarters, dedicated to the traffic in things. There were so many new things, and so many new words naming them, that it was impossible to keep them all straight, and a new class of words came into being to describe things in general—words like gadget, dingus, thingamajig, jigger. Everywhere the commodity teemed with signification—so much so that Marx, in his famous chapter in *Capital* on commodity fetishism, had to shift metaphors every few sentences to do justice to its ubiquity and plasticity as a form of representation. No one entity came so close to being the key to all the mythologies of Victorian life, yet no one mythology seemed to be equal to it. Partly present everywhere but fully concentrated nowhere, the commodity remained both invasive and evasive. Representing commodities was becoming, as Marx saw, a theological problem: how do you go about representing what you take to be the prime mover of a variegated universe?

The problem of creating a stable system of representation for commodities first began to occupy economists in the 1820's, and it culminated in the Great Exhibition of 1851.[2] The Great Exhibition was devised by a think tank expressly to become a sort of semiotic laboratory for the labor theory of value. It assembled the dominant institutions and vested interests of mid-Victorian England to pay homage to the way commodities were produced. But the space it created for commodity production did more than lend it for a time the ceremonial trappings of the central zone of society. The gigantic structure built to house one hundred thousand commodities had been designed to make ordinary glass look like crystal and the shape of a greenhouse look like the outline of a palace. As architecture the Crystal Palace was a magical object; like Pygmalion's statue it dwarfed and captivated its makers. Prince Albert and other luminaries came there to speak of the dignity of production, but the space in which they spoke bombarded the viewer with impressions of a different kind. The Crystal Palace was a monument to consumption, the first of its kind, a place where the combined mythologies of consumerism appeared in concentrated form. It performed a differentiated labor of unification; for the many and various things of the world it supplied a common denominator, a system of objects. The Great Exhibition of Things, the subject of the first chapter of this book, showed once and for all that the capitalist system had not only created a dominant form of exchange but was also in the process of creating a dominant form of representation to go along with it. Capitalism was now consolidating its hold over England not only economically but semiotically. The era of the spectacle had begun.

Descended from the spectacular masques and allegorical processions that celebrated political and economic triumph in the eighteenth century, the spectacle of the Exhibition elevated the commodity above the mundane act of exchange and created a coherent representational universe for commodities. In the spectacle the various contradictory imperatives of capitalism seemed to fit together beautifully. More than anything else, spectacle excelled at making symbolic virtue out of economic necessity. Once products enter a capitalist market, it is notoriously difficult to figure out how, when, or where they were made. In the commodity spectacle of the Exhibition this question, which arguably defined the life's work of Karl Marx, became moot. There manufactured objects were autonomous icons ordered into taxonomies, set on pedestals, and flooded with light. Captions were kept to a minimum; things now spoke for themselves using, as we shall see, a language of their own. Even the smallest and most unalluring objects displayed—bits of clay, clods of dirt, hunks of coal—benefited from the Crystal Palace's greenhouse effect. The spectacle exalted the ordinary by means of the extraordinary, the small by means of the large, the real by means of the unreal; as Horace Greeley, a frequent visitor to the Exhibition, pointed out at the time, "this strange mingling of the real with the shadowy, the apposite with the obsolete, gave additional piquancy and zest to the spectacle."[3] Though the Great Exhibition had not been held for profit, it showed that capital could be much more than monetary or material value. Representing things was a good investment, perhaps the best investment of all: as this book shows again and again, for those who knew how to use it, symbolic capital paid dividends beyond the dreams of avarice.

The spectacle engineered by the Great Exhibition was perfectly suited to legitimate the capitalist system, and the class whose interests it served, in a variety of direct and indirect ways. The Exhibition advanced a peculiarly middle-class vision of restricted equality. Like a modern shopping mall, the Crystal Palace set up an elaborate traffic pattern for channeling people around things. Railways and omnibuses started up special lines to get there. Once you were in, it was hard to slow down and even harder to find your way out. The Crystal Palace was purported to be a place where everyone in England could rub shoulders democratically, a place where social distinction seemed to reside not in persons but in things. The Exhibition turned everyone who entered it into a leisured flaneur, while at the same time it transformed the meticulous flaneur of the Parisian arcades into a manageable consumer of manufactured objects.[4] In a very real sense the Exhibition fashioned a phenomenology and a psychology for a new kind of being, the consumer, and a new strain of ideology, consumerism. The arcade had become an arcadia stocked from floor to ceiling with signs of an abundance achieved by middle-class means, sanctioned by middle-class representatives, and aimed at a middle-class end: the continuing extension and ultimate consolidation of the capitalist system in England.

The dominant system of spectacular representation perfected in the crucible of the Great Exhibition proved to be one of the most powerful and variegated systems of representation ever devised, and it was equal to the demands entrepreneurs made on it for the rest of the century. From the moment the Exhibition opened its doors, the advertising industry saw its future reflected darkly in Crystal Palace glass; and as the century progressed, advertising became the primary beneficiary of, and vehicle for, the commodity spectacle first synthesized in 1851. From the Exhibition advertisers learned that the best way to sell people commodities was to sell them the ideology of England, from the national identity embodied in the monarchy to the imperial expansion taking place in Africa, from the many diseases threatening the national health to the many boundaries separating classes and genders. They became specialists in peddling what Louis Althusser calls "practical ideology," or an imaginary way of relating to a real world.[5] Soon the commodity culture of the advertising industry ranged far and wide over social life in Victorian England. Its productions had the variety of life we associate with Dickens's novels, the fecundity of nature we associate with Darwin's theory of evolution, the totality of effect we associate with Wagner's operas. At once advertisements encapsulated the largest institutions and encompassed the smallest details of Victorian life. By the turn of the century, as we shall see, they went so far as to imagine a single expanded world composed entirely of commodities.

That vision was long in the making, however, and the immediate impact of the Exhibition on advertising was slight. Mid-Victorian advertisers undertook the spectacularization of advertising with modest objectives and paltry means, and for various reasons it took them thirty years to complete it. The year 1851 had found advertising in a primitive state. Most advertising still took place in the streets of London. Few people plied the trade full-time (the 1844 *Advertiser's Guardian* numbered them in the hundreds), and Henry Mayhew did not regard it as a trade distinct enough to merit its own category in *London Labour and the London Poor*.[6] The trade had a few old tricks, a fixed repertoire at least several hundred years old, and nothing more. After the Exhibition the business developed unevenly as advertisers, most of them individual operatives, played with the jigsaw puzzle of spectacle. Most of their productions during this period did not catch on and do not merit our attention, though many have been preserved in that compendium of all the marginalia of Victorian advertising, Henry Sampson's *History of Advertising* (1874).[7] This book concerns itself rather with advertising at precisely those moments in the late nineteenth century when advertisers experimented successfully with spectacle, drawing on the cultural form pioneered by the Great Exhibition to create the most familiar icons of modern advertising. In Victorian England some advertisers were winners, and others were losers. If this is largely a history of the winners, it is because what they won was the right to shape what became and remains our world.

Each of the victorious advertising campaigns that formed the core of Victorian commodity culture began and ended with great sweeping exhibitions of things. They can hardly be called campaigns in the modern sense of the word, for they were not imposed on the market from the top down. Because most Victorian companies retained fairly tight control over their advertising, no single agency had it in its power to create a consolidated imagery of advertisement. Overall it was advertising by social consensus. Like the original exhibition from which they drew continuing inspiration, advertised exhibitions relied on short but influential outbursts of bourgeois self-congratulation. At first they could not exist apart from them. Chapter 2 shows how, for the first time, advertising fully reproduced the cultural form of spectacle in an exhibition of things centered around Queen Victoria's 1887 Jubilee. Chapter 3 traces the development of a specifically imperial exhibition of things centered first around the explorer Henry Stanley's exploits in Africa and, later, around the Boer War. The Jubilee campaign lasted a summer, the others no more than a year or two. But advertising could now draw on new resources to create more permanent exhibitions of things, oriented this time not around the macro-politics of monarchy and Empire but around the micro-politics of the body and gender. Chapters 4 and 5 explain how advertisers dug their pincers deep into the flesh of late-Victorian consumers. Chapter 5 in particular tells how advertisers sucked consumers, especially women, into the vortex of a master-slave dialectic. An extended analysis of a female common reader constituted in and through advertising, this last chapter moves us onto familiar twentieth-century terrain. For by the turn of the century, commodity culture had discovered that it was by the very nature of the knowledge it imparted to consumers that it exerted its greatest control over them. The experience of consumption had become all-encompassing, inseparable from the knowledge of the self.

This series of advertised spectacles perfected the process by which the middle class justified the ways of capital to man. A glance at the notes will show that most of the advertisements analyzed in this book come from middle-class periodicals aimed at middle-class audiences. The icons of Victorian commodity culture all originated in middle-class periodicals. Until the very end of the nineteenth century advertising consisted almost entirely of the bourgeoisie talking to itself. In every epoch, as Marx has said, members of the dominant class produce the dominant representations; what he forgot to add was that, like a wary doctor testing a new inoculation, they first try them out on themselves.[8] Advertising was for many years the self-definition of one class rather than the subjugation of another. The working class eavesdropped, fascinated by the phantasmagoria. A few attended the Great Exhibition; a few more, as George Gissing saw in *The Nether World* (1887), discovered the Crystal Palace after it was moved from Hyde Park to a new location on the outskirts of London.[9] But the primary concern of advertisers was not with influencing a working-class clientele, and for one good reason: the consumer economy had yet to reach them. A mass-produced cigarette was not yet cheaper than a hand-rolled one; new inventions such as sewing machines and typewriters were as yet out of the question for most working people. Some big-ticket items, like pianos and Morris wallpaper, bypassed them entirely. The system of advertised spectacle would extend to mass periodicals that spoke to the working class only after the consumer economy had begun to reach them (the founding of those periodicals, such as Harmsworth's *Daily Mail* in 1896, was itself a sign that it had). In the meantime the middle class equipped itself for the day when its advertisers would mobilize against the working class.

The cultural forms of consumerism, then, came into being well before the consumer economy did. But because most cultural historians have assumed the opposite, that consumerism followed the consumer economy, they have not been in a position to see how vividly the nineteenth century has left its mark on twentieth-century commodity culture. One goes so far as to call the nineteenth century "advertising prehistory," implying that the activities of nineteenth-century advertising somehow fall outside the framework of historical narrative.[10] Little wonder that we have yet to come to terms with the origins of advertising. Almost all the available books about nineteenth-century advertising were written in the nineteenth century. Later books tend to ascribe the formation of truly modern advertising to the decade or decades just before they were written. In the most comprehensive analysis of advertising to date, William Leiss and his coauthors go over a dozen competing theories of how advertising works, derived from structuralism, semiotics, anthropology, Marxism, feminism, and various branches of sociology.[11] Together these disciplines have shed much light on a murky business but, as Leiss is well aware, no one theory has offered more than a partial account of how the medium works. "There is no theory of the media," laments Jean Baudrillard in a similar vein.[12] If there is no theory of the media, perhaps it is because there is no history of the media on which it could be based. The reason we cannot arrive at a clear definition of advertising is that we do not yet know where it came from. Too many historians have taken the concrete facts of advertising's beginning for granted. But the concrete, Marx warns us in the *Grundrisse*, should be the result and not the point of departure for criticism.[13]

Following Marx, the point of departure taken in this book is the crazy material culture of Victorian advertisements. At every point it grounds the history of commodity culture in the analysis of actual advertisements. Writing a history of Victorian commodity culture without examining these advertisements in detail would be like writing literary criticism about books that one has not bothered to read. Admittedly, reconstructing the concrete world of Victorian commodity culture out of an endless and seemingly undifferentiated mass of advertisements has been a long labor, for there were no trails mapped out through this material by previous cultural historians. In many instances it was not worth disturbing the dust that had settled on them, and a record of the false trails made and followed to no avail would take up another volume. Most of the advertisements that appear in this book are reproduced here for the first time, and behind each of them there are countless identical examples. At times I may seem, like a paleontologist, to have reconstructed the animal from a single bone. Someone interested in a full view of the material culture out of which this book springs will find the notes helpful, particularly since the subject has never been integrally treated before, and since the sources relevant to it are of such varying type and uneven quality. Towering above all other sources is the *Illustrated London News*, which from its inception in 1844 led the way in circulation and technology. Right from the start it placed such strong emphasis on the use of printed images that many wondered whether it was seeking to render the written word obsolete (the elderly Wordsworth even wrote a bad sonnet to this effect).[14] Long considered an index to nineteenth-century bourgeois life, it is the closest thing we have to a concordance to Victorian advertising.

Few of the spectacles of Victorian commodity culture originated on the drawing boards of the large London advertising agencies. Though dozens of well-known advertising agencies flourished by the turn of the century, the new commodity culture was not yet dominated by them.[15] Advertised spectacles were powerful because so many advertisers in so many different places acted on them in concert with the aim of keying into the central ideologies of bourgeois life. For most of the nineteenth century the great centralized images of advertising lacked a central point of origin. This troubled most Victorians, who were desperate to attribute human agency to the advertisements they saw everywhere around them. Carlyle, Trollope, Gissing, and Wells all came up with striking portraits of individual operatives at work creating advertisements. The government even knighted the people responsible for Beecham's Pills and Sunlight Soap. But it must be remembered that no one masterminded Victorian advertising, just as no one "genius," a Sir Thomas Beecham or an Edward Ponderevo (the "Napoleon of Commerce" in Wells's *Tono-Bungay* [1909]), invented its basic tropes. Though the system of advertised spectacle began at a certain historical moment—the Great Exhibition of 1851—it did not issue from a pure act of untrammeled human creation. The pattern of Victorian advertising can no more be reduced to a question of simple human agency than can the bizarre layout of a Victorian industrial town.[16]

The problem of attributing human agency to advertised commodities becomes much more pronounced whenever anyone attempts to write about them. The very conditions of language function to invest commodities with many of the attributes of the human agents of history. Language places human beings right at the center of signification, and though this anthropocentrism can be explicit or implicit, it is ever present. Do commodities fly off through the world from the Great Exhibition (as George Cruikshank showed them doing), or do they establish a new model for political economy (as the economist William

Whewell thought they did)? Either way, things appear as independent actors on the historical scene. Classical political economists tried to get around this problem by using what they took to be neutral terms. Even Marx, who wrote the commodity fetishism chapter of *Capital* to call attention to the linguistic attributes of spectacle, did not altogether succeed in demystifying it. He highlighted manifest metaphors like "fetishism" while ignoring the latent anthropocentrism that characterizes everyday speech.[17] Because language has a maddening way of transforming the means of description into a high drama of human agency and intention, a study of the barest facts of commodity culture always turns out to be an exploration of a fantastic realm in which things think, act, speak, rise, fall, fly, evolve. In the nineteenth century Darwin, like Marx, also sought to escape from the creationist language that posited an initiating and intervening creator behind the material world. While revising *The Origin of Species* (1859), he flattened out descriptive passages, removing metaphors that implied the centrality of human beings in the natural order. Just as Darwin sought to minimize a problem he could hardly avoid, this book performs a balancing act. On the one hand it avoids attributing a creationist perspective to commodities, but on the other it makes a detailed historical argument that the commodity became, as Jean Baudrillard has put it, "the one and only form that traverses all fields of social production," a form so central to Victorian social life that it always merited extended description, expanded narratives, and supplemental metaphors.[18]

The approach this book takes to the development of commodity culture in the nineteenth century entails a complex set of interlocking assumptions about the technologies and practices of advertising as an institution. Over the course of the late nineteenth century the advertising industry organized a proliferation of commodity narratives into a stable semiotic canopy for capitalist society, bestowing on this integrated universe an ontological status independent of human activity. The corporate character of Victorian commodity culture, however, did not result from and cannot be traced to the incorporation of the advertising industry so pronounced in the late nineteenth century.

From 1851 to 1914 the advertising industry was transformed beyond recognition as fully modern agencies replaced the early Victorian space brokerages. But this new institutional infrastructure did not leave an easily legible imprint on the archive of actual advertisements. One fact of institutional life in the advertising industry, for example, was the way that English advertisers tried to model themselves after their American counterparts. Most British advertising handbooks quoted Americans extensively; many London agencies organized themselves along American lines; many American agencies opened branch offices in London; H. G. Wells even has the advertiser-hero in *Tono-Bungay* wish that he had been born an American. The Americanization of the business continued into the twentieth century as English advertisers tested Walter Dill Scott's theories of advertising psychology and applied Frederick Taylor's ideas of scientific management to their agencies.[19] But as this book shows time and time again, the advertisements themselves spoke to British concerns using a thoroughly British inflection. American innovations in advertising technologies and practices no more dictated the general pattern of English commodity culture than English innovations in railroad technology dictated how American entrepreneurs would deploy them to colonize the western United States. At all points we must guard against reading the technology of semiotic systems as the epiphenomenon of institutional practices; at best this would lead us into a modern-dress version of the old Marxist idea of the determining economy and the determined culture. So although the subject of this book is the formation of modern commodity culture, and although it contains a great deal of detailed information about nineteenth- and early-twentieth-century advertising, there is little in it about specific advertisers or advertising agencies. Instead the emphasis falls on the underlying typologies in Victorian political culture that contributed to the making of spectacle and the emergence of a distinctively capitalist form of representation. The institution of advertising is considered here not as a point of origin but as a point on a continuum, not as composed of subjects constituting discourse but as composed of discourse inscribing subjects, not as a locus of authorship and authority but as what Michel Foucault has called a mode of "circulation, valorization, attribution, and appropriation."[20]

This book does not follow the development of English commodity culture beyond 1914, but for different reasons than might be supposed. Often critics and historians treat the First World War like a band of scorched earth dividing Victorian from modern Britain. But the system of advertised spectacle did not simply disappear after 1914. To the contrary, it manifested remarkable continuity; a quick flip through the images contained in these pages will confirm that modern advertising still draws on them. Using different vocabularies at different times, various schools of cultural critics have repeatedly pointed to the persistence of spectacle as a generic feature of advertising in the twentieth century. In particular this book draws on the work of Guy Debord, a founding member of the Situationist International and a major theorist of the aborted revolution of May 1968. Laid out in the manner of Marx's "Ten Theses on Feuerbach" as an open sequence of propositions rather than a closed argument, _Society of the Spectacle_ (1967) is the _Communist Manifesto_ of the twentieth century. In it Marx meets Saussure. Marx had viewed the commodity as a slippery thing, "abounding in metaphysical subtleties and theological niceties."[21] Debord brings to Marxist analysis the powerful tool of semiotics, which enables him to see the commodity as a dense locus of signification.

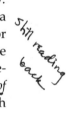

Roland Barthes, in _Mythologies_ (1957), had already set out the basics of cultural semiotics, but he did not detect the presence of a stable cultural form in the capitalist mythologies he analyzed with such penetration. He said that "there is no fixity in mythical concepts" and left it at that.[22] Debord goes beyond Barthes in that he sees a fairly stable cultural form animating all capitalist representation. This he calls "spectacle," or a series of related images in which the consumer sees "the world of the commodity dominating all that is lived." In his ferocious book Debord gives few examples and appears to regard the commodity spectacle as a fairly recent development. But his basic insight is right on target: that the commodity is the focal point and, increasingly, the arbiter of all representation in capitalist societies. This book is intended to take up the analysis where Debord leaves it off, for

he recognizes chronological disparity

at the time Debord saw it at work in France, the commodity spectacle was already one hundred years old. The spectacle and the style of mass advertising that it engendered were products of Victorian commodity culture, and they must be seen, to use Debord's words, as "both the result and the project of the existing mode of production."[23]

Debord's emphasis on the essential unity of a mode of production and a system for representing commodities has a long history within critical theory. Far from being a new kind of numen, economic life has been treated as belonging not only to the realm of what Marx called "social practice" but also to the realm of representations. As early as 1922 Georg Lukács recognized that the problem of commodities offered a common ground between the poles of economic and cultural life. He wrote, "the problem of commodities must not be considered in isolation or even regarded as the central problem in economics, but as the central, structural problem of capitalist society in all its aspects. Only in this case can the structure of commodity-relations be made to yield a model of all the objective forms of bourgeois society together with all the subjective forms corresponding to them."[24] This statement provides an exact formulation of the method that informs this book. In one way or another, all social life under capitalism has been organized around economic representations. This does not mean that the social life of nineteenth-century England was homogenized by the commodity; rather, the commodity was the coordinating frame within which very different forms of social life—economic, political, cultural, psychological, literary—were grouped. It took many years for capitalist society to fully entrust advertising with this all-important cultural work of representing commodities. In 1851 advertising had hardly begun to fashion a distinct institutional identity for itself. The model for the final unification of all representation under capitalism was provided by the trade exhibitions and consolidated by the spectacles of late-Victorian advertising, and they must be seen as both integral institutions of late capitalism and the most familiar products of commodity culture.

But there were certain limits on just how far this unification of representation under capitalism could go. The commodity culture of advertised spectacle was a light show, a complex blend of image, theater, and ideology. It could not and did not constitute or replace social life with a system of signs. Debord avoids making this claim; throughout *Society of the Spectacle* he holds out the hope that the working class and other dominated groups may yet subvert the dominant system of capitalist representation. Following Debord, Jean Baudrillard is right when he says that the commodity has become a culture complete with its own sign system, but wrong when he says that commodity culture has become the only culture there is. So sweeping, so invasive, and so synthetic, spectacle has tricked its twentieth-century viewers into treating it as if nothing else mattered.[25] In the late nineteenth century there were few areas of social life that remained untouched by the massive extension of commodity culture, and advertised spectacle was certainly in the vanguard of this extension every step of the way. For a series of fleeting moments capitalist representation saturated social space with a world of self-referential signs. At its height, however, that saturation never lasted for more than a few weeks—about the life span of a media event today. By the turn of the century advertising had taken precedence over the manufactured object, but even so it remained grounded in real things made by real workers, advertised by real advertisers, and consumed by real consumers. A world dominated by the spectacle of commodity culture is a world awash in representations of commodities, but it is not a world that has ceased to exist.

For a long time now, the project of commodity aesthetics has been caught between the roaring worlds of production and consumption.[26] Some critics have chosen to regard commodities from the standpoint of the producer, others from the standpoint of the distributor and potential consumer. This book does neither, and for one simple reason. In the spectacle production and consumption are paired moments in a single process of commodity representation. Marx repeatedly cautions that we must regard "production as directly identical with consumption, and consumption as directly coincident with production."[27] The vast spectacle figured in Victorian advertising is not the distorted mirror of production: it is the capitalist *mode* of production. What it produces so deliriously are signs, signs taken for wonders, signs signifying consumption. Henri Lefebvre once sensed the delirium in the "consuming of displays, displays of consuming, consuming of displays of consuming, consuming of signs, and signs of consuming" he saw in mid-twentieth-century France.[28] Late-nineteenth-century observers had a hard time understanding the pandemonium of signification they saw embodied primarily, though not exclusively, in the commodity culture of advertising. They wanted to know: Are advertisers producers, distributors, or consumers? Call them what you will, one, all, or none. Spectacle can no more be separated from what Marx called "the regular syllogism" of production, distribution, and consumption than the liturgy of the Mass can be from the theology of the Roman Catholic Church.[29] In the second half of the nineteenth century, spectacle and capitalism became indivisible, a world produced, a world distributed, a world consumed, a world still too much with us.

1

The Great Exhibition of Things

In 1851 a league of nations gathered for a congress in Hyde Park, London. Billed as a peace conference, this congress brought together the representatives of thirty-two nations from Europe, America, Africa, and the Far East. The delegations were housed in a single structure built expressly for them. The building occupied fourteen acres on the north edge of the park, and it contained, not an army of diplomats and attachés, but an assembly of manufactured articles, the largest display of commodities that had ever been brought together under one roof. The United States sent McCormick's reaper and prodigious quantities of ore; the French sent sculpture and artificial arms, hands, feet, legs, eyes; the Germans sent musical instruments and stuffed frogs; the British contributed machines. These things—tens of thousands of them packed into fourteen thousand booths—were the featured attraction at what was called "The Great Exhibition of the Industry of All Nations."[1]

As vast as it was in execution, the Great Exhibition of 1851 had at its root a single conception: that all human life and cultural endeavor could be fully represented by exhibiting manufactured articles. As a kind of surrogate Parliament, it was perhaps the most influential representative body of the nineteenth century. For not only did it erect a monument to the commodity that lasted eighty-five years, but it also prescribed the rituals by which consumers venerated the commodity for the rest of the century. It was the first world's fair, the first department store, the first shopping mall. The Exhibition rooted the commodity in the sense of being near to the heart of things, of being caught up in the progress of people and institutions that dominated Victorian society. Until the Exhibition the commodity had not for a moment occupied center stage in English public life; during and after the Exhibition the commodity became and remained the still center of the turning earth, the focal point of all gazing and the end point of all pilgrimages (Fig. 1). The Great Exhibition of 1851 was the first outburst of the phantasmagoria of commodity culture. It inaugurated a way of seeing things that marked indelibly the cultural and commercial life of Victorian England and fashioned a mythology of consumerism that has endured to this day.

First and foremost, this new way of seeing things was the product of a new kind of place in which things could be seen. After a long competition, the organizers of the Exhibition chose a design by Joseph Paxton, who had made a name for himself as a botanist and architect of greenhouses for the very rich. Paxton submitted a plan that called for a terraced pyramid of succes-

ALL THE WORLD GOING TO SEE THE GREAT EXHIBITION.

FIG. 1. The commodity pilgrimage (Mayhew and Cruikshank, *1851*).

FIG. 2. The palace of consumption (*Tallis's History and Description*).

sively receding stories of glass and iron. The editors of *Punch*
dubbed his three-tiered ziggurat the "Crystal Palace" (Fig. 2).
The name stuck, and with good reason. Though the building
was not crystal but plain glass, and though today it looks to us
more like an overgrown greenhouse than a palace, it successfully embodied the contradictory desires and aspirations which
people in the nineteenth century came more and more to attribute to manufactured things. At one and the same time the
Crystal Palace was a museum and a market: it brought together
a host of rare and exclusive things and promised, in a way that is
very hard to pin down, that each and every one of them would
one day be democratically available to anyone and everyone.
The organizers of the Exhibition did not come right out and say
how this would come about; rather it was the space of exhibition
itself which seemed to assert that, like the feeding of the four

Light again = and similar to the Palace

thousand, an economic miracle was in the making. Under a single ceiling, surrounded by trees and flooded with light, commodities appeared to have come out of nowhere, radiant and ordered into departments that fixed the place of each article and gave it a caption and a numbered place in the catalogue. The Victorians never tired of admiring what the Great Exhibition did to the things they had produced; things had been exhibited before, but in 1851 the exhibited commodity became, for the first time in history, the focal point of a commodity culture.[2]

The exhibition of things had always been what the advertising industry thought it did best, but it had been exhibitionism of a limited kind on a very small scale. In Thomas Carlyle's *Past and Present* (1843), practically all advertising takes place in the streets. Far from being carefully arranged in a clean, well-lighted space, Carlyle's advertisements are part of the unplanned and unregulated contagion of London street life. They spill out onto the streets like untreated sewage as "that great Hat seven-feet high . . . now perambulates London streets."[3] The giant hat sponsored by a Strand hatter was only the latest addition to a crazy street scene catered to by the large and varied class of streetsellers investigated by Henry Mayhew in *London Labour and the London Poor* (1849–54). In a few sentences Mayhew conjures up the pandemonium: "The men are standing in groups, smoking and talking; whilst the women run to and fro, some with the white round turnips showing out of their filled aprons, others with cabbages under their arms, and a piece of red-meat dangling from their hands. . . . Walnuts, blacking, apples, onions, braces, combs, turnips, herrings, pens, and corn-plaster, are all bellowed out at the same time."[4] For all we know he might be describing a market in a painting by Brueghel rather than the scene at Brill, one of over forty open-air markets left in mid-Victorian London. As Fernand Braudel has shown, the sight, smell, and feel of goods in bulk that permeated open-air markets all over Europe changed little from the sixteenth through the early nineteenth centuries.[5] The same can be said for the practices of early Victorian advertisers, who are, despite all their clever little gimmicks, the lineal descendants of the Pardoner with his bottle of pig's bones and Autolycus with his bag of tricks.

After the Great Exhibition of 1851 this traditional kind of advertising became obsolete and increasingly untenable. In an 1863 book called *Advertise: How? When? Where?* William Smith tried to explain what had happened to his business: "How to advertise? That question is very readily answered. Go to the nearest printer's; order a quantity of handbills; let a man deliver them to all the passers-by; send to the daily and weekly papers; and the thing's done. Is it? The thing *was* done thus in the good old jog-trot days of our ancestors, but we live in the nineteenth-century—the age of wonders, of *Scientific Balloon Ascents, Great Exhibitions, and Underground Railways.* So far from the old proverb holding good, there is nothing under the sun that is *not* new."[6] Smith is truly a prophet of modern advertising. In the wake of the Great Exhibition, not only does he assert that advertisers ought to exploit these new technologies so as to monopolize all attention, he is aware that these technologies have permanently altered the conditions of advertising. Spectacle has become paramount. The commodities in the Crystal Palace are no longer the trivial things that Marx had once said they could be mistaken for; they are a sensual feast for the eye of the spectator, and they have taken on the ceremonial trappings of the dominant institutions and vested interests of mid-Victorian England. In his little book, which later went through twenty-three editions, Smith was one of the first in advertising to acknowledge the power of spectacle in organizing and channeling signification around and through manufactured objects.

The central argument of this chapter is that one particular moment of spectacle—the Great Exhibition of 1851—helped to shape the way advertisers represented commodities for the rest of the century and to define the most familiar imperatives of modern commodity culture. No single element of the Crystal Palace was new; the Victorian taste for luxury, ostentation, and outward show had long been reflected on the stage as well as on the street and inside the home. What the Crystal Palace did was to synthesize and systematize these elements of spectacle by putting them all together under one roof in the service of manufactured objects. The Great Exhibition of Things made it possible to talk expressively and excessively about commodities, and it opened up vast areas of social and institutional life that had previously been closed off to advertisers. In 1843 the *Edinburgh Review* had castigated advertisers for fabricating most of their product endorsements, and Carlyle had taken them to task for making "true proclamation if that will do; if that will not, then false proclamation."[7] Eight years later England was flooded with true proclamations affirming the value of things. Famous men like the Prince Consort were now praising commodities; the nations of the earth chose them as their representatives; professional and scientific organizations showed their prowess and charted their progress by displaying them. Every walk of life and every part of the human body now seemed to have some kind of commodity ministering to it. The title page of the one-volume *Official Catalogue* may have insisted that "the earth is the Lord's, and all that therein is," but it would have been altogether more fitting and proper had the Exhibition taken Ecclesiastes 5:11 as its text: "Where much is, there are many to consume it; and what hath the owner but the sight of it with his eyes?"

I

The commission that planned the Exhibition puts one in mind of Swift's Academy of Projectors: given all they wanted to accomplish, it is remarkable that they managed to accomplish anything at all. Because the planning commission was unsure how many articles would ultimately be exhibited, it wanted "a *big* place": a third of a mile long, a hundred yards wide, and three stories high.[8] Because it wanted a building that could be taken down after the event was over and moved somewhere else, the behemoth was supposed to be portable. Because the commission was on a tight schedule, the building had to be composed of prefabricated material—iron and glass rather than brick and mortar—that would be ready at once to house exhibits. And because a prominent member of Parliament objected to cutting down trees on the site, the building was adjusted at the last minute to accommodate a grove of elms. Official histories of the Exhibition do their best to make the architect Joseph Paxton look like the presiding genius of the place, but the truth is that a committee created the Crystal Palace. Far from being the product of a single imagination, it was at once an improvisation, a compromise, and a synthesis. Like the great Gothic cathedrals whose terminology the planners never tired of invoking—an aisle was a "nave," a gallery a "transept"—the Crystal Palace was in a very real sense a collective enterprise. In an age that valued authorship highly, here was a building that had something of everyone in it. Though it was a space built expressly to be filled with property, it seemed to belong to everyone.

The view of the Crystal Palace the Victorians liked best was the view from a distance. From a distance it could be seen as a purely magical object, a building begotten, not made. The iron framework looked less like a network of columns and girders supporting the building than a series of delicate lines adorning nearly one million square feet of glass suspended in midair. Like glass skyscrapers today, the Crystal Palace reflected its surroundings, and unless you got very close to it, you could not see in and catch a glimpse of the thousands of commodities it contained. At a distance the building closed itself off to outside scrutiny; it seemed to say that you had to enter it in order to be initiated into its mysteries. Indeed most Victorian engravings represent the outside of the building as if it were opaque rather than transparent (Fig. 3). But this opacity did more than conceal the Crystal Palace's commodities; it placed them in a kind of casing that duplicated on a grand scale the little cases and slipcovers that affluent Victorians used to protect specialty items like pocket watches, thermometers, cutlery, and umbrellas. Viewed from the outside, the Crystal Palace was both an heirloom and a humidor, conferring sentimental value on the things it contained and preserving them in perpetuity in a gigantic glass case.[9]

The outside of the building was a far more orderly sight than the inside, which was impossible to take in at a single glance. John Ruskin was not a fan of the Crystal Palace, but in one sense it offered precisely the profusion of new sights which he had thought essential to "the Gothic spirit," namely, "a series of forms of which the merit was, not merely that they were new, but that they were *capable of perpetual novelty.*"[10] Designed around a single corridor, the "Grand Aisle," ringed with a mezzanine and

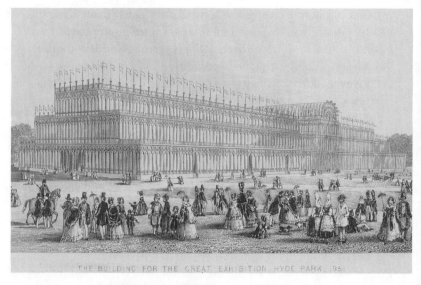

FIG. 3. A magical object (*Tallis's Illustrated London*).

divided in half by a semicylindrical vault, the interior was essentially one long gallery of novelties. As in Edgar Allan Poe's "The Masque of the Red Death" (1842), the novelties changed as you went from room to room, and with equally bizarre results. At the west end of the building, which was reserved for English articles, you began with mirrors that recalled Versailles. Above there was a basilica-sized organ surrounded by daguerreotypes, clocks, firearms, and hanging globes. Moving eastward, you followed the path of locomotives set on railroad tracks and passed dioramas of cities, models of churches, and booths displaying fabrics, furs, and tools of every size and description. To the north of the Grand Aisle you generally saw machinery; to the south, raw materials and produce. Before leaving the English half of the building, you passed sculpture and furniture and entered a little enclosure called the "Mediaeval Court," the handiwork of A. W. N. Pugin. In the central court statues, flowers, and palm trees were littered around a crystal fountain. It was as if the planning commission had decided that it was impossible to make representative selections from among the things of the world and so had put them *all* on display. In the eighteenth century the plates from Diderot's *Encyclopedia* had shown individual objects placed in huge empty rooms reserved especially for them; in the nineteenth century these bare spaces were filled by a dense vegetation of things packed together so tightly that the largest conservatory in the world could now barely hold them.[11]

If visitors expected the foreign half of the Crystal Palace to measure up to the English half, they must have been sorely disappointed. Because the planning commission had decided to let each participating country do whatever it liked with its allotted space, there was not even a pretense of order on the east side. Next to the virtual encyclopedia of manufactured objects crammed into the English half, the foreign half looked like a disheveled cabinet of curiosities. In rapid succession strollers along the Grand Aisle passed the characteristic national products of thirty-two nations: Egyptian carpets, Turkish embroidery, Roman mosaics, German porcelain, Russian furs, and India rubber. But for every foreign item on display there were a dozen comparable items in the English section, and even the *Official Catalogue* of the Exhibition had to admit that the foreign half of the building was at best a mutilated copy of the English half. One of the big draws of the eastern half was supposed to have been the architectural styles of the various national exhibitions, but even these seemed familiar to the English, who after all had built their own French Gothic churches and French Renaissance hotels, Venetian Gothic museums, Grecian clubs, Egyptian houses, and Moorish baths. Surveying the interior space of the exhibition, an article in *Household Words* went so far as to claim that there had really been two exhibitions, "The Great Exhibition and the Little One."[12] Or more accurately, little ones: for the exhibition layout essentially balkanized the rest of the world, projecting a kind of geopolitical map of a world half occupied by England, half occupied by a collection of principalities vying for the leftover space (Fig. 4).

If the interior layout of the Crystal Palace exemplified the characteristically Victorian confusion of styles that Pugin once called a "carnival of architecture," the articles on display verged on riot.[13] Like the editors of today's *Encyclopaedia Brittannica*, the planning commission issued both a short and a long version of

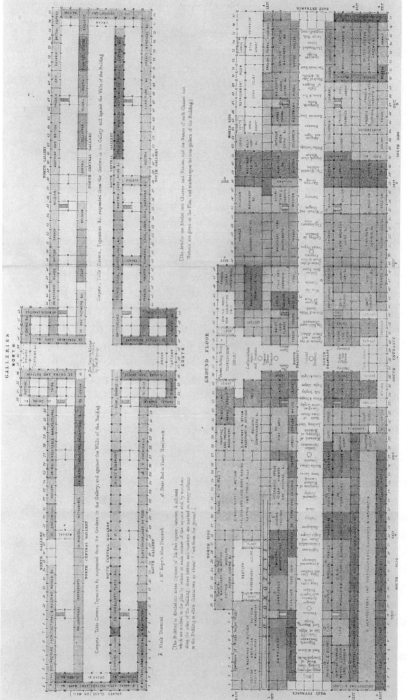

FIG. 4. The world balkanized (*Catalogue*).

its *Official Catalogue*. The short one offered descriptions so terse as to be unintelligible, while at four volumes the long one was too heavy to be carried around the Exhibition and so was really only a souvenir. As the inscriptions fixed to each exhibit were brief and, many complained, often misleading, visitors were left to their own lights to make what they could out of what they saw. As Horace Greeley testifies, the result was often a blur: "The aisle itself, farther than the eye can reach, is studded with works of art; statues in marble, in bronze, in plaster, in zinc; here a gigantic Amazon on horseback, there a raging lion, a classic group, or a pair of magnificent bronze vases enriched with exquisite representations of scenes from the master-singers of antiquity. Busts, Casts, Medallions, and smaller Bronzes abound; with elegant Clocks, Chandeliers, Cabinets, &c."[14] Many visitors besides Greeley ended their accounts of the Exhibition with an encompassing "et cetera." Far from appearing to visitors as an exact census of a known and knowable world of goods, the commodities in the Crystal Palace appeared to be expanding profligately in every direction possible.

This abundance and variety of the things of the world both awed visitors and accustomed them to what can be called a phylogeny of manufacture. In effect, though hardly by intention, the Crystal Palace advanced a prescient vision of the evolutionary development of commodities. Under one roof commodities appeared in the endless variety of forms that Darwin later saw in the natural world. In *The Origin of Species* (1859), Darwin predicated his theory of natural selection on his observation of the fecundity of the natural world. Wherever he looked, Darwin saw profusion, variety, mobility, and adaptation. This was because "each species tends by its geometrical ratio of reproduction to increase inordinately in number" so that "each large group tends to become still larger, and at the same time more divergent in character." Darwin further explains that this increase is intensified by domestication, so much so that cultivated plants and animals "generally differ more from each other, than do the individuals of any one species or variety in a state of nature." Like domesticated species in Darwin's world, the commodities in the Crystal Palace exemplify plenitude and multifariousness and resist being resolved into a straightforward order. Well-supervised and carefully tended in their garden environment, the things of the world have become so abundant that they have made it difficult to draw "any clear distinction between individual differences and slight varieties."[15] They have become, as we have seen, hyperproductive to the point of riot.

The superabundance of articles in the Crystal Palace may have foreshadowed some developments in evolutionary theory, but in 1851 it primarily brought to mind a different sort of hyper-productivity. More than anything else, the Exhibition projected an image of *surplus.* In a speech given on opening day, Prince Albert had said that "the products of all quarters of the globe are placed at our disposal, and we have only to choose which is the best and cheapest for our purposes."[16] Albert took for granted an almost unlimited productive capacity and made the problem out to be one of simply choosing how to deploy existing resources of production. In recent years historians have shown that this vaunted productivity was something of a science fiction. It turns out that the Victorians were very fond of overestimating their own achievements; that they had a tendency to conflate scale with surplus, to assume that because the production of textiles, coal, iron, machinery, hardware, foodstuffs, clothing, houses, ships, and a host of other goods had gone up, there was more than enough of everything to go around. Nothing could have been further from the truth. Far from being an actual cornucopia, the Crystal Palace was an extraordinary collective bluff that succeeded in presenting itself as what one historian has called "a ceremonial threshold to a new period in which contentment as well as prosperity seemed more widely enjoyed compared with the insecure and often unhappy years of the 1830s and 1840s."[17] By seeming to make the general happiness and welfare of the country into the byproduct of the extraordinary number of goods on display in one building, it made Bentham's felicific calculus concrete in a way that it never had been before. Contentment could now be easily measured, and satisfaction fully gauged, by taking the pulse of things.

The truth, then, is that the Great Exhibition of 1851 actually helped to create the sense of surplus that it is so often cited as evidence for. It palpably embodied the vehement hope that one day there would no longer be not enough, but too much, and too much for everyone. The air was thick with predictions, and *The Economist* was one of a dozen magazines prophesying that "every future improvement in society will radiate in some unknown or known way from the Great Exhibition." Horace Greeley was a little more specific about the shape of things to come: "Not until every family shall be provided with a commodious and comfortable habitation, and that habitation amply supplied with Food and Fuel not only, but with Clothing, Furniture, Books, Maps, Charts, Globes, Musical Instruments and every other auxiliary to Moral and Intellectual growth as well as to physical comfort, can we rationally talk of excessive Production."[18] Like so many visitors to the Crystal Palace, Greeley imagines transferring everything it contains into the already cramped confines of the Victorian home. Though the building had been laid out on a monumental public scale, complete, as the *Edinburgh Review* pointed out, with "its post-office—its branch bank—its telegraph—its miniature railroad—its little army—its police," it mostly set people to dreaming about what home life would be like once it had been overrun with and circumscribed by things.[19] Several writers advanced the idea that it modeled the kitchen of the future. Paxton gave speech after speech proposing that his design be used to improve the houses of the poor, and *The Economist* looked ahead to the day when "the land will be everywhere adorned with crystal palaces" (5). These panegyrics made it look like the coming utopia would primarily be the result of a big construction job whose aim it would be to clear away the slums and replace them with "the light and elegant, the cheerful and airy, the cheap and wholesome style of building of the Crystal Palace" (5). So awestruck were people by the design of the Crystal Palace that they actually began to believe in the transformative power of interior decoration, whereby the arrangement and presentation of manufactured objects becomes not only a model for human habitation but also a blueprint for social change.

Faced with the widening spiral of utopian claims the Victorians liked to make for the Great Exhibition of 1851, it is worth remembering that they were responding to a single building and a finite number of manufactured things. That building may have produced the impression that commodities were running riot and would soon overrun the country, but that impression was as meticulously manufactured as any precision instrument on display in the Exhibition. The Crystal Palace combined museum, laboratory, factory, railway station, workshop, theater, auditorium, restaurant, and greenhouse, but in a crucial sense it was also something quite different from any of these. For not only did it assemble thousands of manufactured objects under one roof, but it amalgamated them and created a coherent representational universe for commodities. The *Illustrated London News* was right to say that "the whole work comes well together, and, from whatever point it is viewed, the vastness of the structure, the extent of the arrangements, and the variety of objects displayed, all go to make one complete whole."[20] The Crystal Palace combined work, leisure, nature, and culture and dispensed them in a single confined space. Out of the apparent disorder of things it established an equilibrium and provided a working model of a consumer society by creating a sophisticated space for interacting with merchandise that Jean Baudrillard has called "a phenomenology of consumption."[21]

This phenomenology of consumption can best be described as a set of purposive procedures for producing consumption. The Crystal Palace did not isolate production from consumption; to the contrary, it successfully integrated the paraphernalia of production into the immediate phenomenal space of consumption.[22] News article after news article reminded viewers that the things they were seeing had been produced. Of course the way these articles had actually been produced differed drastically from the way the Exhibition re-produced them. Aside from a few moving mechanical parts, the commodities in the Crystal Palace were at a standstill; no one could possibly mistake the Crystal Palace for a factory. Nothing happened at the Great Exhibition but the sight of things just sitting there, mute and solid. The design of the building, however, produced a kinetic environment for inert objects. Like a prototypical department store, it placed them in a climate-controlled landscape, it flooded them with light, it isolated them in departments, it channeled people through them, and it turned them into the focal points of aesthetic and linguistic contemplation. Its peculiar ambience charged things with special significance and made it difficult to perceive them as static. In many different and complementary ways, as we shall see, the Crystal Palace succeeded in producing a space that drove consumers to distraction. The Exhibition began by creating a polyvalent landscape for commodities. Back in 1843 John Ruskin had admired landscape paintings "in which all the details of an object are seen, and yet seen in such confusion and disorder that we cannot in the least tell what they are, or what they mean." There is no better description of the Crystal Palace's phenomenology of consumption than Ruskin's insistence that landscapes be "no cold and vacant mass" but "full and rich and abundant," so much so that "you cannot see a single form so as to know what it is."[23] Inside the Crystal Palace it was impossible to draw the line between the many and various things put on display; in such a space things seemed to lose their distinctness and enter into a vast space of association in which everything, even the most mundane articles, appeared in a novel light. In a more homely way Thackeray said the same thing in a bit of doggerel called "Mr. Maloney's Account of the Crystal Palace":

> With conscious pride
> I stud insoide
> And looked the World's Great Fair in,
> Until me sight
> Was dazzled quite,
> And couldn't see for staring.[24]

Being inside the Crystal Palace was an almost hallucinatory experience: you felt overpowered by sweetness and light. Paxton's design had liberated the enclosure from seasonal fluctuations in temperature, and the result was a landscape of perpetual spring (a result not lost on Jules Jaluzot, who some years later named his Parisian department store "Printemps").[25] Essential to this landscape was the light the glass ceiling let in: so much that a canvas barrier had to be erected to keep the reflected light from blinding visitors. Without light, commodities were confined to the dim alleys of London streets explored by Mayhew, consigned to the junkshops Boz visits in *Sketches by Boz* (1836), or relegated to the dark corners of Krook's rag-and-bottle shop in *Bleak House* (1851). Illuminated by light, commodities appeared autonomous and untouchable. The organizers of the Exhibition had done their best to bring people as close as possible to things without actually allowing them to touch what they saw; some barrier, a counter or a rope or a policeman, always intervened to assert the inviolability of the object. If, as Roland Barthes has remarked, touch is the most demystifying of the senses, and sight the most magical, then the Crystal Palace both extended the sway of sight over all commodities and signaled the rise of a new imagistic mode for representing them.[26]

The magical appearance of commodities was further reinforced by the way they were classified. Like everything else in the Crystal Palace, the classification system was the result of a compromise, and it did not make for a perfect fit. Back in 1850 Prince Albert had originally proposed that the Exhibition divide articles in three categories, but in the end he settled for four: "1. Raw Materials. 2. Machinery and Mechanical Inventions. 3. Manufactures. 4. Sculpture and Plastic Art generally" (*Catalogue*, 22–23). But the planning commission had other ideas, and it tacked on twenty-nine extra categories, each of which had the virtue, according to Horace Greeley, of relying on divisions "which had been determined by commercial experience to be most convenient" (14). In other words, the Great Exhibition had two more or less separate systems of classification. The Prince Consort was interested in creating an ideal taxonomy for things and in telling the public how they were made; the planning commission wanted to divide finished articles into departments for the sake of presenting them to consumers in the most convenient way possible. Like an eighteenth-century philosophe, Albert wanted a watertight logical arrangement, while, like the managers of nineteenth-century department stores, the planning commission envisioned a system, as the *Illustrated London News* put it, "by which articles of a similar kind from every part of the world could be disposed in juxta-position."[27] The consuming public could not have agreed more wholeheartedly with the commission's departmentalization of things, flocking to exhibits that featured small numbers of finished articles and virtually boycotting the Portuguese and Spanish exhibits, which had made the mistake of following Albert's scheme by overdoing their raw materials and highlighting tons of copper, kegs of snuff, and bushels of olives.[28] Each of the national exhibits further obliged the public's taste for alluring consumer goods by arranging, as one visitor observed, "its most enticing products in front, so that they shall be seen from the grand aisle, putting its homelier though in some cases intrinsically more valuable productions in the back-ground" (Greeley, "Crystal Palace," 11).

The products most foregrounded by the Exhibition, and most admired by its visitors, best epitomized its consumerist phenomenology: gadgets. A gadget is a mechanical device so specialized as to be practically useless, and the Crystal Palace contained more gadgets than any other type of article. The *Illustrated London News*'s description of the range and variety of this misplaced ingenuity is right on target: at the Exhibition "we may look at a tissue which nobody could wear; at a carriage in which nobody could ride; at a fireplace which no servant could clean if it were ever guilty of a fire; at a musical instrument not fit for one in fifty thousand to play; at endless inventions incapable of the duties imputed to them."[29] You could also see a "Sportsman's Knife" that no sportsman would ever handle, a baroque version of a Swiss Army knife containing, according to the *Catalogue*, "eighty blades and other instruments . . . with gold inlaying, etching and engraving, representing various subjects, including views of the Exhibition Building, Windsor Castle, Osborne House, the Britannia Bridge, etc." (Fig. 5). At times the *Official Catalogue* of the Exhibition reads like the archive of a patent office, and in fact the Exhibition gave impetus to a movement that had been trying for years to get the government to establish a patent office to keep track of all the gadgets inventors were coming up with. So prevalent were gadgets at the Exhibition that one visitor commented that the most practical machines on display—machines that printed newspapers, folded envelopes, and wove cloth— looked like unwieldy gadgets when contrasted with "the hand-

FIG. 5. The useless object (*Catalogue*).

icraft methods with which most of the spectators were familiar."[30] If the machine is commonly taken to be the emblem of
mid-Victorian industrial society, then the gadget—a thing fabricated not to be used but to be admired—can stand as an emblem of the late-Victorian commodity culture prefigured in the
Great Exhibition of 1851. In a very real sense the crowds that
jammed the Crystal Palace to admire artificial foods and substitute cutlery and replacement noses were already behaving exactly according to the code of connoisseurship Oscar Wilde formulated in 1891: "We can forgive a man for making a useful
thing so long as he does not admire it. The only excuse for
making a useless thing is that one admires it intensely."[31]

In the Crystal Palace, however, this admiration was short-
term. For though the Exhibition had been engineered to instill
admiration through a massive phenomenal assault on the senses
of the consumer, it had also been set up to keep people moving.
Because so many people visited the Exhibition during the summer of 1851 (sixteen million by the official estimate), and because
the Crystal Palace's police force (four hundred strong) liked to
keep traffic going at a good clip, visitors were virtually forced to
acquire a limited attention span. Like it or not, they had to adjust themselves to the serial rhythm of the place; being set loose
in the Crystal Palace was the Victorian equivalent of flipping the
TV channel and sorting through various kinds of programmed
information. Like today's television viewer, the Exhibition spectator was free to pick and choose from a limited spectrum of prefabricated choices. Allowed a certain amount of mobility within
a confined space of exhibition, the spectator could formulate
what were essentially consumer preferences, and indeed many
firsthand accounts of the Exhibition read like nineteenth-century
versions of *Consumer Reports*. Some people liked the stuffed
frogs, some the gas stoves, some the plaster casts, but in the end
it hardly mattered what you liked. Nothing more than a coat of
mail, a divan, a vest, and some fans caught Gustave Flaubert's
fancy when he visited the Exhibition.[32] Regardless of what you
ultimately fixed your gaze upon, the Crystal Palace turned you
into a dilettante, loitering your way through a phantasmagoria
of commodities. As Walter Benjamin first pointed out over fifty

years ago, people in the mid-nineteenth century were experiencing for the first time "the intoxication of the commodity around which surges the stream of customers."[33]

On most days the customers who surged around the commodities exhibited in the Crystal Palace were solidly middle-class. More than any other, the middle class was the audience at which all the persuasive powers of the Exhibition had been directed, and with good reason. Even at mid-century the English middle class preferred to save its money rather than spend it; it preserved a view of capitalism that owed a lot to utilitarian political economy, which had preached thrift, hard work, and prudence.[34] Getting the tightfisted middle class all worked up about being consumers was easier said than done, and despite all the fuss made in the press, there were many holdouts. A prosperous trader like Curtsy Sandboys, hero of Henry Mayhew and George Cruikshank's *1851: or, The Adventures of Mr. and Mrs. Sandboys, Their Son and Daughter, Who Came Up to London to Enjoy Themselves and See the Great Exhibition* (1851), looks on the Exhibition as Ebenezer Scrooge looks on Christmas. When he first hears about it he views it as a wasteful expenditure of time and money: objecting to "the moral pollution of the metropolis," he would just as soon decline "the privilege of participating in all the amusements and gaieties of the capital at its gayest possible time."[35] The remainder of *1851* shows how much disciplining it takes to turn Curtsy Sandboys into a compliant consumer. His neighbors try to convince him to go, and when they fail, they band together to deprive him of "the necessaries of life" (21). All of a sudden he cannot conduct business, cannot buy food, cannot get his horse shod, cannot even get his own shoes mended. By dint of his refusal to attend the Exhibition, Sandboys soon finds himself and his family reduced to a state of near-poverty. He has no alternative but to attend, which he does with so much reluctance that every catastrophe that London can visit upon out-of-towners is visited upon him. He loses his luggage, gets swindled by a city slicker, has his pocket picked, and spends time in jail. Only after he acquiesces in the Exhibition, joining a crowd of people "streaming along the road, like so many living rays, converging towards the Crystal focus of the World" (128), does his lot improve. From then on *1851* reads like a conversion narrative, and accordingly Mayhew and Cruikshank interrupt their story with a fifty-page encomium which confirms that at the Exhibition "there was a sense of reverent humility forced upon the mind . . . that filled the bosom with the very pathos of admiration" (137).

This disciplining of reluctant consumers was also directed at the working class, which, for the simple reason that it had never had much experience with consumer goods, was even less disposed to revere the sight of them. The planning commission had had high hopes that the Exhibition would teach the working class to respect what Mayhew and Cruikshank called "that glorious exchange of commodities, without which society cannot exist" (17). To encourage working people to attend, the commission announced a series of what were called "Shilling Days," or days when people could be admitted at one-fifth the usual price. The Great Exhibition, however, could not discipline those who chose not to attend it. The *Illustrated London News* was sad to report that "the gay, glancing, fluttering tide of bonnets and ribbons, and silks, and satins, and velvets, had vanished, and the blank was filled up by no adequate substitute of meaner, or coarser, or more commonplace material." The Exhibition was "anything but overcrowded," and the best face the magazine could put on the first Shilling Day was to remark "the utter absence of anything like rude crushing, or confused and disorderly thronging round particular points of interest," and to praise the crowd for being "orderly, perfectly manageable, and good-humoredly amenable to rule." Though there were as yet very few people in this crowd, and though they were "more prone to touch, feel, and finger the goods than they ought to have been," the working-class crowd at the Great Exhibition proved to be every bit as docile as the middle-class crowd.[36] In the Crystal Palace the working class no longer looked like the indigenous ally of the class that had rocked Europe in 1848. It was now just another segment of the market; it had become a customer.[37]

As yet, however, it was a customer in spirit only. For though the Great Exhibition laid the foundation for modern commodity culture by publicizing commodities in the most highly structured and phenomenally dense space of exhibition the world had ever seen, it did not attempt to sell them to anyone. From the outset the planning commission had stated unequivocally that "the object of the Exhibition is the display of articles intended to be exhibited, and not the transaction of commercial business; and the Commissioners can therefore give no facilities for the sale of articles, or for the transaction of business connected therewith." [38] At one and the same time the Exhibition conjured up a vision of commodities and banished from sight the reality of their exchange. It is certainly ironic that the event most responsible for changing the overall orientation of consumer to commodity should repudiate any connection with the actual exchange of commodities. In all fourteen acres there was not one price tag to be found. Yet a price tag would have made it impossible for most people to see commodities with the kind of phenomenal immediacy that the greenhouse environment afforded. A price tag would have intervened with the information that the objects were beyond the reach of all but the very rich. In the absence of a price tag, the gaze of the beholder was directed instead to the immediate sensual attributes of the commodity on display. The Great Exhibition thus fostered what can be called a transparency of exchange: though it was not set up to sell things, it let things sell themselves.

The fact that there were no price tags, however, did not mean that the Exhibition prevented visitors from imputing value to the goods they saw. Taking the planning commission at its word, one historian has called the Exhibition "innocent of commercial purpose." [39] Far from it: the Exhibition was like a space of auction in which the price of an article is not fixed but floated. At the Exhibition people browsed through the articles and quietly calculated the value of everything they saw. This guesswork was compulsive and universal: almost every account of the Exhibition contains a long passage in which the writer speculates on possible values. Almost in spite of itself the Exhibition became a functioning microcosm of mid-Victorian capitalism. The French stalls were staffed by salesmen. Promises were large, piracy was rampant. "On every side," said Horace Greeley, "sharp eyes are watching, busy brains are treasuring, practical fingers are testing and comparing" (18). Because the 1850 Act for the Protection of Copyrights of Design did not apply to mechanical inventions, it was often hard to tell who had invented what. At times, complained the *Illustrated London News*, there were "so many claims to inventions by parties who never invented anything" that the Exhibition did little more than "deck a wilderness of daws in peacock plumage."[40] In such an environment many manufacturers became adept at camouflage, and even the *Catalogue* had to admit that the reason descriptive captions were so vague was that the typical exhibitor desired "to reveal as little as possible of the specific character of his articles" (1: 25).

As prevalent as it was, however, this imputation of value ran largely under the surface of the Exhibition; inside the Crystal Palace it was no more than a ripple in the tranquil and transparent space of Exhibition. Though the planning commission frustrated many people by shutting its eyes to the fact that, as one critic put it, "not a single article will be exhibited that has not been expressly invented or manufactured to be sold,"[41] the Exhibition was in fact all the more influential for having tried to impede the imputation of economic value to commodities. The Exhibition succeeded precisely because it elevated the commodity above the mundane act of exchange. In the Crystal Palace a commodity was not merely an object of exchange; it was, as we have seen, a concentrated aesthetic assault on the senses of the consumer, a consolidated image, a visible ideal, and an object of contemplation. Other nations had held exhibitions before, and later in the century the French and Americans were to hold them on an even larger scale. But it was the Great Exhibition which invented the mold that systematized the representation of commodities and provided a scale model of a consumer society. Around merchandise the Exhibition created modern merchandising, which was both a way of talking about commodities and, increasingly, a way of looking at them.

The fact that in a particular brief period—the summer of 1851—this new merchandising became located and embodied in the Crystal Palace tells us something important about the requirements of Victorian culture and its changing view of commercial activity. The measured and harmonious merchandising that went on inside the Crystal Palace was radically different from the traditional buying and selling that went on outside it, not only in the nature of its appeal, but in the status it conferred on the sellers of things and the diversity of information it used to signify the things themselves. In the outdoor markets of eighteenth- and nineteenth-century England, advertisers and other sellers had traditionally been considered nuisances, a step above derelicts and vagrants. Selling was grimy, as the term "sales pitch" still vividly testifies, and when John Ruskin opened a tea shop on Paddington Street he refused to hang a sign outside his shop to tell the world that he was open for business.[42] In the indoor world of exhibition, selling was an exalted activity, and salesmen were an established and visible part of society. Though the organizers of the Great Exhibition would have emphatically denied it, many Victorians would have agreed with the *Westminster Review* when it said that the real purpose of the Exhibition was to gather together "the commercial travellers of the universal world, side by side with their employers and customers, and with a show room for their goods . . . such as the world has never before beheld."[43] The Exhibition proved once and for all that the best way to sell things to the English was to sell them the culture and ideology of England, its plans for commercial dominance, its dreams of Empire, its social standards, and its codes of conduct. Once the advertising industry discovered what this new kind of merchandising could do for commodities, the commerce and culture of England were never again the same.

II

In 1851 this new mode of merchandising had yet to be translated into a set of practical procedures for selling things to the public at large. The Crystal Palace may have excelled at displaying mechanical wizardry, but it largely excluded the articles common to everyday life. The closest the Exhibition came to what we now consider consumer goods were once-in-a-lifetime purchases like furs and diamonds; overall it allotted very little space to those ordinary articles that are affordable, sustain life, and need to be frequently replaced. The Coleman's Mustard booth had few visitors, and a display of soap packaged in bright boxes provoked many disparaging comments. At the time few people thought that these standardized articles could in any way contribute to the spectacle of Exhibition, though there were some who foresaw that they might benefit from it. In years to come, as we shall see, advertising both redefined the scope of what was considered a necessity, expanding it immensely by introducing new products, and changed the way people related to ordinary articles by making them seem quite extraordinary. At mid-century, however, these commodities did not yet have a secure and prominent place in society. The Great Exhibition may have exalted the commodity as an ideal, but it made no effort to show under what conditions commodities were actually sold in the streets of London, a few paces from the phantasmagoria at Hyde Park.

For most of the population flooding London's streets, selling was a euphemism for begging. Among the large and varied class of streetsellers investigated by Henry Mayhew in *London Labour and the London Poor* (1849–54), daily life was a struggle for survival, and survival meant keeping above the line that divided London labor from the London poor. The poverty line varied from place to place, from season to season, and from trade to trade, but Mayhew makes it clear that even in the best of times making a living on the streets was an uncertain and unrewarding business. "It's only another way of starving," says one of his informants (11). The street people picked up work wherever they could find it and drifted from trade to trade. Those who stuck to a single occupation often did so out of sheer tenacity, for many of the traditional street occupations were dying out, and many more were being forced out of business by new police regulations. The street performers complained of dwindling audiences. Buyers and finders scoured the metropolis for old clothes, glass, broken metal, and waste paper, sometimes hoarding this stuff, sometimes selling it to people like Krook, who in Dickens's *Bleak House* runs a "general emporium of much disregarded merchandise." [44] These scavengers participated in what, for want of any alternative, was essentially an informal sanitation system that used the working poor to carry off and recycle the city's garbage. As London gradually made other arrangements for disposing of its refuse, these people were forced out of business. The only street people in *London Labour and the London Poor* who appear to be holding their ground are the streetsellers, who, according to Mayhew, eke out a living by selling eight kinds of articles: fish, vegetables, eatables and drinkables, used books and stationery, secondhand articles, live animals, minerals, and manufactured articles.

Of all the streetsellers cataloged by Mayhew, only the last group actually deals in newly manufactured commodities, and he finds that this is the most varied and most prosperous class of all. The sellers of manufactured articles survived for the simple reason that they had adapted their trade to the dictates of mass production and had begun to sell cheap standardized items. They dealt exclusively in cheap and readily available consumer goods such as blacking, hardware, china, linen, haberdashery, snuffboxes, combs, and pincushions—things not much in evidence at the Great Exhibition. Though these vendors tried to fit up their stalls to promote "the exhibition of their various goods" (53), they did not often succeed in showing them off to their best advantage. "Some of the stalls consist merely of a few boards resting upon two baskets" (52); these vendors "expose their wares as tastefully as they can" (53) (Fig. 6). Others "use merely baskets, or trays, either supported in the hand, or on their arm, or else they are strapped round their loins, or suspended round their necks" (53). In each instance Mayhew makes it quite clear that the poverty of the seller totally governs his impression of whatever the seller happens to be selling. Though the manufactured objects displayed were often bright and new, Mayhew cannot ignore "the sunken eyes and other characteristics of semi-starvation" that he sees on every face. In the world of the London streetsellers there is no trace of the euphoria of the Great Exhibition; as one trader tells him, "The Great Exhibition can't be any difference to me" (74).

None of Mayhew's streetsellers advertise. For them selling is a means of subsistence and a form of bondage. All across London, streetsellers were not out to make a profit but were trying to stay alive; theirs was a dwindling subsistence economy trapped within the expanding capitalist system. Mayhew esti-

THE COSTER-GIRL.

"Apples! An 'aypenny a lot, Apples!"

[*From a Daguerreotype by* BEARD.]

FIG. 6. Streetbound selling (Mayhew, *London Labour and the London Poor*).

mated that no more than a quarter of them owned the stock they traded or the stand over which they presided. Few of them displayed a competitive attitude toward their street brethren, and fewer still charged anything other than the long-accepted price for what they sold. Nor did they in any way dissociate them-

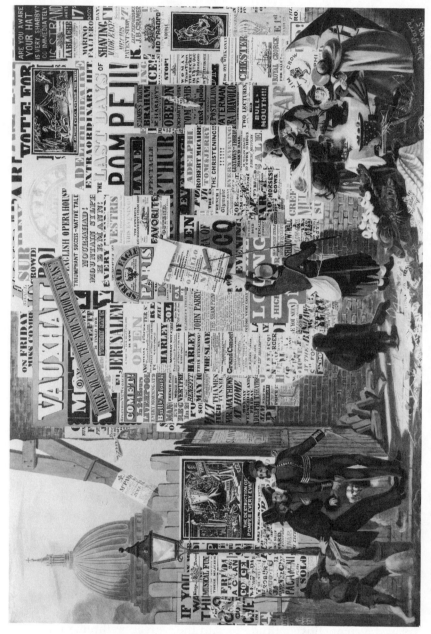

FIG. 7. The commodity marginalized: mid-Victorian advertising (John Orlando Parry, *A London Street Scene* [1835])

selves from the goods they sold; they carried them around and never let them out of their sight; and when asked, most of them even identified themselves by the names of the articles they sold (452–53). The way they made themselves known was to cry out a formulaic sentence or two; you always heard them before you saw them, and unless you were interested in buying what they were selling, you might never see them at all. Since streetsellers catered mostly to the working poor, middle-class people would often pass them by without even looking at them. Again and again mid-Victorian accounts stress that the streetsellers belong not to the sights but to the sounds of London. Mayhew under-scores the primacy of this oral mode of publicity: "The street-seller cries his goods aloud at the head of his barrow; the enter-prising tradesman distributes bills at the door of his shop. The one appeals to the ear, the other to the eye" (12). Though it sur-vived in the form of advertising jingles, the appeal to the ear was always in danger of being lost in the sensual confusion of the city. Unlike the grand aisles of the Great Exhibition, the streets of mid-Victorian London did not provide an antiseptic ambience for commodities; in the open air a commodity was still preemi-nently an inert thing handled by human beings, an everyday item available for purchase, and an object of use.

The sort of advertising that Mayhew sees on the London streets seems equally remote from the orchestrated procession of commodities in Hyde Park. Though this advertising was as removed from the traditional methods of streetselling as written is from oral culture, it nevertheless relied on a small number of fixed patterns of seeing and articulating the commodity. Most mid-Victorian advertising was not a replacement but an exten-sion of traditional streetselling, for it took place on the streets and depended on human intermediaries to pass the word. Sur-veying the streets, Mayhew finds advertising embodied in bark-ers, bill deliverers, billstickers, sandwich-board men, and ad-vertising van men. An 1834 painting by John Orlando Parry shows a typical down-to-earth scene (Fig. 7). At the center a bill-sticker prepares to paste up his latest poster, while on his right a street vendor stokes her grill with a bellows. On his left a middle-class man whisks by in too much of a hurry to glance at the wall or to notice that his pocket is being picked. Plastered pell-mell with posters, the wall itself is hard to read, and the street people, many of whom are illiterate, pay no attention to it.[45] Instead they are absorbed by the activity of the billposter, who clearly works for one of the big London theaters. Much mid-Victorian advertising was an offshoot of theater advertising, and the billposter may actually be employed by William Smith, author of *Advertise: How? When? Where?* (1863), and for many years manager of the Adelphi Theater (well represented here). In this scene, however, Smith and others like him have not yet discovered the potential of commercial advertising. Theater and show ads relegate the commodity to the sidelines; at the edge of the wall one can barely make out ads for a patent razor and a sale of horses and cows. Here advertisers have not selected the space for permanence or maximum visibility but have taken the first available empty wall and smeared it with print.

Parry's painting underscores the degree to which, in the years before the Great Exhibition, the commodity had yet to consolidate a complete hold over the cultural life of England. On this weatherbeaten wall all manner of goods and services are shuffled together indiscriminately. All at once the consumer is told to go to a play, to vote for someone, to buy something. Each of the posters tries to outdo the others by using loud colors and big print. Although the wall provides a space in which elements of theater, politics, and commerce can overlap, it is always in flux and does not privilege any one element. Overall it looks about as finished as the construction site upon which it borders. By contrast, the Great Exhibition represented the material world as an unchanging configuration of consumable objects—as a kind of still life.[46] Emphasizing the phenomenal immediacy rather than the historical contingency of the material world, the Crystal Palace placed the commodity at the center of cultural life and invited visitors to lose themselves in a utopia of visible commodities. In Parry's painting the commodity does not call attention to itself; it finds a place only at the margin of representation. Hardly visible and nearly illegible, it occupies a minuscule part of a scenic backdrop to the undirected street life of mid-Victorian London.

An extended gloss to Parry's painting can be found in an 1855 book called *The Language of the Walls*. Following the model of nineteenth-century philology, which based the study of language on the spoken word and which sought to probe language as a living human archive, the London walls reverberate with dialogue. In an unusual step for a Victorian book about advertising, the author, James Dawson Burn, decides to remain anonymous (thus losing all the free advertising provided by publication), calling himself "One Who Thinks Aloud." From the outset Burn intends his book to be a catch-all for collective utterances; he comes right out and says that "there is nothing in heaven above, and in the earth beneath, or in the air we breathe, but will be found in the universal Language of the Walls." Reading the walls becomes for him an exercise in comparative philology; as a reader of announcements he is looking for something very much like the root of Indo-European languages and, as an amateur archaeologist, he believes that he has found the key inscribed monumentally on brick and stone. On the walls Burn reads not so much the present but the past: "the Language of the Walls presents us with an *epitome* of this history of civilization—the progress of commerce—a chronicle of passing events—and a *multum in parvo* of all things." There Burn thinks he has discovered a kind of Rosetta stone enabling him laboriously to plot out the structural affinities between the various languages of commerce, politics, religion, theater, the press, and the police. But much remains undiscovered. As a reader of walls he directs his gaze at a Babel of deciphered and undeciphered languages inhabiting a common space of representation, a space which often leaves us "not a little puzzled." He sees other possibilities in the way that the walls "open up to the vulgar gaze the *arcana* of man unmanned"—in the way the hoardings, or billboards, sometimes figure a self-sustaining system of objects—but in the end they remain nothing more than the writing on the wall.[47]

The mid-Victorian hoarding brought the problem of how to represent the commodity into particularly sharp relief, if only because advertisers frequently found their offerings squeezed out of it. Although advertising handbooks were full of before-and-after pictures that showed hoardings displaying exclusively commodities (Fig. 8), most advertisers thought the situation was

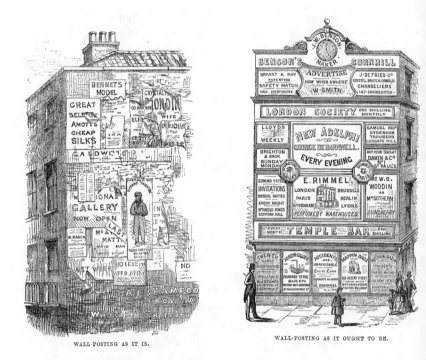

WALL-POSTING AS IT IS.

WALL-POSTING AS IT OUGHT TO BE.

FIG. 8. Advertising before and after (Smith, *Advertise*).

hopeless and began experimenting with different ways of placing commodities before the public eye. Sometime in the 1830's an enterprising advertiser hit upon the idea of parading big mock-ups of commodities around in carts, and by the 1840's the streets of London were clogged with the effigies of things. Best remembered today because in *Past and Present* (1843) Thomas Carlyle decided that one of these effigies—a seven-foot hat (Fig. 9)—embodied the vanity of mid-Victorian capitalism, these huge mock-ups removed the commodity from the pandemonium of the hoarding, swelled it to fantastic proportions, and put it on parade.[48] Whereas the wall-bound commodity was easily lost in a welter of detail, the gigantic commodity distinguished itself from its surroundings. Exaggerated umbrellas, Cheshire cheeses, tubs of butter, and sides of bacon flaunted the assumption that commodities were fashioned on a human scale to serve human needs. Like killer tomatoes from a B-movie, these objects rebelled against the limited uses to which people put them by becoming grossly obese and taking to the streets, where, if Carlyle's response is any indication, they usually inspired laughter and derision. Thus, though intended to show how important commodities were, these gigantic commodities were actually only a carnivalesque inversion of the low regard in which everyday articles were commonly held. Much to the chagrin of mid-Victorian advertisers, the commodity's status remained the same.

Despite all the stunts, tricks, and gimmicks that advertisers used to dress up their offerings, the representation of the commodity remained remarkably stable for the first half of the nineteenth century. Advertisers were more or less free to advertise in any way they wished—more because no laws yet existed regulating truth in advertising, less because they still had to pay a tax on the printed matter they circulated. But they could not escape from the traditional ways and means that had conventionalized

FIG. 9. The vehicular hat (Smith, *Advertise*).

the representation of things for centuries. They might swell the size of a bowl until it resembled the hollowed-out rock in which Rabelais's Gargantua ate his gruel. They might parade a loaf of bread around like the display of the host in a liturgical procession. They might tout the virtues of the same "Sovereign cordials" that Defoe says abounded during the plague year of 1664. Or they might cry out some stock phrase that Londoners had heard for centuries (the streetsellers' cries that Edmund Gosse remembered hearing as a child in London in the 1850's had changed remarkably little from those recorded by Pepys in his *Diary*).[49] Try as they might, however, they could not transcend a repertoire of representation that had been fixed in early modern Europe. Mayhew had the right idea when he called his streetsellers "primitive tradesmen," for they inhabited a world that manifested a remarkable structural continuity over a long time span. In this Mayhew did not attempt to set advertisers apart from streetsellers, and he denied advertising its own distinct category in his massive inventory of London trade, lumping advertisers together with a variety of other "Distributors of Production."[50] For all their emphasis on novelty, mid-Victorian advertisers also remained trapped within an economy of representation that Claude Lévi-Strauss has called "bricolage," that is, an activity that circumscribes creative expression by making it rely on "a heterogeneous repertoire which, even if extensive, is nevertheless limited."[51]

The analogy to bricolage is worth pursuing because it helps us to understand why so much mid-Victorian advertising looks raw and incomplete to us. A bricoleur is an artisan who makes do with whatever materials are available, and the bricoleur's primary activity is to adapt an activity to serve new purposes while preserving it more or less intact. Thus a tool invented to till the soil might be used to cut wood, or thread used to weave clothing might be used to bind foodstuffs. As adept as the bricoleur might be at making a few instruments perform a large number of diverse tasks, Lévi-Strauss nevertheless sees bricolage as a restricted and constricting activity. He finds that the bricoleur's "universe of instruments is closed and the rules of his game are always to make do with 'whatever is at hand,' that is to say with a set of tools and materials which is always finite and is also heterogeneous because what it contains bears no relation to the current project, or indeed to any particular project." Rather that set of tools and materials is "the contingent result of all the occasions there have been to renew or enrich the stock or to maintain it with the results of previous constructions or destructions."[52] In much the same way the primary activity of mid-Victorian advertising involved the displacement and redistribution of a stable aggregate of elements. The shape of a mid-Victorian advertisement was not determined by the object for sale, by the circumstances of the sale, or by the audience at which the advertisement was directed; rather it was the result of a kaleidoscopic sort of experimentation in which the elements of previous advertisements were shifted slightly to produce a slightly different effect. Nineteenth-century advertisers tinkered as best they could with a few simple components—posters, bills, walls, carts. Thus a bill handed out on the streets was folded into a striking shape like a piece of origami; dogs rather than horses were pressed into service to pull carts; slogans were scrawled on the pavement instead of the wall. In *Martin Chuzzlewit* (1843–44) Pecksniff so overuses the limited possibilities of his "form of advertisement" that Dickens admits that his method of advertising often "seemed to have no particular reference . . . to anything."[53] In each of these cases the limited economy of bricolage drastically reduced the margin for experimentation, and the result was the stagnation of selling so much in evidence in Mayhew's London. Advertisements came and went, but advertising continued unperturbed, much as it had since the eighteenth century, when Samuel Johnson, in a flash of insight that has often been misunderstood, wrote that "the trade of advertising is now so near to perfection that it is not easy to propose any improvement."[54]

Not until well after the Great Exhibition did the limited economy of bricolage begin to break down in the advertising industry. The little hard evidence we have suggests that the advertising industry made a killing during the summer of the Great Exhibition and that it was heartily sorry to see the Crystal Palace close its doors in September of 1851. But it contributed nothing to the phantasmagoria of Exhibition. During the Exhibition summer advertising remained on familiar ground, repeating and re-combining stock phrases, formulas, and narrative segments according to the dictates of the moment. The claims made on a July 1851 advertising page of the *Illustrated London News* did not differ in essentials from those made ten or even twenty years earlier. Many of the advertisements did take their cue from the Exhibition, offering a "GRAND EXHIBITION of WATCHES" or a "GRAND EXPOSITION of RICH and COSTLY SILKS," but the form of the advertising sheet, with its serried ranks of announcements squeezed into small boxes, remained rigidly fixed by convention. Though many of the commodities for sale here were consumer goods (silver plate, cameos, silks, and needles) and though many were exactly the sorts of things on display inside the Crystal Palace (artificial teeth, jewelry, works of art), the medium through which they were represented could not be adapted to register their newfound significance. Commodities barely disturbed the general configuration, which allotted at least half the page to a great variety of miscellaneous announcements. Despite its wide circulation, the advertising page was really just another version of the hoarding, and it is no accident that it looked a lot like the ideal hoarding of the future that advertising handbooks were always promising to erect.

A great deal more could be said about the various ways that advertisers went about publicizing their wares in the first half of the nineteenth century, but by now it should be clear that the economy of mid-Victorian advertising was one of diminishing returns. The hoarding and the advertising page were centrifugal spaces that directed attention away from the axis of representation. The confusion of the hoarding did not present itself as a sight to be contemplated in and of itself; rather people read it like a kiosk, to find out what was going on elsewhere so that they could move on and go about their business. Such a space may have had obvious utility as a means of publicity, but it ultimately repelled rather than attracted attention because, as the *Quarterly Review* recognized in 1855, it "reflects every want and appeals to every motive which affects our composite society."[55] As we have seen, a commodity on a hoarding was at best one small part of a big picture, whereas in the Crystal Palace the commodity was all there was to be seen. The real novelty of the Great Exhibition is that it constructed a centripetal space of representation that took the commodity as its center and axis. In the Crystal Palace the commodity was something more than the sum of its parts: it was now the key to all the mythologies of Victorian society, the master fiction around which society organized and condensed its cultural life and political ideology.[56] Freed from the exigencies of the mid-Victorian marketplace, the commodity had become a cynosure, a monument, a palace, and a shrine, and soon it would set about remaking the world in its own spectacular image.

III

The Great Exhibition of 1851 represents a pivotal moment in the history of advertising, for the particular style it created for the commodity ultimately transformed the advertising industry and contributed to the formation of a new commodity culture in Victorian England. Many firms considered the Exhibition the best publicity they had ever had, and for years afterwards advertisers venerated the event without understanding exactly what it had done to their business. In *Advertising: How? When? Where?* William Smith saw clearly enough that "the Great Exhibition seemed to give an immense impetus to advertising," but he immediately qualified this by adding that "there has not been the improvement in the various modes of appealing to public notice that we might have expected" (7). Smith goes on to complain about the flimsy paper, poor graphics, and bad grammar of most advertising in the 1860's. The advertising industry took a long time to realize that the Great Exhibition had created a new cultural form for the representation of commodities. Though at different times and under different circumstances the industry attempted to recover something of the charisma the Great Exhibition had temporarily conferred on commodities, it was not until the 1880's that commodities were again able to achieve a monopoly of signification in the public sphere. In part, the Great Exhibition had exalted commodities because it had been an event designed expressly to exalt them. But if for a short period of time the Exhibition also brought about the apotheosis of the commodity, it was because it had managed to synthesize and refine a particular cultural form for the representation of manufactured things: spectacle.

The Victorian taste for spectacle is well known and has been well documented.[57] It consisted primarily of a rhetorical mode of amplification and excess that came to pervade and structure public and private life in the nineteenth century, and it originated in the legitimation crisis that followed in the wake of the French Revolution and the Napoleonic Wars.[58] In the eighteenth century carefully orchestrated displays of secular and sacred power had been the prerogative of ancien-régime monarchs. In the nineteenth century, most of the rituals that fixed a king firmly at the center of a long-standing hierarchical order had disappeared even in England, where the monarchy remained embodied in the moribund figures of George III and George IV. But the need for legitimating the new bourgeois order remained, and the class that came to dominate the nineteenth century found it was better to update the old forms of spectacle than do away with them altogether or invent new ones. Since most societies, even societies undergoing revolutions, find it much easier to assert some kind of continuity with the past rather than to break cleanly from it, most forms of legitimation, even the ones employed by revolutionary leaders like Lenin and Mao, must at the very least conjure up the shade of the past in order to banish it forever into oblivion. Even in the extreme examples contained in books like *Brave New World* and *1984*, where old ways have continued outside the pale of new social orders, societies do not succeed in manufacturing a total break with the past, thus putting totally new wine in totally new bottles. What they have done, and what the bourgeoisie in nineteenth-century England did with notable success, was to put new wine in old bottles. The high style of the eighteenth-century spectacle survived, but in a new and specialized context. In a variety of ways nineteenth-century consumers were witnessing the modulated transformation of the remnants of the high style into the basic tropes of a new commodity culture.

The transformation of spectacle into a new kind of political

advertisement/
↑ *theater*

theater came at a time when the high style of representation had
fallen into general disrepute. It had been many years since people
gathered to hear oral recitations of heroic poetry or masques
staged at court. Early in the nineteenth century the last remaining bastions of the high style crumbled as the dramatic postures
of sentimentalism lost favor, the gothic novel went into a steep
decline, and the romantic poets eschewed declamatory verse
and espoused a pared-down aesthetic. In the historical novel
Walter Scott relegated the mode of excess to the distant past and
encapsulated it in what he called "a style . . . neither alarming
our credulity nor amusing our imagination by wild variety of incident." [59] The expressionist rhetoric of spectacle no longer seemed
to have any place in human relations. Far from dying out, however, the mode of excess became a mode of producing the *material* world, and material culture became a drama that played to
packed houses. The 1820's saw the invention of dioramas, epic
versions of the built world advertised with every ounce of hyperbole the showmen could muster. The popular refuge of the
high style, the opera, set the standard for lavish sets, props,
backdrops. [60] The commission that planned the Great Exhibition
began by experimenting with spectacle as a new kind of hard
sell and ended up discovering that the hardest sell of all was the
high sell. Designed explicitly to aggrandize the commodity, the
Exhibition contributed to the formation of a commodity culture
in which highly artificial literary structures and extravagant
modes of expression served to publicize and stylize manufactured articles. In years to come, the spectacles of late-Victorian
advertising would return again and again to the outmoded conventions of the high style to declaim the commodity; one 1890
advertisement would go so far as to show an African costumed
like a character in an Inigo Jones masque and gesturing like a
singer in a Purcell opera. [61]
    The high style of early-Victorian spectacle may well be the
most reliable surviving index to the formation of commodity culture in the years before the Great Exhibition. As political theater
the spectacles of the early and mid-nineteenth century bore only
a superficial resemblance to the royal progresses, public pag-
eants, and elaborate rituals of the eighteenth. Display, extrava-

gance, and excess survived—but less for the sake of those who staged the spectacle than for the sake of the spectacle itself. The certainty that the means of spectacular representation signified anything in particular had disappeared, and increasingly it was the means themselves that mattered. And the means were industrial. People thronged to theatrical performances that featured floods, train crashes, shipwrecks, tempests, sunsets, mountain ranges, and horse races on giant treadmills. Academy paintings featured public buildings—docks, warehouses, bridges, factories, gasworks, railway stations, hotels, banks, office blocks. Whatever the medium, the use of graphic and often melodramatic spectacle was one way of representing the industrialization of England. Since the 1830's the fruits of industrial capitalism had resisted easy categorization and, as Catherine Gallagher has shown, had in fact quite confounded the usual antinomies of Victorian social thought.[62] In the midst of this confusion spectacle functioned as a kind of experimental theater for industrial capitalism, not only by accustoming audiences to technologies but also by making the technologies themselves into a form of entertainment. Indeed, if you take away the machines and buildings from Victorian spectacular theater and art, there is not much left to look at. "We go not so much to hear as to look," admitted one Victorian theatergoer.[63] In a way that proved to be very influential, these early Victorian spectacles compelled people to contemplate the material culture of a country in the throes of industrial development.

The purveyors of spectacle were astonishingly inventive about astonishing the early Victorian public. Over the years they cooked up various combinations of lighting, sound, scene painting, transparencies, cutout scenery, models, lanterns, projections, dioramas. In the Victorian theater the stage manager became a technician whose job it was to create what we now call "special effects." The primary result of these effects was to institute a continual escalation of representation. This escalation had its own logic of one-upmanship: everything had to outdo what had come before it, and in turn, everything had to be outdone by what came after it. The spectacles of the early Victorian stage conditioned their audiences always to expect more—and more and more. For example, the adoption of panoramas and dioramas as scenic backdrop did not satisfy audiences for long. Pretty soon the technicians invented moving panoramas, painted on a single canvas and rolled between two large scrolls mounted vertically at each end of the stage. By 1848, three years before the Exhibition, the moving panorama had become an exhibition in itself, and one of the year's most sensational events was the debut of a 3,600-foot-long moving panorama depicting a journey down the entire length of the Mississippi River.[64] Indeed, one reason Prince Albert's idea for a Great Exhibition was so well received is that by the late 1840's the escalation of spectacle had gotten so out of hand that it was evident nothing short of a massive collective effort could possibly come close to satisfying the well-nigh universal public craving for monster displays of special effects.

These special effects popular on the Victorian stage all had in common, as has been suggested, the elevation of a form of technology into a form of culture. They fashioned what can quite literally be called a technology of representation. According to the logic of this technology of representation, the means for producing the world became the means of representation. Thus the Victorian stage put machines on the stage, and after a time the machines *became* the stage. The great innovation of the Great Exhibition of 1851 was that it took this technology of representation to its logical conclusion. Recall that the Exhibition had been organized to feature not machines but the things machines were used to make. By placing a spotlight, not on the means for producing the world (machines), but rather on the things produced (commodities), the Exhibition proposed that the ends of production, the things produced by all the burgeoning forms of industrial technology, become the ends of representation. If, as has been argued, the Exhibition can be seen as having brought about the apotheosis of the commodity, it did not do so by elevating it above the social world. The Exhibition commodity was many things, but it was not transcendent. Under glass, lit by the light of the sun and touched by the scrutinizing gaze of the public, the Exhibition commodity was an encyclopedia of representation. It was everything that could or should be represented; it established new boundaries for representation; and, in the eyes of many beholders, it was representation itself, balled up and made visible as a lump sum.

The perimeters of representation the Exhibition defined for the commodity outlasted the year of Exhibition and, as will be shown, proved to be remarkably influential in shaping capitalist representation over the next sixty years. The first thesis of Guy Debord's *Society of the Spectacle* (1967) says it all: "The entire life of societies in which modern conditions of production reign announces itself as an immense accumulation of *spectacles*."[65] The Exhibition was a clear indication that the capitalist system had not only created the dominant form of exchange but was also in the process of creating a dominant form of representation to go along with it. In the Crystal Palace there was monumental architecture and elaborate scenery, and there were fountains, locomotives, gasworks, and more—all meticulously staged. The Exhibition not only placed itself at the aesthetic confluence of these popular forms of spectacle; it also succeeded in making commodity culture virtually coterminous with the symbolic apparatus of spectacle. If the spectacles of early-Victorian England can be seen, as has been suggested, as having provided the cultural form for a kind of technology, then the Exhibition rounded out the form by supplying it with a perfectly matched content: the commodity. During and after the Exhibition the commodity was fused indissolubly to a technology of representation, and the result was that the commodity became a much more complex form than it ever had been before.

Out of this disparate array of popular technologies of spectacular representation the Great Exhibition fashioned a new high style suited to commodities, a style that became the basis for Victorian commodity culture. In particular, the Exhibition was responsible for synthesizing what can be seen as the six major foundations of a semiotics of commodity spectacle: the establishment of an autonomous iconography for the manufactured object; the use of commemoration to place objects in history; the invention of a democratic ideology for consumerism; the transformation of the commodity into language; the figuration of a consuming subject; and the invention of the myth of the abundant society. None of these elements was new; as many studies have shown, each originated in the seventeenth or eighteenth century.[66] The point is that taken together, these six elements now constituted a complex signifying system that set the mid-Victorian commodity apart from earlier forms of the commodity and made it loom large in the cultural and political life of nineteenth-century England. As the successive chapters of this book will show, it was out of this spectacularization of the commodity—a process that began during the Exhibition and proceeded in fits and starts over the next sixty years—that modern advertising was born.

The first element of this semiotics of commodity spectacle was the establishment of an autonomous iconography for the manufactured object. In the revolutionary year of 1848, updated versions of the French Revolution's "Declaration of the Rights of Man" were much debated. The English response to all this revolutionary fervor was to begin to confer the privileges of bourgeois individualism on manufactured things. In the Crystal Palace, commodities appeared to be at sovereign liberty to do whatever they wished. They seemed to have rights. Like the classical subject of individualism, the various objects on display in the Great Exhibition tended to be described with an intensity all out of proportion to their use to or value in society at large. Panegyrics devoted to gimcracks took up pages and pages of the *Illustrated London News,* and not even the stodgy *Westminster Review* could resist genuflecting at the bright new altar of English manufacture. And just as the privileged individual subject tended to lend itself to idealism, commodities on display in isolated cases in the Crystal Palace were routinely lionized as the manufacturers (read "creators") of the visible external world. Accordingly, time and again objects were described not as the result of human activity but as the cause of it. The close philosophical parallel here (one never very far from bourgeois individualism) is solipsism, a view according to which the solitary self is the only reality.[67] In the Crystal Palace, the consumer was confronted with a multiplicity of solipsistic things, each of which simultaneously announced its existence and refused to recognize the existence of all others. At the Great Exhibition commodities were always sliding from autonomy into solipsism, and each and every commodity had its cult of viewers (the German stuffed frogs were the most prominent of these commodity cults).[68] Here, if we look closely enough, we can catch a glimpse of our own billboard-cluttered world, a world strikingly encapsulated by Guy Debord in the sixty-sixth thesis of *Society of the Spectacle*: "Every given commodity fights for itself, cannot acknowledge the others, and attempts to impose itself everywhere as if it were the only one."[69]

②   The second element of this semiotics of spectacle was the use of commemoration to place objects in history and, ultimately, to replace history. A commemorated event is one that never took place. Commemoration is memory that has been placed in a state of suspended animation, and the sad fact is that the force of this suspension is often powerful enough to blight what is remembered beyond the range of recognition or the possibility of recovery. We can see a complex phenomenology of commemoration at work in the Exhibition, an event whose position in history eluded most Victorian observers. Certainly the Exhibition made history—but in both senses of this double-edged phrase. As shown at some length, the Exhibition synthesized a new spectacular mode for the representation of commodities, thereby opening a new public arena for them, an arena that would ultimately become crowded with advertisements. But, crucially, the Exhibition had been intended to be a comprehensive reinterpretation of recent industrial history. "At last," proclaimed the *Westminster Review*, "came Prince Albert to proclaim that England should no longer be misunderstood."[70] Here the social unrest of the 1830's and 1840's becomes a simple misunderstanding, not a fact but an error. The purpose of the Exhibition was not to mark any one event but to act as a historical corrective to this misunderstanding, and the way it went about correcting history was to obscure it. The little cards, so hard to read, that accompanied each exhibited article rarely told their readers when and where the article was invented, much less who used it and for what purposes. Unlike a museum, the Exhibition made it extremely difficult to pinpoint the origins of individual objects. Instead the space of Exhibition revised the past by making it wholly present. "By annihilating the space which separates different nations," wrote William Whewell approvingly, "we produce a spectacle in which is annihilated the time which separates one stage of a nation's progress from another."[71] In the Crystal Palace, everything, all the history-making machines from over the past fifty years, was simultaneously present and uniformly new. By encapsulating the past in the glossy shell of the present, the Exhibition both commemorated the past and annihilated it.

The third element was the invention of a democratic ideology (3) for consumerism. The Exhibition rarely confronted the reality of class difference; instead it advanced a utopian vision. This vision was not so much of a classless society as of a society in which everyone was equal in the sight of things. Commodities provided a common ground for everyone. It did not matter whether or not people had them, because now the assumption was that they all wanted exactly the same articles. Formerly the wealthy tended to cultivate idiosyncratic tastes in privacy; think of Horace Walpole erecting Strawberry Hill at great remove from prying eyes. The great innovation of the Exhibition is that it offered to compensate the have-nots with a vision of what the haves had, and correspondingly, it offered the haves a precise vision of what they needed to possess. For all its vaunted comprehensiveness the Exhibition actually limited the field of possible consumption by restricting it to a set number of possibilities. Without exception, everyone had to be satisfied with these possibilities, either by owning these things, or, for the overwhelming majority, by gleaning some kind of aesthetic compensation from the sight of them.

Furthermore, by an interpretive sleight of hand, mid-Victorian critics managed to make this aesthetic compensation seem more desirable than any material compensation. In an 1851 lecture Horace Greeley characterizes this compensation by contrasting certain unnamed countries in which "the arts are mainly exercised to gratify the tastes of the few" to Britain, in which the arts "supply the wants of the many." Developing his point, he goes on to say that "there Art labours for the rich alone; here she works for the poor no less" ("Crystal Palace," 18–19). What the poor are supposed to get out of the Great Exhibition are not higher wages but higher thoughts. Mayhew and Cruikshank's *1851: or, The Adventures of Mr. and Mrs. Sandboys* makes this substitution explicit: "The Great Exhibition is a higher boon to labour than a general advance of wages. An increase of pay might have brought the working men a larger share of creature comforts, but high feeding, unfortunately, is not high thinking nor high feeling" (132). But for all this emphasis on the life of the mind, Mayhew and Cruikshank, like Greeley before them, offer no examples of the sort of elevating sentiments they want to cultivate. Even though the comedy of their novel results from the fact that Mr. and Mrs. Sandboys steadfastly refuse to be elevated, the writers persist in believing in the compensatory value of the spectacle they are consuming. The sight of goods in such numbers was still quite new, and it would take many years before a consumer like Nancy Lord, the heroine of George Gissing's *In the Year of Jubilee* (1894), would be able to find satisfaction in the spectacle of commodities in a department store.

(4)   The fourth element was the transformation of the commodity into language. Ever since Swift parodied nominalism in *Gulliver's Travels* (1726), wave after wave of skeptics had been on the lookout for any tendency to confuse, elide, or equate words and things. In a passage of biting satire, Swift ridicules the proposition that "in reality all things imaginable are but nouns" by showing a group of intellectuals who have carried the idea to its logical and absurd conclusion. "Since words are only names for *things*," they decided that "it would be more convenient for all men to carry about such *things* as were necessary to express the particular business they are to discourse on."[72] So at Swift's Lagado, speakers are compelled to sink under the weight of their referents. After many years of having been the butt of philosophers like Hume, Gibbon, and Bentham, this old equation of words and things was more or less defunct, but Horace Greeley revived and updated it to express what he saw going on in front of him at the Great Exhibition. His new twist is worth quoting at length:

The objects there, the symbols, instruments, and manifestations of beauty and power, were utterances,—articulate utterances of the human mind, no less than if they had been audible words and melodious sentences. There were expressed in the ranks of that great display many beautiful and powerful thoughts of gifted men of our own and of other lands. The Crystal Palace was a cabinet in which were contained a vast multitude of compositions—not of words, but of things, which we who wandered along its corridors and galleries might con, day by day, so as to possess ourselves, in some measure and according to our ability, of their meaning, power, and spirit. ("Crystal Palace," 25–26)

Greeley is careful to avoid overtly equating words with things. For him, beauty is power manifested in language, which is a discourse that originates in things. The Crystal Palace is a text for the times, what Greeley calls "a settled common language" in which "the manufacturer, the man of science, the artisan, the merchant" can "speak of the objects about which they are concerned" (25–26). The Exhibition has dispelled the Babel of the marketplace, replacing it with a language that appears to originate in the things themselves.

Nowhere is this attribution of language to things made clearer than in a little 1851 *Household Words* article called "The Catalogue's Account of Itself," in which it is the catalogue of commodities that speaks. The *Catalogue* functioned as a kind of rhetorical handbook to the new speech of things, and this article sheds some light on the grammar of this reified speech. From the beginning the talking *Catalogue* admits that "my manner of speaking is extremely terse."[73] Extreme simplicity of syntax characterizes the new grammar; here language appears to revert to its primitive use as a form of inventory. Coordination replaces subordination. Quantification replaces qualification. In a revival of eighteenth-century orthography, nouns leap from lower to upper case, not only in the *Catalogue* but in dozens of exhibition accounts. The talk is of "Saws, Files, and Hammers; Stoves, Grates, and Furnaces; Bedsteads, Chairs, and Lanterns" (Greeley, "Crystal Palace," 11). The aim is "precision, uniformity, or coherence," as the submissions of some fifteen thousand exhibitors, "most of them authors for the first time," are "pruned" in such a way that they no longer contain any verbs ("Account," 521, 522). The result (this one from the *Catalogue* itself) is "Fire Escape. Percussion carbine musket, with rotary primer. Omnibus passenger register. A mileometer. Small weighing machine. Cannon, with improved percussion-lock" (1: 467).

Running parallel to, and in many cases augmenting, the transformation of the commodity into language was the fifth element of the new semiotics of commodity spectacle, the figuration of a consuming subject. In the Crystal Palace, the traditional Cartesian distinction between the perceiving subject and the perceived object changes shape. From Descartes onward, the human subject's gaze was fixed on a complex external world composed of many sorts of objects—the natural world, cultural artifacts, other human beings. At the Great Exhibition anything that interferes with the direct perception of manufactured objects has conveniently fallen away; there is a contraction of perception as the subject becomes the exclusive consumer of *material* objects. Now the basic phenomenology of perception is oriented around property. This microcosm of the visible world may not be owned by any one person, but the basic fact is that it, and every single thing in it, can be owned. The act of perceiving becomes a proprietary act: to perceive something becomes inseparable from perceiving its value. Not that it matters what the exact value is of what one perceives. As has been indicated, the Great Exhibition was all the more successful because it refused to fix values. Much of the most lionized merchandise in the Crystal Palace was "priceless"—a perfect term for the new consumerist phenomenology, because a priceless object is an icon of pure property. By fixing the gaze of the perceiving self upon commodity icons, the Great Exhibition did for capitalism what none of its apologists over the previous two hundred years had been able to do: it established the philosophical precedence of manufacture and elevated things to the status of the ultimate reality.

If the Great Exhibition shifted the axis of perception toward an objective phenomenology of property, it also introduced an operation that objectified on a large scale the traditional distinction between the perceiving subject and the perceived object. Usually the subject/object distinction is treated as a small-scale interaction between a single subject and a single object. By contrast, the Exhibition multiplied the possibilities of perception by figuring a consuming subject who accorded fundamentally with the theory and practice of the burgeoning nineteenth-century science of statistics. Today "statistics" brings to mind the calculation of numbers, figures, chances, and types based on a survey of vast and amorphous populations. In the nineteenth century, however, the modeling of the generic, typical, or average self by no means inhibited the figuration of distinct individualities. In Mayhew's *London Labour and the London Poor* the individual and the type share a reciprocal space of representation in which the specific always implies the series and the series always invokes the specific. From its inception, the Exhibition was both a *project* involving the construction of a massive facility and a *projection* involving the construction of seriated consuming selves from calculations of numbers, figures, chances. The Planning Commission, as we have seen, spent a lot of time amalgamating two different constructions of the prototypical visitor, a middle-class version and a working-class version. Throughout the Exhibition Summer turnstiles kept a running count of visitors, and the figures were widely published and closely examined for evidence of trends. It is no accident that Mayhew, the great tabulator of mid-century London street life, found the Exhibition such a congenial subject for fictional treatment. *1851* is one long "composite" portrait of a nineteenth-century consumer, a novel in which we can see both the individual constituting the norm and the norm constituting the individual. Curtsy Sandboys is the first fictional attempt (though not a very successful one) to represent the statistical consumer. He comprises what Francis Galton, inventor of composite photography, called in 1894 a "total heritage," total because he includes "a greater variety of material than was utilised in forming his personal structure."[74] Every visitor to the Exhibition both embodied a social typology and displayed controlled deviations from the type, and the result, soon to be visible throughout Victorian advertising, is a generic but individuated consumer who maintains a personal ensemble of traits and desires that nevertheless can be deduced from the population as a whole. As yet few female consumers appear in *1851*, but as we shall see in Chapter 5 the construction of a female consuming subject in late-Victorian England was greatly to extend this foundational figuration of a statistical consuming subject.

(c)

Each of the preceding elements of this new semiotics contributed to the invention of the sixth and most visible element, the myth of the achieved abundant society. In many ways this myth accomplished a startling reversal, shattering as it did one of the chief dogmas of classical economics. For someone like Adam Smith, the capitalist system owed its dynamism to its expansionist tendencies, to the fact that capitalism's reach always exceeded its grasp. He continually pressed for the reinvestment of accumulated capital lest the members of society "leave nothing behind them in return for their consumption."[75] Like Malthus and Ricardo after him, Smith firmly believed that achieved abundance was the vanishing point of the capitalist system, and he took it as axiomatic that it was in the nature of things that prosperity always be just around the corner. But the Exhibition altered this scheme of things. As every child in England knew, the innovation of the Great Exhibition was that it announced the long-awaited arrival of a millennium of prosperity. The country may still have been on the threshold of abundance, but now that abundance, far from being a distant fruit of generations of diligent labor, seemed more tangible than it ever had been before. In reality, of course, all one had to do was walk a few miles from Hyde Park to see that this Exhibition was another in a long series of capitalist annunciations, and there were many who perceived the incongruity. Nevertheless, the Great Exhibition succeeded where other official annunciations had failed for the simple reason that it used commodities themselves as the medium for the announcement. The commodities on display in the Crystal Palace seemed to have arrived as the vanguard of permanent prosperity, and the English press and people welcomed them as liberators.

The use of the commodity as a semiotic medium—as icon, commemorative, utopia, language, phenomenology, annunciation; in a word, as *spectacle*—so striking in the year of Exhibition, would have surprised earlier theorists of the commodity. For until the middle of the nineteenth century, the English commodity did not have a particular form of representation that it favored above all others. When classical economists turned to describing the workings of the commodity, they tended to do so in rather colorless terms. In Adam Smith's *Wealth of Nations* (1776), the commodity is simply a form of exchange subject to the laws of supply and demand, which Smith considers akin to the laws of nature. One of his formulations makes this equation in a striking way: "the market price of every particular commodity is . . . continually gravitating towards the natural price" (162). Here the "natural" price is described in Newtonian terms as the product of as unquestionable and omnipresent a force as gravity. Clearly Smith believes himself to be describing the workings of the commodity in essentially neutral terms. In a way that has since become difficult for us to understand, Smith regards the commodity as a featureless channel of exchange, and separates the cultural and economic worlds into entirely different realms.

Though Adam Smith liked to regard the commodity as a medium and a conduit rather than as a social force and a cultural form, the commodity was no more neutral a channel than the Suez Canal. The commodity has always had a local habitation and a name, and it has behaved differently under different historical circumstances. Black cloth sold for public mourning in England, whales killed for hoop skirts, trinkets swapped for land with American Indians, Manchester cloth traded in the Punjab: the value of these commodities cannot be understood as an economic abstraction.[76] To his credit, Smith admitted that social forces played a big part in structuring the demand for these articles, but he paid absolutely no attention to the particular cultural forms that the articles themselves assumed. Once made, he considers commodities "work done" (162) and consigns them to the market, where they move about according to the laws of supply and demand. The very examples he uses—like pins—make it difficult to look at the commodities as anything other than trivial things. In *The Wealth of Nations* the commodity is not a cultural force in its own right, and it is certainly not a spectacle.

The spectacularization of the commodity did not happen all at once, but during and after the year of the Great Exhibition many observers perceived that something untoward was happening to manufactured things. The Exhibition was far and away the most visible manifestation of a general sea change in commodity relations that soon caught the eye of the foremost social observer of

the mid-nineteenth century, Karl Marx. By the time Marx wrote
his famous analysis of the fetish character of commodities in
Capital in the 1860's the situation had changed dramatically from
Adam Smith's time. In a variety of striking and subtle ways,
Marx's text registers a new spectacular mode for the representation of things. The various metaphors Marx uses to describe
commodity relations—metaphors that seem to go haywire—actually make a great deal of sense when understood as an imagi-
native response to the spectacularization of the commodity that
we have been tracing. Throughout his text, Marx develops a
number of different strains of metaphor, each of which appears
to contradict the others, but all of which turn out to be quite
complementary when seen as the constitutive elements of a new
semiotics of commodity spectacle.

Marx uses three distinct kinds of metaphors to evoke the
complex of commodity relations: metaphors of transcendence,
of community, and of sensory experience. Each set of metaphors
leads us into the next. Marx's metaphors of transcendence are
perhaps the most familiar of the three; he speaks of "the mystical character of commodities" and evokes "the mist-enveloped
regions of the religious world." His metaphors of community
evoke what happens when commodities become so detached
from their producers that they "appear as independent beings
endowed with life, and entering into a relation both with one
another and the human race." A conduit of economic exchange
thus becomes a means for articulating exchanges other than economic, and so Marx says that there now is "a social relation between the products" themselves. And how do people react to
this fantastic society of commodities? In a striking phenomeno-
logical metaphor, Marx suggests that these autonomous objects
excite our sense perception in such a way as to make them look
ineluctably objective. Just as "the light from an object is perceived by us not as the subjective excitation of our optic nerve,"
so too does the commodity appear to be "the objective form of
something outside the eye [of the consumer]." [77] Here the metaphors of transcendence express the apparent autonomy and
ahistoricity of commodities; the metaphors of community stress
the common political and linguistic ground that commodities
create; and the metaphors of sensory experience evoke the new

consumerist phenomenology, which establishes the commodity as the privileged datum of sense experience.

Taken together, all three kinds of metaphor approach the commodity not simply as a form of exchange but as a powerful and essentially unstable form of representation. For the sake of clarity Marx's nucleus of metaphors has been divided into three categories; in the text they move as quickly as a chain reaction. The important point, though, is that Marx is aware that the commodity can no longer be viewed as an exclusively material form of exchange. By summoning a complex of images to illustrate the commodity's workings, Marx illustrates that the commodity relies on and functions through a mercurial array of representations. For Marx, the commodity form is no longer a dissociated conduit for economic exchange. Though he certainly devotes a lot of space to showing that the commodity form establishes a medium of incongruous equivalence for qualitatively incommensurable goods and services, he also admits that the commodity banishes this incongruity by embedding it in a form of representation. The quick succession of images that Marx uses makes it clear both that there is no particular and inevitable form of representation that the commodity favors and that the form it currently favors, the form which finally unites the polyvalent imagery of *Capital*, is spectacle.

Though by the early 1860's the new semiotics of spectacle was able to exercise a powerful hold over Marx's description of commodity relations, it took some time to catch on in the advertising industry. This slow but sure movement toward spectacle in advertising can be traced in Trollope's 1861 novel, *The Struggles of Brown, Jones, and Robinson*. The story follows the exploits of a trio of entrepreneurs who open up a department store and begin to experiment with various ways to use advertising to better their business. Most of their creations would not have been out of place in a sensation novel or on the melodramatic stage:

RUIN! RUIN! RUIN!
Wasteful and Impetuous Sale

By resorting to the sensational trope of exclamation, the proprietors of Magenta House can get the public's attention, but they cannot hold it. The store finally folds. They circulate bills falsely offering to sell clothing below cost; they publicize exotic articles they do not actually stock; and they sweet-talk customers into accepting shoddy substitutes. Chicanery, charlatanism, and quackery rule, and the sole aim of the advertiser is not to get exposed. At one point in the story Brown and Robinson decide to lure customers by announcing that the store has just acquired "Eight thousand real African monkey muffs." Afraid that eight thousand customers might show up wanting to buy these things, "Brown begged almost with tears in his eyes, that [the plan] might be modified. 'George,' said he, 'we shall be exposed.' 'I hope we shall,' said Robinson. 'Exposition is all that we desire.'" [78]

The moral of *The Struggles of Brown, Jones, and Robinson* could not be clearer: just ten years after the Great Exhibition closed its doors, the aim of advertising was no longer exposure but exposition. Exposing goods to public view was, as has been shown, traditionally a dirty business that Henry Mayhew consigned to a low rung on the ladder of streetsellers. What Trollope's advertisers also lacked, and what, in spite of all their efforts, they never seem able to achieve, was precisely what an exposition like the Exhibition supplied so prodigiously: a consolidated rhetoric of public representation. The "sensation advertising" of the 1860's was a step in this direction, for it drew upon a literary form familiar to a mass audience. [79] At the same time, however, it lacked central authority and stable form. At the Great Exhibition it was impossible to tell the commodity apart from the dominant institutions of mid-Victorian life, and from the medium—spectacle—through which these institutions were being represented. Representation came stamped with the imprimatur of social consensus, and what is more, it seemed to be intrinsic to things, to inhere in them. The commodity spoke for itself and for England. By contrast, in the sensation advertising of the 1860's the commodity did not speak at all: it was still a trivial thing, so trivial that it had to be hidden away, veiled with outrageous rhetoric, deprived of its attributes, and offered for public consumption as something other than an article of manufacture.

In years to come, the great developments in English advertising would coincide with a series of great exhibitions of English culture, politics, and ideology. The Great Exhibition created the mold from which these later exhibitions of commodity culture were cast, and each of these later exhibitions can be seen as issuing from it in some way. Planned under the patronage of the royal family, the Exhibition was both a macrocosm and a microcosm. It assembled products from all over the world, but it also contained the most up-to-date medical and scientific instruments, textiles, fashions. It was the world's largest enclosed space, but it contained the world's smallest compass. The subject of later commodity exhibitions might be large or it might be small, but every one of them relied on the common rhetoric of public representation—spectacle—that had been pioneered at

1) mid-century. The 1887 and 1897 Jubilees of Queen Victoria gave the commodity a triumphal progress through the streets of London and fixed a ready-made image of royal power and prerogative to manufactured things. The various Imperial Exhibitions of

2) the 1890's summed up an immense effort, largely carried on through advertising, to sell imperialism to the domestic public.

3) Patent medicine advertisers followed the lead of Victorian physicians in turning the most private ministrations of the body into the subject of spectacular public scrutiny. And the great seaside

4) resorts of the late nineteenth century became a locus of spectacle as the female body, clothed and unclothed, was put on parade in a series of advertisements designed to arouse male spectators. The basic argument of this book is that out of these four discrete exhibitions, macrocosmic and microcosmic, representing monarchy and empire, the healthy body and the female body, came all the familiar imperatives of modern commodity culture, with its emphasis on status, exoticism, health, and female sexuality. Beginning in the 1880's, these later exhibitions would heighten, extend, and finally consolidate the rhetoric of public representation visible in the raw during the year of the Great Exhibition. For in 1851, as Horace Greeley saw, the space of Exhibition still had "an unmistakable aspect of haste and rawness,—an odor born of green boards and fresh paint,—and although an infinity of carpenters' work still remained undone, yet the Exhibition was plainly there, and only needed time to perfect its huge proportions, and stand forth the acknowledged wonder of the world" ("Crystal Palace," 6).[80]

Between exhibitions, the spectacular commodity continued

to coexist peacefully with the earlier and increasingly obsolete forms of the commodity. The Exhibition had created a rhetoric of public representation, not a grammar, and much experimentation with the elements of spectacle contained within the transparent walls of the Crystal Palace lay ahead. Many were aware, as the *Westminster Review* pointed out, that "the general system of shopkeeping seems on the eve of change," but few dared to hazard a precise prediction about what this system would look like, and there was much nostalgia for the good old days (whenever they were) when the hard sell was still soft.[81] The Exhibition was not a blueprint but a prototype, a model on which later stages of development are based and against which they can be judged. For the eighty years that it remained standing, the Crystal Palace was a symbol of the generation of 1851. A second Great Exhibition, held in 1862 and intended to be a carbon copy of the first, was a bust, and the advertiser William Smith admitted that "in the amount of attendance attracted, and indeed in most other respects, the Exhibition of this year shows but poorly when contrasted with its forerunner of 1851" (*Advertise*, 109). After 1862 planners quietly dropped the idea of holding an exhibition every ten years. Though other Great Exhibitions of Things did come along from time to time, it turned out that the greatest exhibitions of all were topical and took nearly everyone by surprise, just as the first one had.[82] What the first Exhibition heralded so inimitably was the complete transformation of collective and private life into a space for the spectacular exhibition of commodities. The shape of things to come had come.

2

The Image of Victoria in the
Year of Jubilee

For a brief and dazzling moment during the summer of 1851, England had a center. Bounded in a nutshell within the Crystal Palace were things, things, and more things, which together embodied and propounded a vision of social life as a vast assembly of exchangeable artifacts. In one place the commodity had in its special custody the official cultural and political life of England. The Great Exhibition began by creating an official rhetoric of public representation for the commodity and ended by making the commodity into the one rhetoric of all representation. That rhetoric, which has been designated spectacle, adumbrated an emerging commodity culture and contributed materially to fashioning, for the first time in history, a dominant machinery of specifically capitalist representation. Commodity representation now became synonymous with the phenomenology of possession guided by the presence of bourgeois authority. In the Crystal Palace, capitalism was not, as the classical economists had claimed, a natural state of affairs; it was a sanctioned state ideology affirmed by representatives from all walks of Victorian life. Led by Prince Albert, the nation joined together to proclaim a new dominion of things.

In 1851 this dominion seemed genuinely new. "We sadly lack a new stock of public images," wrote Disraeli in 1847. "The current similes, if not absolutely counterfeit, are quite worn out." [1] The commission that planned the Exhibition must have considered itself forewarned, for it relied only incidentally on established institutions such as Parliament, the military, and the monarchy. At the opening ceremony the finished product utterly dwarfed the dignitaries of mid-Victorian England; the Crystal Palace seemed to lend them dignity instead of the other way around. The monarchy in particular seemed shut out of a space structured so as to let everyone in. After the turbulence of 1848 the commission was understandably reluctant to orient its Exhibition around a display of royal prerogatives. Like Louis Napoleon, whom Marx characterized as a stick figure playing a comic role in a farce, Victoria and Albert seemed to be vestiges of an elite that, however much it might approve of the new commodity culture, faced imminent extinction. The new dominion of things lacked a ruler; democratic plurality rather than charismatic singularity was the ordering agent of the commodity spectacle.

Judging from the minor role she played during the Exhibition, Queen Victoria would not appear to be a very promising subject for a new direction in English commodity culture. Staid, portly, and retiring, she often seemed to be the consort rather than Albert. As late as 1886 an advertising handbook called *Successful Advertising* explicitly counseled its readers to avoid using the royal arms and, implicitly, to search out a new stock of public images.[2] At the beginning of 1887 Rider Haggard published *She*, a gothic tale of a charismatic queen who seemed in every respect to be the exact opposite of the reigning English monarch. Just a few months before the image of Victoria was revived and extended during the Jubilee summer, it was universally considered to be the debased coin of the realm. To the extent that she now stood for anything, she seemed to represent a precapitalist form of exchange. In an 1884 history of signboards, the chapter dealing with the royal arms went so far as to stop its narrative at the beginning of the nineteenth century.[3]

In 1887, the year of Victoria's first Jubilee, the advertising business made an all-out effort to reclaim this moribund official figure for the greater glory of the commodity. All the institutions that had made the British empire the most powerful in the world gathered together at the foot of Victoria's throne to bask in their mutual prosperity. It was the biggest ball that England had ever seen, and all the participants came masked as Queen Victoria. The army dressed her as a warrior queen; the House of Lords as a diplomat queen; the Corporation of London as a citizen queen. Advertisers, too, masked their offerings with her image and created a consumer queen. In doing so they further consolidated the commodity spectacle that had been modeled by the Great Exhibition of 1851 and, for the first time, extended it in its entirety into the realm of advertising. The Jubilee was celebrated around the world, and everywhere it was celebrated, it gave commodities a strong sense of national and international purpose. At the height of the Jubilee summer, commodities were again rooted in the sense of being near the heart of things, of being caught up in the progress of people and institutions that dominated Victorian society. For many years afterwards the Jubilee exerted a pervasive influence on English advertising because it had made it possible for commodities to speak with more, and broader, authority than ever before.

The broad charismatic authority with which the Jubilee vested Victoria had two distinct components, each of which contributed materially to the resulting spectacle of advertisement. As vibrant and unexpected as it seemed at the time, the spectacle of Jubilee did not just erupt out of nowhere. It took hold because it created a staging ground capable of uniting two very different conceptions of authority that had long shared a common space of representation in Victorian England. At one and the same time Victoria was both the reigning monarch—a temperamental Hanoverian with an absolutist personality—and the presence presiding over the largest bureaucracy the world had ever seen. From the time of the Great Exhibition the Queen's name had been invoked to sanction collective undertakings for which she was not actually in the least responsible. Eleven years before the Jubilee Disraeli had proclaimed Victoria Empress of India, sovereign monarch of a civil service. This new image of Victoria Imperatrix embodied authority from above (in the body of the sovereign) even as it advanced authority from below (in the name of various institutions). As we shall see, Max Weber would later incorporate this dual authority in his concept of "charisma," and this chapter argues that the Jubilee taught advertising a lasting way of exploiting this dual authority on behalf of the commodity. In Jubilee advertising, things took on a very strange sort of charisma—partly immaterial, partly material. The result was a spectacle of the widest scope embodied in the narrow compass of what can only be called kitsch.

I

So orderly was the procession on the June day in 1887 when seventeen princes joined the official celebration of Victoria's Jubilee—fifty years as queen—that the English public, taken by surprise, could hardly believe its eyes. Ten state carriages, each drawn by six cream-colored horses, preceded Victoria's carriage and carried some of her close relations: Battenbergs, Bernadottes, Bourbons, Bourbon-Parmas, Braganzas, Coburgs, Glucksburgs, Hapsburgs, Hesses, Hohenzollerns, Mecklenburg-Strelitzes, Romanoffs, Savoys, and Wittelsbachs. The princes followed, riding three abreast in full dress uniform in front of the Queen's carriage. A troop of the First Life Guards brought up the rear of the procession, which began at Buckingham Palace and ended with a thanksgiving service at Westminster Abbey. Together they followed a carefully planned route through the affluent West End of London, where the municipal authorities had decked the roadways with festoons and flags, wreathed the lampposts with garlands, and adorned house fronts and shop windows with red cloth and legends in crimson letters (Fig. 10). At the Abbey an expertly drilled choir sang a "Te Deum" as the Queen, dressed in black satin with a white bonnet and the broad blue ribbon of the Garter, slowly walked through the nave to the dais. The total effect of this brief spectacle, the first of many processions, jamborees, reviews, gun salutes, bell ringings, dinners, tableaux, and toasts, exceeded all expectation (which had not been high). The *Illustrated London News* spoke for the nation when it called the events of the first day of Jubilee "the grandest State ceremony of this generation; one, indeed, practically unique in the annals of modern England." [4]

This was no exaggeration. Prior to 1887 most of Victoria's ceremonial appearances had been completely unrehearsed. At her coronation in 1837 the clergy lost their place in the order of service while attendants talked through the ceremony. At the wed-

THE QUEEN'S JUBILEE THANKSGIVING FESTIVAL IN LONDON, TUESDAY, JUNE 21.

THE ROYAL PROCESSION IN REGENT-STREET.

FIG. 10. The Jubilee Day procession of June 21, 1887 (*Illustrated London News*, June 25, 1887).

ding of the Prince of Wales in 1863 commentators noted "the poor taste of the decorations, the absence of outriders, and the extraordinary shabbiness of the royal equipages."[5] After Albert's death in 1861 Victoria became a virtual recluse, with the result that whatever royal ceremonies continued to be conducted *in absentia* became shabbier still. The invocation of the queen at the opening of Parliament degenerated into a mumbled litany. By 1871 Walter Bagehot could write that "there has never been a moment when what we may call the *showy* parts of the Constitution have been in less general favour than they are now."[6] When Victoria made a rare appearance to open Parliament in January 1886, reporters remarked on the "old-fashioned paraphernalia" of the six-carriage procession and regretted that it "was spoilt by the damp and the drizzling sleet."[7] In the weeks before the big day in 1887, the London periodical press was full of speculation that the Jubilee, like all of Victoria's previous public appearances, would be less than satisfying. The political cartoonists of the day showed the British lion rigged out and brushed up as a poodle. *Punch* ran a bit of doggerel called "Preparing for the Jubilee" that warned its readers to brace themselves for "this huge anniversary rout." The *Times* helped to sour expectation by complaining about the planned route, remarking that the procession "must pass along the narrow roadway of Parliament-street. This mean street, flanked by grimy and ignoble buildings, has always been considered unworthy of its surroundings, and is practically incapable of decoration."[8] Victoria herself was so apprehensive that it took several months for her inner circle to convince her to participate in ceremonies that reflected so little of the melancholy cast of mind that had caused her to be nicknamed the "Widow of Windsor." "The day has come," goes her first recorded remark on Jubilee Day, "and I am alone."[9] Nevertheless, she did her best to play the part, wearing dresses she found bulky and stifling, packing her social calendar to the breaking point, officiating over galas she found sadly evocative of happier days with Albert, and confessing astonishment to her diary when the crowds displayed an enthusiasm that she had in no way incited. In all, it is hard to imagine a less charismatic center of attention.

Though the Jubilee organizers did their best to supply Victoria with some charisma of their own devising, they were never able to confer on her the sacred aura of sovereign power that they really desired. Well before the long procession wound its way through the streets of London, preparations had been underway in the Office of Works to insure that the Jubilee would come off like clockwork. A chorus of three hundred voices from the best choirs in England was selected and trained; the officiating clergy rebuilt the Abbey's organ and revived elaborate vestments; the order of procession for Jubilee Day was arrived at and made public weeks ahead of time.[10] At the center of serried ranks of retainers, attended by ladies-in-waiting and maids of honor, escorted by plumed guards and turbaned lancers, Victoria was supposed to complete the effect by regarding events around her with a remote patrician calm. Instead she was nervous and fidgety, prompting observers in the crowd to call her "an old body like ourselves" and "a little old lady coming to church."[11] To the further chagrin of her relatives she had opted to wear, not the long robes of state, but a simple black satin dress. In such attire she could only appear all too human in the public eye, a point reflected in George Gissing's *In the Year of Jubilee* (1894), when Lionel Tarrant, a critic of Jubilee, refers to "the colour of the queen's bonnet, and of her parasol" as if he were discussing the wardrobe of any common matron.[12] All the pomp and circumstance in the Empire could do nothing to conceal the fact that Victoria was a domesticated monarch whose public image resided not in the trappings of the upper class but in the middle-class ethos of frugality, self-denial, hard work, and civic responsibility. For all the attention lavished on her, she continued to lack charisma as expressed in Weber's words, that "certain quality of an individual personality by virtue of which he is set apart from ordinary men and treated as endowed with supernatural, superhuman, or at least specifically exceptional powers or qualities."[13]

Weber's concept of charisma enables us to bring the Jubilee into sharper focus. For by no means did Weber restrict his definition of charisma to the glamour of a single personality. Though most charismatic figures do provide a cultural focal point around which an ideology (here, the middle-class work ethic) is defined and legitimated symbolically, Weber emphasized that they could serve other functions as well. In recent years sociologists and anthropologists have called attention to another dimension in Weber's concept of charisma by stressing, in Clifford Geertz's words, "the connection between the symbolic value individuals possess and their relation to the active centers of the social order." These centers consist "in the point or points in a society where its leading ideas come together with its leading institutions to create an arena in which the events that most vitally affect its members' lives take place."[14] In other words, Victoria did not have to be inherently charismatic to exercise a kind of acquired charisma by becoming a semiotic lodestone for events that occurred around her and conferred charisma on her. Like the exhibits in the Crystal Palace, many of the Jubilee's leading events were designed primarily to show how smoothly Victorian institutions functioned, and though they were held in Victoria's name, they had little or nothing to do with her. The "Children's Jubilee" marshaled the organizational energies of the school boards, who divided twenty-six thousand school-children into six brigades and directed them in three columns to Hyde Park, where each child received a bun, an orange, and a Jubilee mug. Salvation armies of all denominations put on dinners for the poor in iron-transomed auditoriums as spacious as model prisons. There were even special spectator sports, boxing matches staged in outdoor amphitheaters to make them easier to police.[15] The more recent the institution, the more it relied on the Jubilee to justify its existence. On Jubilee Day the House of Lords played their immemorial role to the hilt, just as they had done at the celebration of George III's Jubilee in 1809; but it was the events sponsored by the great Victorian bureaucracies of education, philanthropy, sport, and commerce that made the Jubilee what it was.

The acquired charisma that Victoria took on during the Jubilee did not simply create a new Victoria out of thin air. Rather it fashioned a new image out of the debris of her old one. The Jubilee organizers were perturbed that they could not persuade Victoria to discard her black mourning dress and wear a bright new costume, but they need not have been. Jubilee events took on added strength from the fact that their focal point had an otherworldly appearance. Queen Victoria may not have manifested the inherent charisma we most readily associate with Weber's concept, but she relied on many of the same symbolic strategies to suggest what Weber called a "personal experience of heavenly grace," a grace that emanated from her dead husband. Victoria was not what Weber called "a God-willed master,"[16] but for over twenty-five years she had been devoted to one. Since Albert's death she had superintended the cult of the dead Prince Consort, a cult that far exceeded typical nineteenth-century mourning practice and for which she was the chief priest and intermediary. As a permanent mourner Victoria was not a charismatic hero but a charismatic-hero-worshipper along the lines of Carlyle's *On Heroes, Hero-Worship, and the Heroic in History*, which promulgated the doctrine that "Worship of a Hero is transcendent admiration of a Great Man. . . . No nobler feeling than this of admiration for one higher than himself dwells in the breast of man." [17] Victoria's admiration for her dead husband, however, did not merely take the form of "transcendent admiration" prescribed by Carlyle. She was determined to fill the material world with the tokens of transcendent admiration. First she appointed herself interior decorator of his tomb. Then she commissioned others to erect cenotaphs, shrines, commemoratives of all sorts. The members of her household had to keep up his rooms and lay out his possessions as if he were still alive. The queen made it clear to everyone that she subscribed to the popular view that imagined the immaterial world of heaven in the most material terms possible. She surrounded herself with people who shared the same views, and a few years after Albert's death her attending chaplain, Norman McLeod, contributed a paper called "Social Life in Heaven" to a collection entitled *The Recognition of Friends in Heaven* (1866). [18]

The showy modern monarchy had, in fact, been quietly in the making during these years of retirement. Back in 1872 Walter Bagehot had observed how a "middle-aged lady is about to drive, with a few little-known attendants, through part of London, to return thanks for the recovery of her eldest son from fever, and the drive has assumed the proportions of a national event." Bagehot captures the moment when a very old idea took on modern dress. For the past ten years he had been carrying on a crusade against republicans who had argued that the monarchy was not worth the annual price of four hundred thousand pounds from the exchequer. Against these claims that the reigning monarch was nothing more than a very spendthrift private citizen, Bagehot summoned up the people who "regard the sovereign as something separate, and as it were, awful; as the most national thing in the nation; as a person not only entirely above themselves, but possessed of powers and rights which they do not give; as an ultimate authority which never changes, never passes away, and never can be overcome." [19] The being Bagehot describes possesses more than acquired charisma. She has an inherent charisma that connects her not only with the nation at large but with another realm: the old fiction of the king's (or queen's) two bodies, according to which the monarch has a material body, limited in scope and subject to decay, and an immaterial body, limitless, changeless, and ethereal.

The fiction of the queen's two bodies can best be described as an early way of distinguishing between inherent and acquired charisma. The queen's material body consists of the significance she had acquired as a living member of the material world; her immaterial body consists of the significance she had inherited and so possessed inherently by virtue of being queen. In his classic study *The King's Two Bodies* (1957) Ernst Kantorowicz makes it clear that the two bodies provided "an important heuristic fiction which served . . . to bring into agreement the personal with the more impersonal concepts of government."[20] The interesting feature of the queen's two bodies as a nineteenth-century fiction, however, was the subordination of Victoria's immaterial to her material body. The two did not exist in agreement, as they once had hundreds of years before; now Victoria's immaterial body existed primarily to heighten and accentuate her material existence. Even her staunchest advocates conceded that her immaterial body carried little political weight. Bagehot articulated a wide consensus when he wrote that "actual power must reside in a committee of great officers elected by the representatives of the people . . . whilst formal power must rest with a great personage."[21] When it came right down to it, the balance tipped toward Victoria's material body—toward her acquired charisma rather than her inherited or inherent charisma. Victorian observers may have detected an element of the immaterial in their queen, but by the 1887 Jubilee, as we shall see, what they primarily saw in her was a heightened manifestation of materiality that can be called a *transcendent materiality*.

The Jubilee succeeded not only in reviving the monarchy but in taking it in a new and recognizably modern direction. The basic argument of this chapter is that the Jubilee used traditional intimations of the immateriality of royal power to confer a vast and often uncontrollable significance on the material world. The Jubilee advanced a mediumistic vision of things according to which the material world became a vehicle for occult forces which were thought to stand outside of it. This peculiar vision of the

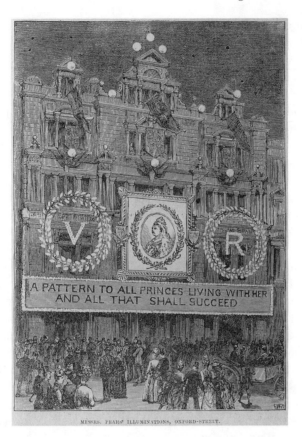

FIG. 11. The Pears' illuminations (*Illustrated London News*, July 2, 1887).

transcendental life of objects—a vision in which objects seem, like the queen, to have two bodies—provided the template for one of the largest spectacles of commodity culture in the nineteenth century (Fig. 11). Commodity culture put Victoria's two bodies to work in a variety of ways as insignia, souvenirs, and icons. Though there was much in commodity culture that would not have been sanctioned by the Jubilee organizers or recounted reverently in the *Illustrated London News*, the commodity culture of the Jubilee closely replicated the twin-bodied charisma that made the event truly unprecedented. What began with the limited charisma of a single personality ended with the limitless cha-

risma of a thousand manufactured objects as the Jubilee image
of Victoria sought and found coordinated representation in an
extraordinary array of commodities at once material and immaterial—commodities whose various attributes came to embody
what we now call kitsch.

In a limited way commodity culture had long experimented
with the drawing power of charisma. In 1843, for instance, the
Edinburgh Review discovered that Mr. Cockle's Antibilious Pills
were recommended by, among others, ten dukes, five mar-
quesses, seventeen earls, eight viscounts, sixteen lords, one
archbishop, fifteen bishops, the adjutant-general, and the advo-
cate-general.[22] The irony of these advertisements was that most
of these figures were comparatively unknown before they appeared in the advertising columns and that the ones conferring
celebrity were not the "celebrities" but the people publicizing
them. In any case these early advertisers rarely rested their attention long enough on any one celebrity for the public to develop a sense of that celebrity apart from his or her status as the
endorser of a given product. Advertisers had discovered their
own power to invent certain kinds of personalities and confer a
limited kind of charisma on them, but they were not yet able to
address, let alone appropriate, known celebrities who possessed
an acknowledged charisma by virtue of their high social status.
In *The Language of the Walls* (1855) James Dawson Burn has a
chapter on "Theatrical and Clerical 'Stars'" in which he notes
how "these bright orbs generally possess an amazing power of
attraction, particularly as regards drawing money out of the
pockets of the people." As examples he mentions Jenny Lind
and Tom Thumb. Burn thinks that the celebrity of these personalities is a form of self-advertisement but not a form of advertisement proper. He considers them little better than "quacks" and
"mountebanks" and does not see how their celebrity could possibly benefit anyone other than themselves and "the coffers of
[their] managers."[23] Depending as it did on a limited economy of
self-representation and restricted as it was to the walls of London, this machinery of celebrity did not exude or embody charisma. It did not transform the image of a single self into a fungible ideological construction capable of traversing a wide arena

FIG. 12. A mid-Victorian purveyor to the queen (Smith, *Advertise*).

of social space. The stars of the mid-Victorian hoardings were celebrities who lacked not only the inherent charisma of a supernatural figure but also the acquired charisma that later made the Jubilee image of Victoria so powerful.

When advertisers made use of Victoria's image in the years before the Jubilee conferred an immense new charisma on her, they tended to treat her as one of these second-order celebrities. One historian has found that Victoria was included among a stock of images that nineteenth-century show promoters drew upon to construct and publicize their exhibits; another, that her image filtered into advertising soon after her coronation in 1837. Nevertheless, there was no general agreement among advertisers as to how to go about using her image. In one advertisement Victoria might appear as the butt of low comedy (Fig. 12); another ad might try to provide a glimpse into her private life; another still might draw on Victoria's coronation portraits to produce an image of unreachable magnificence.[24] All of these had much more in common with the petty commodity productions of eighteenth-century street vendors than with the carefully crafted industrial productions of twentieth-century advertising agencies. Inventive as they often were, mid-Victorian advertisers had not yet settled on a systematic way of representing celebrities so as to keep them before the public eye as long as possible. So ephemeral did the editors of the *Edinburgh Review* consider most advertisements that they devoted a portion of their 1843 article on "the advertising system" to remarking the rarity of "*standing* advertisements."[25] Even to most advertisers the image of Victoria offered at best a very restricted form of high visibility.

The rapid conglomeration of commodities around Victoria's Jubilee image made advertisers sit up and take notice. Nobody *planned* to use the queen's image to sell perfumes, powders, pills, lotions, soap, jewelry, and cocoa; most Victorian businesses were run by entrepreneurs too suspicious of one another to entrust their publicity to the nascent advertising agencies.[26] So during the Jubilee summer when hundreds of advertisers independently flooded the market with one of several forms of the image of Victoria, the result was striking and unexpected. Upon what was in fact a disorderly, far from integrated, and only minimally regulated glut of competing advertisements, the image of Victoria impressed a general categorical image. As often happened in the nineteenth century, the people who ran the new advertising agencies were the last to see what was actually happening. Luckworth Crewe, an advertising agent in Gissing's *In the Year of Jubilee*, shows how completely some advertisers misread the Jubilee. Like most of the characters in the novel, Crewe does not care for royalty; he calls them "expensive humbugs." Spectacle for its own sake he considers a waste. Though Crewe is bristling with schemes and rumors of schemes, known already as "Jubilee speculation," he does not participate actively in them. Rather he confesses to having just missed investing in "a really big thing,—a Jubilee drink,—a teetotal beverage; the kind of thing that would have sold itself." Undaunted, he goes on to confess his surprise that the Jubilee had fostered such an excellent commercial climate: "I didn't expect much from Jubilee Day . . . but that only shows how things turn out—always better or worse than you think for. I'm not likely to forget it."[27]

Crewe misreads the Jubilee because it depended on a sudden and unorchestrated social consensus, a consensus he neither foresees nor foreordains. He tends to view advertising as something imposed from the top down rather than improvised from the bottom up. Overall Crewe would have heartily agreed with advertiser Thomas Smith's 1886 statement that "like the Nasmyth steam hammer, advertising can be used with crushing, irresistible force," but he would have been blind to Smith's collateral and vastly more influential observation that "it can also be reduced to small and limited, though adequate, power." [28]

In adopting the Jubilee, many advertisers like Crewe came up with too little too late. But it is not hard to see why they kicked themselves for not having seen it coming. From day one the Jubilee offered them an opportunity to tailor their offerings to a popular event, much as they had been doing during the Christmas sales at the big London department stores. [29] Just as today fast-food restaurants cluster together in strips to promote mutual prosperity, it was an article of faith among late-nineteenth-century advertisers that all their offerings stood to benefit from these repeated liturgies of consumption. Moreover, the idea that an advertising campaign benefited from a consolidated imagery had already taken hold in the 1880's. Louis Collins's *Advertiser's Guardian* (1885) and the anonymous *An Advertiser's Guide to Publicity* (1887) both called for advertisers to concentrate on a single topical theme; both agreed on the value of illustrations, especially sharp and striking engravings; both admitted, in the words of the *Advertiser's Guide*, that the purpose of any ad was to appeal to the greatest "number of people who can be persuaded." [30] These advertisers believed that they needed to cast as wide a net as possible over a public that, in an emerging national market, remained largely unknown to them. To reach so many at once, advertisers knew that they had to search for a single common denominator that would offer them a way to extend their campaigns as a thin layer over all but the furthest reaches of the kingdom. The basic program of these practical guides—a program permanently impressed on advertising by the experience of the Jubilee—was simple: find an image so universal, so familiar, so fungible, that it would sell anything.

II

This movement toward a consolidated imagery of advertisement took the form of kitsch. Kitsch may be defined as elaborately aestheticized commodities produced in the name of large institutions (church, state, empire, monarchy) for middle-class home use. Kitsch is short-order charisma, charisma that has obviously been recently manufactured. In kitsch the world of the Great Exhibition (a world of great institutions capable of conferring charisma) has been shrunk to palm size: it is the miniature attempting to signify the gigantic by compressing the public sphere into the narrow compass of small objects designed for private consumption.

In late-nineteenth-century commodity culture all advertising aspired in some way to the condition of kitsch. In the late 1880's advertisers had just begun to experiment with sentimental kitsch (as in the Millais painting, "Bubbles," the rights to which Pears' Soap had purchased for a large sum) when the Jubilee came along and melded the typologies of sentimental, religious, and political kitsch (Fig. 13). The Millais painting prompted a debate about the "art" of advertising that raged for many years, and in due course the painting proved to be very influential. Later advertisements produced by the new advertising agencies were likely to be sentimental scenes that depicted a private moment and deemphasized the materiality of the commodity, as in this painting where the bar of soap had been added almost as an afterthought.[31] In stark contrast Jubilee kitsch saturated the space of advertisement with public significance; in a great variety of ads individual commodities appear so overburdened with significance that they seem in imminent danger of collapsing under the weight of their own materiality. In the Great Exhibition commodities had been grouped together to signify the social; in Jubilee kitsch the materiality of discrete objects signifies the social and then some. Queen Victoria was the great-grandmother not only of miniature Washington Monuments and piggy banks of the Statue of Liberty but of mosaics of the Mormon Tabernacle and honorific portraits of the eternal Elvis.[32] In *Illustrated London News, Graphic, Penny Illustrated Paper, Queen, Theatre Annual,*

FIG. 13. Sentimental kitsch (*Illustrated London News*, December 10, 1887).

Athenaeum, and *Punch,* a cosmic material culture came popping out of the very pores of print. By midsummer 1887 the Jubilee had transformed the reigning monarch into a cultural frame for a new spectacle of commodity culture, the spectacle of kitsch.

The word *kitsch* comes from the German word *kitschen,* "to put together sloppily."[33] A kitsch object has not been carefully crafted to instill a want or inculcate a need. It is an unfinished object improvised to meet an immediate, short-term demand. The new economy of rapid-fire consumption it represents can be usefully contrasted with the old economy of bricolage so prevalent in the years before and after the Great Exhibition of 1851. Recall that early Victorian advertisers were what Lévi-Strauss has called bricoleurs—adepts at making objects serve multiple purposes and masters of adapting old techniques to new uses. The essence of their method was conservation. Jubilee kitsch, however, was garbage-in-the-making. Whereas the techniques of bricolage were good for the *longue durée,* kitsch objects belonged to one moment and one moment only. Instant souvenirs, they passed immediately from the present into the past, figuring all time as potential nostalgia for what was past, passing, or about to pass. They signified, as Susan Stewart has written, "the constant self-periodization of popular culture," the determination that objects bear the weight of signifying different phases of collective identity.[34] Jubilee kitsch performed two distinct operations, as we shall see: it trivialized collective life by reducing it to a series of commodities that lacked any use value, and it collectivized trivia by making the commodity—the very entity that Marx once called "a trivial thing"—into a validated repository of historical memory.

Most definitions of kitsch see it as an utterly unsuccessful form of representation. For Matei Calinescu, kitsch "always implies the notion of *aesthetic inadequacy.*"[35] It would be more accurate, however, to see kitsch as an outmoded rather than an inadequate form of representation. The term entered English at the beginning of the twentieth century to describe the leftovers from nineteenth-century commodity culture. In a 1912 essay Roger Fry says that all bad taste shares "a large amount of futile display."[36] He goes on to catalog the exhibited contents of a typical

Victorian sitting room—stained glass, potted plants, "Greco-Roman" molding. Almost everything that Fry considers dates from the second half of the nineteenth century, the *locus classicus* of commodity exhibition. What needles Fry, however, is not the great exhibitions themselves but the tendency of the nineteenth-century bourgeoisie to put on more or less permanent mini-exhibitions in their homes. For these interiors produced to cater to the home use of the Victorian middle classes did not simply disappear after those tastes became unfashionable. Produced in greater numbers than ever before, numbers so great that they could not be ignored even once used, these commodities continued to merit a name and a position in the hierarchy of classification. The modern idea of "kitsch" came into being to designate the goods that had once played a prominent part in Victorian social life. In various guises our idea of kitsch comprises every article that was ever exhibited in the nineteenth century and signifies our determination that Victorian commodities are no longer capable of performing the cultural work they once did. When in *Lady Chatterley's Lover* (1928) Connie pulls a small Victorian medicine chest out of a lumber room junkheap, she finds its detail and workmanship incomprehensible.[37] Because the voluptuous taste of the bourgeoisie seems to us to be a compendium of the weakest features of nineteenth-century life, we have forgotten how powerfully it once figured in the Victorian material imagination. In the 1860's and 1870's kitsch began as a simple descriptive term for the products of a fully modern mode of commodity manufacture, and that is how it will be used here. Far from being trivial things, the varieties of kitsch constructed a complex representation of the material spaces which the nineteenth-century bourgeoisie charged with a heavy burden of significance. Though Jubilee advertisers certainly did not invent kitsch—by definition, the whole world they lived in was destined later to become kitsch—they helped to demarcate one of its most lasting icons, Victoria, the consumer queen.

In 1887 three related kinds of kitsch flooded the market with the image of Victoria: insignia, souvenirs, and icons. The last developed out of the first two, and it alone took on charisma and became a major trope of advertising.

As an insignia the image of Victoria had long been public property. The arms and profile of Victoria combined the emblems of rank, office, membership, and nationality and appeared prominently on mail boxes, postage stamps, newspaper mastheads, and against the dark brown paint of government offices. These were seals of approval in a world where the authority of the English crown offered something like a guarantee of quality. The genius of Jubilee kitsch was that it extended this guarantee to encompass objects representing all aspects of everyday life. Entrepreneurs stenciled emblems, etched mottoes, and embroidered patches on banners, samplers, rugs, plates, cups, spoons, terra-cotta, bookmarks, toys, games, dolls, jump-rope handles, medals, bracelets, brooches, trinket boxes, and scent bottles. A few pence would buy a Jubilee balloon from Cremer's on Regent Street. "JOHN BULL, a real jubilee game" went for a shilling. For five shillings Percy and Company offered the "Jubilee Bangles," a charm bracelet with facsimiles of every coin issued during Victoria's reign. Three pounds bought a gold enameled Jubilee brooch, encrusted with a miniature likeness of the queen, from the Goldsmiths' and Silversmiths' Company of Clerkenwell. A real aficionado could, for fifteen pounds, commission a Jubilee portrait cut in onyx from W. Schmidt of Hatton Garden. One advertiser in the *Times* offered to convert "a splendid variety of good things"—meaning almost anything—into Jubilee kitsch.[38] Together these insignia seemed to promise a familiar world wherever one went, a world created by manufacturers, populated with commodities, and depicted in the idiom of the brand name. As an insignia of Jubilee the crown appeared to be less a political institution than a vast benign commissary dispensing the English way of life.

The idea of "insignia," however, took on an extra meaning in the nineteenth century, and this points to the role the Jubilee played in establishing an imaginary meeting ground between public and private life in the late nineteenth century. Early in the century the word went from denoting a badge of rank to connoting a distinguishing sign inscribed on an individual, as when a grieving person was said to be displaying "the insignia of sorrow." An insignia could now summon up the extremities of both

The "JUBILEE" SCENT BOTTLE.

May be purchased throughout the Empire.
Wholesale only of
S. MORDAN & CO., LONDON.

FIG. 14. The Jubilee scent bottle (*Graphic*, March 5, 1887).

public and private life. This union of extremes can be seen in S. Mordan and Company's Jubilee Scent Bottle (Fig. 14), a rounded bottle molded with the profile of the young Queen Victoria and topped with a screw-top crown. Nothing could be more public than this container, with its crown and profile, and nothing more private than what it contains, perfume to be applied to the human body. Yet as far apart as container and contents appear to be, they have come together as one and the same object. In a very real sense the bottle elides the relation between public and private domains with the relation between the container and the thing contained. The key point here is that as an article of kitsch, the bottle brings together the public and private realms that nineteenth-century people had such a hard time reconciling in theory or in practice. The bottle arrives at the status of kitsch because it places a manufactured object at the unlikely intersection of the vast heraldry of the crown (a public insignia) and the small procedures circumscribing the care of the self (a private insignia). At the impossible but frequently imagined point of juncture between public and private insignias in the nineteenth century, we almost always find the signs of commodity kitsch.

In the second kind of Jubilee kitsch, souvenirs, the commodity comes very close to buckling under the weight of the significance attributed to it. A souvenir is an insignia that has been made to bear the weight of history. Souvenirs had been much in evidence at the Great Exhibition, which had celebrated the labor theory of value by expending large amounts of labor to produce catalogues (including one four volumes long) commemorating itself. The first Jubilee souvenirs were also publicly produced and appeared early in 1887, when foundation stones for Jubilee statues of the queen were being laid at the rate of one a week; by spring the country was littered with them. These statues caused great stirs wherever they were planned, in Worcester, in Windsor, in London; newspapers everywhere carried proposed designs of elaborate monuments, domed, pedimented, turreted, colonnaded, ornamented with urns and friezes and ceremonial staircases.[39] These ponderous monuments were full of doors that did not open, staircases that led nowhere; though they often looked like palaces, they were designed to be uninhabited; like many articles on display in the Crystal Palace, they were great big gadgets. Jubilee souvenirs were miniature versions of this monumental public gadgetry, and though they were sold everywhere, they attached themselves to locations and experiences that were not for sale.[40] Like the commodities in the Crystal Palace, which seemed all the more valuable because they did not have price tags stuck on them, Jubilee souvenirs also depended upon the fiction that they existed outside the cash nexus. Most Jubilee souvenirs did this by moving history into the private time of childhood, and the most heavily advertised souvenirs were scaled-down plates, cups, glasses, spoons—indeed, the most widely reported event of Jubilee came when Victoria presented a schoolgirl with a Jubilee mug. The problem for advertisers was that because these souvenirs were so small, they tended to figure history as an illegible spiral of events. The spokes on the wheel separating events on a Jubilee plate make the events it depicts downright circular in motion.[41] Destined to be forgotten, or at least soon to occupy a position on the margin of materiality as a piece of junk, the souvenir comes very close to being either unreadable (as with the four-volume Exhibition *Catalogue*) or illegible (as with most Jubilee souvenirs). Lacking a Crystal Palace to confer significance on them, Jubilee souvenirs by themselves take on the impossible task of narrating the events of Victoria's reign in the compass of a ten-inch plate, and the result is the amnesia of the commemorative.

Of all the forms of Jubilee kitsch, by far the most influential for future advertising was the icon. Jubilee insignia and souvenirs were limited by the very materiality of the articles themselves; they were restricted to the life span of an object, and though that span might be extended or revived, it could not traverse as wide a field of social practice as the iconography of the consumer queen. In essence, as we have observed, Jubilee iconography was a revival of a very old idea, that the reigning monarch has two bodies—one material, the other immaterial, the one advancing authority from below and the other embodying it from above. Weber's concept of charisma essentially modernized this very old idea, and so did the icons of Jubilee kitsch. Jubilee insignia and souvenirs had searched unsuccessfully for common ground to connect the public and private extremities of Victorian life; the Jubilee icons found it. Today the quintessential icons of kitsch are pulsating neon baby Jesuses and electric crèches. The icons of Jubilee kitsch took a decisive step in the direction of religious kitsch by locating that point of juncture between private and public existence at the intersection of the material and ethereal bodies of the monarch. The Great Exhibition had stocked a public universe with public objects. The Jubilee icons fused an intensely private material world with a universal public one, and the result was a durable and recognizably modern spectacle, the spectacle of the consumer queen.

The medium through which the consumer queen made her

most widely advertised appearance was, suitably enough, artificial black velvet. Black velvet was an immaterial material: not only was it widely used as upholstery in the everyday bourgeois interior, but it was also the required color of mourning dress and the universal appurtenance of cultic funerary practice.[42] If nothing else, Jubilee Day offered spectators a staggering display of velvet: corporation members in gowns of mazarine blue, archbishops in copes of purple, peers in uniforms of scarlet, princesses and countesses in gray, the Abbey itself in crimson and indigo. But it was Victoria's own personal preference for black velvet that inspired Jubilee velvet advertising. In some of these advertisements there appears to be nothing regal, numinous, or ethereal about Queen Victoria. One shows her receiving a gift of flowers from an obeisant subject (Fig. 15). Clad in her trademark black satin dress with white bonnet, Victoria stands off to one side, upstaged. At center, her back facing us, a lady bows deeply, herself upstaged by the lush folds of velveteen draped across the lower half of the advertisement. This ad reverses the usual relation of high fashion: whereas in fashion designer-originals usually set the standard for a large number of imitations, here the imitation overwhelms the original. Victoria is shown sidelined by an imitation of a dress she actually wore during the Jubilee ceremonies. For all the splendor it purports to depict, then, this ad actually places the queen in the position of an ordinary consumer admiring an imitation purchased at a place like the "Jubilee Fashion Club" Luckworth Crewe establishes in *In the Year of Jubilee*. It weighs her down with materiality and makes her look like a pale imitation of an imitation. As a consumer queen she is at best a figurehead for fabric, which in this ad comes very close to consuming her.

When we look more closely at the Jubilee velvet ads, however, we find that their materiality is replete with signs of transcendence. The "Louis" Velveteen ad avoids inscribing fashion directly on the queen's body. Unlike modern advertisements showing celebrities actually wearing the clothes they are endorsing, the queen consents to the product without actually trying it on. Though other Jubilee ads also surround Victoria with material objects, they too never attempt to inscribe them on her body.

THE
"LOUIS" VELVETEEN.

The strictest examiner may try every test of touch and sight without discovering that these are other than the Genoa Velvets they so closely resemble, while the peculiar arrangements resulting in the Fast-woven Pile enable them to stand interminable wear that would ruin real velvets at four times the price.

Special attention is drawn to the colours, which for brilliancy, depth of tone, and magnificent appearance are quite perfection.

Note well! The word "Louis" in connection with this Velveteen, is spelled "L-O-U-I-S," and in no other way.

Every yard of the genuine bears the name "Louis," and the wear of every yard, from the cheapest quality to the best, guaranteed.

MAY BE HAD FROM DRAPERS THROUGHOUT THE KINGDOM.

FIG. 15. The consumer queen's material body (*Illustrated London News,* April 23, 1887).

Even in the midst of commodities the consumer queen retains an element of transcendence (invariably she wears the widow's outfit identifying her as the chief priestess of the Albert cult). She appears as the final arbiter of the choices consumers make in an ad for "My Queen" Vel-Vel in an August number of the *Graphic* (Fig. 16). Here she sits in judgment, a lady-in-waiting at either side, as a saleswoman kneels before her unrolling a bolt of heavy fabric from a box labeled "My Queen" Vel-Vel. The scene is crammed with all the weighty clutter of a high Victorian household, much of which had found its way into the Great Exhibition of 1851—an overstuffed chair and pillow, a wooden screen carved with festoons, lace curtains, a potted palm, a timepiece with cupids, and an end table with a basket of flowers. Victoria's attendants fix their attention on the long ribbon of artificial velvet;

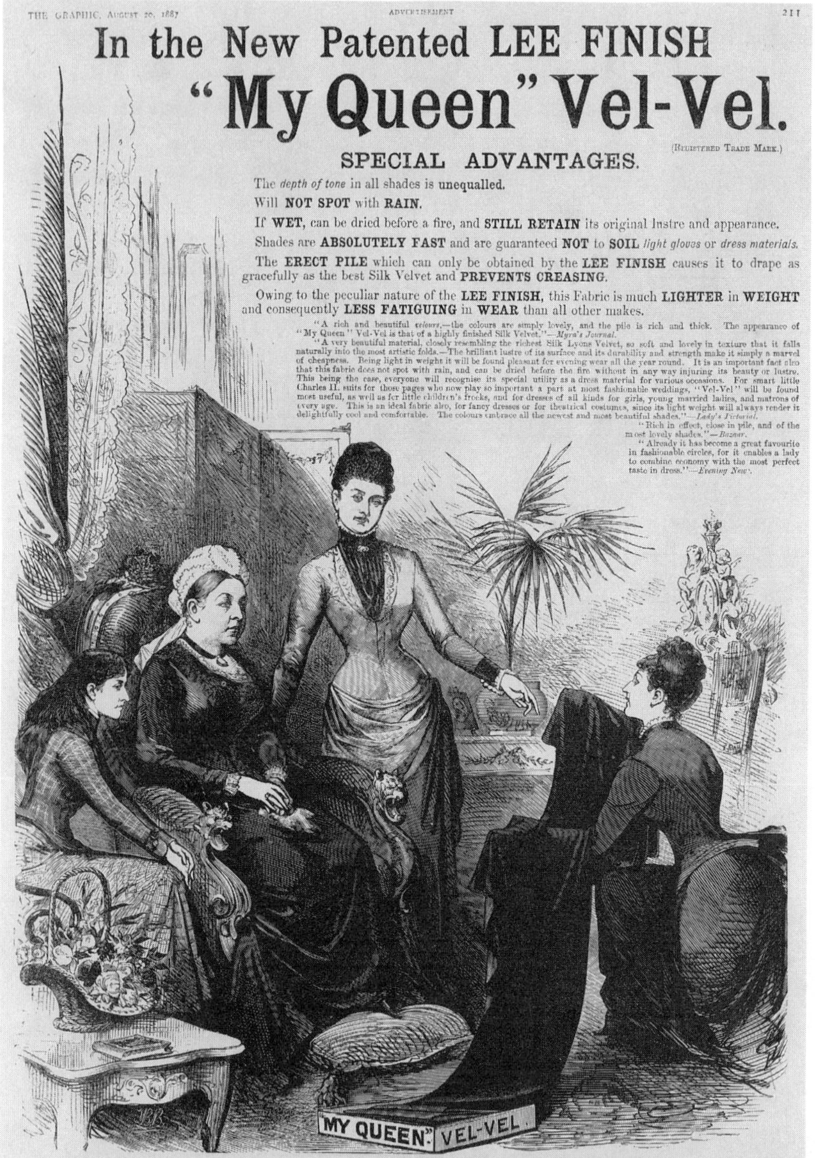

In the New Patented LEE FINISH
"My Queen" Vel-Vel.

(REGISTERED TRADE MARK.)

SPECIAL ADVANTAGES.

The *depth of tone* in all shades is **unequalled**.

Will **NOT SPOT** with **RAIN**.

If **WET**, can be dried before a fire, and **STILL RETAIN** its original lustre and appearance.

Shades are **ABSOLUTELY FAST** and are guaranteed **NOT** to **SOIL** *light gloves or dress materials*.

The **ERECT PILE** which can only be obtained by the **LEE FINISH** causes it to drape as gracefully as the best Silk Velvet and **PREVENTS CREASING**.

Owing to the peculiar nature of the **LEE FINISH**, this Fabric is much **LIGHTER** in **WEIGHT** and consequently **LESS FATIGUING** in **WEAR** than all other makes.

"A rich and beautiful *colours*,—the colours are simply lovely, and the pile is rich and thick. The appearance of "My Queen" Vel-Vel is that of a highly finished Silk Velvet."—*Myra's Journal*.

"A very beautiful material, closely resembling the richest Silk Lyons Velvet, so soft and lovely in texture that it falls naturally into the most artistic folds.—The brilliant lustre of its surface and its durability and strength make it simply a marvel of cheapness. Being light in weight it will be found pleasant for evening wear all the year round. It is an important fact also that this fabric does not spot with rain, and can be dried before the fire without in any way injuring its beauty or lustre. This being the case, everyone will recognise its special utility as a dress material for various occasions. For smart little Charles II. suits for those pages who now play so important a part at most fashionable weddings, "Vel-Vel" will be found most useful, as well as for little children's frocks, and for dresses of all kinds for girls, young married ladies, and matrons of every age. This is an ideal fabric also, for fancy dresses or for theatrical costumes, since its light weight will always render it delightfully cool and comfortable. The colours embrace all the newest and most beautiful shades."—*Lady's Pictorial*.

"Rich in effect, close in pile, and of the most lovely shades."—*Bazaar*.

"Already it has become a great favourite in fashionable circles, for it enables a lady to combine economy with the most perfect taste in dress."—*Evening News*.

MY QUEEN" VEL-VEL

In the new "LEE" FINISH, the Patentees have most successfully overcome the drawbacks common to all makes of Velveteen and Cotton Pile Fabrics finished by the ordinary process, producing at a much lower cost, and bringing within the reach of all purses, the beautiful fabric "MY QUEEN" VEL-VEL, which has been pronounced by connoisseurs to be equal in appearance to and wear better than the best Lyons Silk Velvet. The Wear of every yard is guaranteed, and for the protection of the public every yard is stamped with the registered Trade Mark, "MY QUEEN" VEL-VEL. "MY QUEEN" VEL-VEL can be obtained from all the best Drapers throughout the United Kingdom, from 1s. 6d. to 5s. 6d. per yard.
Sole Proprietors: FELSTEAD & HUNT, 41, St. Paul's Churchyard, LONDON. and 9, Fountain Street, MANCHESTER.

FIG. 16. The consumer queen's ethereal body (*Graphic*, August 20, 1887).

one of them, standing, indicates the queen's preference with a slight motion of her left hand (even as a consumer Victoria speaks by proxy). Victoria appears to be in a trance, her gaze trained at some distant object, her face and mind blank as she sits in state. Describing how Disraeli inspired in Victoria "a portentousness almost ridiculously out of keeping with the rest of her make-up," Lytton Strachey conjures up the awesome materiality of the consumer queen that we see here: "Her very demeanour altered. Her short, stout figure, with its folds of black velvet, its muslin streamers, its heavy pearls at the heavy neck, assumed an almost menacing air."[43]

In this advertisement, as in Strachey's description, the materiality of the bourgeois interior has been transfigured by the presence of the consumer queen's two bodies, to return to Kantorowicz's conception: the phenomenal body of the reigning monarch and the numinal body that partook of the animating spirit of kingship. The two velveteen ads form a kind of diptych showing the consumer queen's two bodies at work. In the first, Victoria's material body appears in the ascendant as she manifests the acquired charisma conferred on her by the Jubilee events; in the second, her immaterial body etherealizes everything surrounding it as she manifests the kind of inherent charisma that people once thought went hand in hand with the immaterial component of queenship. In the first, Victoria has been upstaged by the splendor of manufacture, much as she had been when she toured the Crystal Palace back in 1851. In the second, Victoria is a kind of one-woman Crystal Palace: she elevates the commodities that surround her into a space of representation in which many of the tropes formerly used to structure the ritual display of religious emotion have been redeployed to summon up the transcendental stimulus of the material world. In Victorian culture at large these tropes of transcendence frequently appear where one least expects them—even in the work of Karl Marx, where the many metaphors of transcendence that tear the commodity fetishism chapter of *Capital* to the breaking point bear striking and complementary witness to what can be called a reification of transcendence, or an embodiment of transcendental signification in the dead matter of material culture.

Such transcendent spaces of materiality were common at the Victorian court, particularly in the years after Albert's death, and they drew upon certain typologies common in sentimental religious culture. A well-known 1862 photograph of the Blue Room in Windsor Castle (Fig. 17) shows the room in which Albert died. Here the sentimental fascination with transcendence goes hand in hand with the sentimental fascination with the transcendental life of dead matter. The paraphernalia of death, however, do a lot more than preserve Albert's memory by objectifying it monumentally. Like the Victorian cemetery, such paraphernalia construct an objectified site of contact with another realm. The Blue Room is not only a monument to Albert's memory but an altar to Albert's living presence as enshrined in things. Albert's material body may be dead, but his immaterial presence lives on in this tableau, which places the twin-bodied charisma of kitsch at the still center of sentimental culture. The basic structure of kitsch, then, had long been built into the glum world of Victoria's court. Long before the Jubilee her court was an open-air mausoleum that inspired and articulated devotion to things using the means and methods of the sentimental valuation of the dead. Jubilee advertisers did not have to look very far to find models upon which to base their icons. Victoria's own fixation on Albert's memory had effectively transformed any material sign of that memory into a breviary of kitsch, a regular program of devotions that the *Times* once called "a sort of religion."[44]

The peculiarly sentimental admixture of material and immaterial bodies can be seen a bit more clearly in the way Jubilee advertising addressed women. All forms of Jubilee kitsch associated Victoria's image with common domestic articles largely used by women. In many ads she performs the services of housework and shopping: for Sapolio she appears as a domestic servant who shines the crown jewels as the midnight oil burns;[45] and for "My Queen" Vel-Vel she appears engrossed in buying a fabric ideal for, as the caption promises, "little children's frocks, and for dresses of all kinds for girls, young married ladies, and matrons of every age." As advertisers evidently recognized, the image of a domesticated consumer queen possessed a special appeal for women consumers. For though shopping had long

FIG. 17. The Blue Room at Windsor (Royal Collection, Windsor Castle).

been a principal domestic activity for middle- and upper-class women, it had yet to be elevated to the sacred status of their other occupations, notably homemaking and motherhood. Indeed the Angel of the House was likely to become a demon the moment she set foot in a department store: an illustration from Anthony Trollope's novel about the department store trade, *The Struggles of Brown, Jones, and Robinson* (1870), depicts consumption as hysteria as two women customers vent their anger on a male sales clerk who has just told them that the store has run out of a sale item (Fig. 18).[46] In contrast to this all-too-familiar topos of a mob of semihysterical women tearing apart the very merchandise they have come to buy, the image of the consumer queen conferred an enormous and immobile calm on the hustle and bustle of department store shopping. For "My Queen" Vel-Vel, Victoria sits in a strictly formal pose, silent while all around her attendants labor in her service. The queen's ethereal body

FIG. 18. Consumption as hysteria (Trollope, *Brown, Jones, and Robinson*).

has been mobilized here to make shopping into something more than a material activity. Her transcendent presence both legitimated consumption for women by offering them the queen's stamp of approval and lured even more women into department stores by leading them to believe that there they, too, would be treated like royalty.

The paradigmatic status of the consumer queen's body for female consumers can also be seen in some of the conventions of the central organ of sentimental culture, the domestic novel. In *The English Constitution* (1867) Walter Bagehot makes it clear that he regards the Victorian court as a sort of domestic novel aimed at female consumers: "A *family* on the throne is an interesting idea also. No feeling could seem more childish than the enthusiasm of the English at the marriage of the Prince of Wales. . . . The women—one half the human race at least—care fifty times more for a marriage than a ministry. All but a few cynics like to see a pretty novel touching for a moment the dry scenes of the grave world."[47] Like the Victorian court, the domestic novel legitimated female consumption by advancing and exploiting exactly the same tension between the material and immaterial components of commodity culture. Middle- and upper-class women had long been avid consumers of the domestic novel, a genre that embodied the very sense of material security and transcendent benevolence that the queen's two bodies so prodigiously enshrined. Novels like Maria Cummins's *The Lamplighter* (1854) and Mary Jane Holmes's *Tempest and Sunshine* (1854) offered exactly the mixture of "peace and security" that Victoria herself, in one of her letters, mentions craving in the years following Albert's death. Though intimations of an eternal peace spread through these books like incense, evidence of material security is ever-present. In a preface to Cummins's novel, Mrs. Gaskell remarks that domestic novels "reveal all the little household secrets; we see the meals as they are put on the table, we learn the dresses which those who sit down to them wear."[48]

The last item on Gaskell's list looms particularly large in the genre's representation of domestic life. Though populated with suffering heroines, elderly philanthropists, and routine spinsters who seize almost any pretext to deliver a homily, a domestic novel like *The Lamplighter* instantly drops its mantle of piety the minute a noteworthy garment appears on the scene. Since, like soap opera viewers today, many Victorian women read domestic novels just to keep abreast of the latest fashions, Cummins does not hesitate to show her heroine, Gerty Flint, engrossed at the sight of "the most remarkable toilet she had ever witnessed," here "a reticule of unusual dimensions and a great variety of colors, a black lace cap, a large feather fan, a roll of fancy paper, and several other articles."[49] This aggregate of articles steps beyond the realm of fashion and enters the saturated space of materiality we have defined as the condition of kitsch. Though Cummins soon has her heroine disavow any interest in clothes, Gerty remains an avid, if unwitting, consumer of high Victorian kitsch. In heroines like Gerty, the domestic novel offered its readers models of pious consumption that predisposed them to react favorably to the dual imagery of Jubilee kitsch. Though at times domestic novelists deliberately placed material and immaterial realms in a relation of mutual exclusivity, when it comes right down to it the pious gaze which they longingly fix on a higher realm can always be pivoted to illuminate a lower realm replete with belongings. The two realms repel each other—like a pair of magnets.

III

It requires a readjustment of our hierarchy of cultural forms to imagine kitsch as central to social representation in late-Victorian England. Today's kitsch comes nowhere near the animating centers of society; we have relegated it to the periphery of representation and downgraded it to the status of illegitimate theater. In an underhanded way we still pay tribute to the power once embodied in Victorian kitsch by devoting a lot of time and energy to collecting it, but these collections do not come close to capturing the major role that kitsch items once played in Victorian culture. In 1887 the iconography of Jubilee kitsch was out-and-out legitimate theater where the queen's two bodies came together in what Marx called "the fantastic form of a relation among things." [50] The image of Victoria incarnated relations among things by imposing on them a sentimental typology that simultaneously summoned up two complementary consumer worlds, the material world of the Victorian court and the ethereal world of the beyond (in sentimental culture, a luxurious and well-stocked afterlife had already become a model for the easy-street daydreams of commodity culture). The icons of Jubilee kitsch melded immanence with transcendence, acquired with inherent charisma, bodied with disembodied authority, and so established abiding patterns of representation for commodities. Though by autumn the public's appetite for Jubilee kitsch had waned, the unprecedented popularity of the image of Victoria had permanently altered the landscape of English commodity culture, and few of the advertising campaigns that had been current before Jubilee survived for more than a few years after it.[51] Long after the Jubilee had come and gone, the image of Victoria continued to exert a powerful influence over English mass advertising, spurred on, as the *Illustrated London News* once remarked, by "such help as capital, enterprise, and mechanical skill can afford."[52] Because of the Jubilee, the spectacle of advertised kitsch became almost as influential a medium for advertisers as the printed word.

Jubilee kitsch, then, must be seen as pioneering a new kind of cultural production: the *advertised* spectacle. As we have seen, the commodity spectacle of the Great Exhibition had never been successfully translated into the discourse of advertisers. In 1851 the commodity reached an artificial apotheosis in a carefully monitored laboratory space. In the decades after the Exhibition the advertising industry gained in sophistication as it experimented in various ways with disparate elements of the commodity spectacle. The production of domestic articles had slowly been on the rise since mid-century, and the advertising industry picked up on the common but unsubstantiated claim that there was now enough of everything for everyone. The 1860's saw sensation advertising, which drew on a popular literary form to affirm commodities in a striking and topical way. The 1870's saw the establishment of major department stores, which further commercialized the space of exhibition. Not until the Jubilee, however, when the image of Victoria became a common text and a prevailing context for the nation, did advertising and spectacle meet. The result was that the advertised image of Victoria became a kind of repository for the semiotics of commodity culture, advancing the spectacularization of the commodity and making it loom even larger in the cultural and political life of nineteenth-century England.

Victoria's image introduced both a human and a divine element into the iconography of the manufactured object. The Great Exhibition had located objects in a cavernous and evacuated space, where they appeared to be levitated above human reach and beyond human ken. This elevation, however, was anything but transcendent. It relied upon things themselves to figure a culture of commodities that appeared to take in the entire visible world. During the Great Exhibition the commodity embodied all of culture; during the Jubilee it embodied all of the cosmos. In the Crystal Palace the commodity was a secularized icon of the Victorian sublime; in Jubilee kitsch it was an article of faith. Part of the appeal of the queen, however, was that, like the autonomous objects that were constantly being placed at her disposal, her body was not only eternal but contingent. Whether Victoria is seen inspecting cloth or as a figure on a screw-top jar, the great desideratum was an exact balance of immanence and transcendence. As we have seen, in Jubilee kitsch Victoria preserved both phenomenal and numinal bodies: as a living woman she moved among things as a consumer and animated them with her living touch, but she also relinquished her physical body and animated them with her sovereign touch (the touch of the sovereign, once thought to cure scrofula, now confers eternity on a universe of manufactured objects). The image of Victoria thus performed a dual operation: not only did it vivify things, it also placed them in a separate realm and made them apparently immune to decay. The queen's two bodies have become the commodity's two bodies, and the ambivalence at the heart of the commodity—what in another context Marx calls the tension between its status as "object of utility" and "bearer of value"—has become the essence of kitsch.[53]

Victoria's image, though sometimes spectral, was not completely devoid of history. The Jubilee itself served to counterbalance the synchronic autonomy of the consumer queen by placing her in a diachronic relation to historical time. Victoria had, after all, been on the throne for fifty years, and throughout 1887 the periodical press was full of references to events that had transpired during that time. But even at the points where Victoria's image seems to be firmly embedded in historical time, the ground turns out to be shifting and uncertain. Her image both exuded and expelled history. It did not distill tradition; as David Cannadine has shown, it invented it. Retrospective articles written during the Jubilee framed the events of the past fifty years firmly within the perimeters of Victoria's reign, but in such a way that the past took on significance solely in relation to her. The Jubilee periodized her reign, but it also made it into a convenient block of time to be commemorated all at once. The putative event commemorated actually took place, but the commemoration was all out of proportion to the "event" observed. Anniversaries—like the Jubilee, the centenaries of the American and French revolutions, as well as party congresses, proclaimed political holidays, and the Olympics—were an invention of the late nineteenth century, and they contributed to the dissolution of the sense of historical time that Henri Lefebvre has called "the decline of the referentials." [54] The breakdown of the certainties of space and time that was later to occupy philosophers and physicists such as Bergson and Bohr was prefigured in the twisted historicity of Victoria's image.

Lefebvre attributes the decline of stable referentials to science and technology, which changed the perception of static and mobile, light and dark, absolute and relative. Another reason for the decline was that the commodity had established itself as a fluid object of universal reference. Having everything refer to commodities was like having everything refer to nothing at all, for a commodity was not a fixed and absolute point of reference but a mobile and fungible form of exchange. The ascendant commodity not only corroded the sense of historical time but also made it more and more difficult to settle on any one way of representing commodity relations. The Great Exhibition had skirted this problem by creating a certain kind of language for the commodity. (As we have seen, the 1851 Exhibition *Catalogue* spoke this language of things.) The image of Victoria was much harder to pin down, for it combined language and image in a way new to English commodity culture. In Jubilee advertising, Victoria did not speak; as a consumer, she was spoken for. Jubilee ads muted the speech of the consumer and substituted in its stead the voice of the advertiser. In this way Victoria's image was a model of irreferentiality: it burst the confines of traditional iconography and made it possible for any language to be attached to any image. By the mid-1890's, as we shall see, advertisers were regularly superimposing their slogans over standardized images drawn from every sphere of public and private life.

If, as an irreferential icon, Victoria's image laid itself open to a range of interpretations, it also at times moved along a razor's edge of signification. Like any powerful icon it invited and withstood contradiction, and in Jubilee advertising no tension is more evident than that which the queen's image established between society's center and its periphery. The authority of society's center, Edward Shils writes, "has a tendency to expand the order which it represents toward the saturation of territorial space."[55] Advertisers placed the queen at the center and the consuming public at the periphery, but they also made it very difficult to locate authority in either sphere. For a brief period Victoria's image effortlessly traversed social space, but it only did so because it was the bearer of middle-class values. It asserted the hegemony of the upper class but placed that class wholly within the domain of middle-class consumers. In Jubilee advertising class lines wavered even as they were being upheld. During 1887 the authority of Victoria's image was constantly expanding, but it no longer had any constituency. The only kind of community her image figured was a community of consumers—a community then so vast, invisible, malleable, and evanescent that it could hardly be said to have existed at all. The image of a Hanoverian shopper had melded center and periphery, scrambling the class system to such an extent that all classes now appeared to have one thing, and one thing only, in common: the imperative to consume.[56]

Regardless of what class she represented, Victoria contributed to gendering the consuming subject and situating her firmly within advertising. Recall that during the Great Exhibition anything that interfered with the direct perception of manufactured objects conveniently fell away; there was a contraction of perception as the subject became the exclusive consumer of material objects. In Jubilee advertising the only thing Victoria is capable of doing is staring at kitsch. The Crystal Palace had developed an architecture that pioneered a phenomenology of consumption. Victoria takes this phenomenology one step further: she is the prototype for a consumer whose mind has been manipulated to such an extent that she has been placed in a passive state of complete receptivity. By 1902 Walter Dill Scott, in *The Psychology of Advertising*, would attempt to base all advertising on a theory of the essential passivity of the perceiving subject. The problem with Scott's model of the consumer, however, was that it lacked specificity. It figured the consumer as a jumble of faceless attributes like "perception," "association," "memory," and "will" (unlike Freud, with whom he is often paired, Scott did not rely on case studies).[57]

In marked contrast, there was no mistaking the consuming subject that Victoria figured: she was a woman. Long after Jubilee kitsch had lost its universal appeal, the image of Victoria remained a prototype for a female consuming subject. In *Queen Victoria* (1921), written when the image of the consumer queen still lingered in living memory, Lytton Strachey conjures up the essential elements. He describes Victoria as an obsessive consumer, "a woman not only of vast property but of innumerable possessions." Even more importantly, Strachey pictures a being at once material and ethereal, ordinary and remarkable, familial and fantastic when he describes "the superabundant emotionalism, the ingenuousness of outlook, the solid, the laborious respectability, shot through so incongruously by temperamental cravings for the coloured and the strange, the singular intellectual limitations, and the mysterious essential female element impregnating every particle of the whole."[58] The contradictory being he describes is the female consumer, and his description of her does not differ much from the traits ascribed to the female consumer in *Advertising to Women*, a guidebook to merchandising published a few years after Strachey's biography of Victoria.[59]

The commodity spectacle of the Great Exhibition had mostly left the last act of consumption up to the imagination of the consumer. The advertised spectacle of Victoria had more to say about the afterlife of objects. It advanced a proximate vision of what Thorstein Veblen, in *The Theory of the Leisure Class* (1899), would later call "conspicuous consumption." Proximate because, in Jubilee advertising as well as in real life, Victoria does not use the articles surrounding her merely as symbols of affluence. Jubilee commodities are not pawns in the social gambit of status seeking and status maintenance but icons of transcendent materiality. Victoria was less a conspicuous consumer (after all, she never bought anything in her entire life) than a conspicuous collector. She collected everything she came into contact with, and everything she collected took its place within an intricate economy of self-classification. Her contemporaries readily acknowledged what a large role the queen's storerooms played in constituting her inner life, a life for which bourgeois interiority and the bourgeois interior were indistinguishable. In *The Private Life of the Queen* (1897) a member of her household wrote that "to attempt to depict the inner life of the Queen, to shadow forth her haunts and habits, her temperament and characteristics, and to omit all mention of her linen-room, store-cupboard, and the places where her glass and china find resting place, were to render this record woefully incomplete."[60] For Victoria things possessed genealogical import; she had given orders that nothing ever be thrown away. Every dress she had ever worn was preserved and arranged in chronological order. As they wore out, carpets and drapes were replaced by identical copies. Photographs documented the life-stages of every close relation, and photographs documented the life-stages of every single object in her possession (shots taken from several angles, bound in albums, numbered by room, position, and principal characteristics).[61] As a collector Victoria had an unerring instinct for kitsch. Only incidentally did she collect objects approved by the institutions of art and sanctioned by the canons of taste. Rather she homed in on the transcendental details of everyday life. Because she wanted the life of objects to be replete with intimations of immortality, she surrounded herself with miniatures, porcelains, and paintings of dead husband, servants, and dogs. The vast archive of objects that she created aspired in its entirety to the synchrony of eternity, an abundant hermetic world of dead matter in which, as Lytton Strachey put it, "the fate of every object which had undergone this process was irrevocably sealed."[62]

The image of Victoria, then, translated the terms of the commodity spectacle into the discourse of advertisers. It brought to life the iconography of the manufactured object; it placed historical time at the disposal of the commodity and virtually invented modern commodity kitsch; it synthesized language and image; it simultaneously effaced and upheld social class; it inculcated passivity among consumers; and it figured abundance as a hermetic collection. But apart from the many ways in which it replicated and refined the commodity spectacle so much in evidence at the Great Exhibition, the decisive factor about the Jubilee image of Victoria was that it permanently established the advertised commodity as a pervasive commodity culture. Though advertising had long occupied a prominent place in English public life, that place was far from systematized. Mid-Victorian photographs and engravings show the hoardings plastered pell-mell with posters, bills, and flyers as each commodity fights for itself, refuses to acknowledge the others, and attempts to impose itself everywhere as if it were the only one.[63] In contrast to these striking images of collective disunity—the very stuff that led Thomas Carlyle, in *Past and Present* (1843), to use commodities like Morrison's Pills to exemplify the principle of "Laissez-faire, and Every Man for Himself"[64]—the Jubilee image of Victoria unified and routinized the semiotics of commodity culture and created a lingua franca for late-Victorian advertisers.

An inextricable mesh of image, theater, and ideology, Victoria's image nevertheless cannot adequately be reduced to the terms of language. As language, as we have seen, commodities tended to conform to certain set procedures of articulation. For the sake of argument these procedures can be usefully conceptualized as a "rhetoric" of the commodity, but it must be remembered that Jubilee advertising often operated in a realm for which language offered at best an incomplete analogy. Drawing on the eclectic charisma of Jubilee kitsch, commodities actually became something other than language. For want of a more precise phrase, they became a *system of signs*. The rapid-fire succession of metaphors Marx used in the commodity fetishism chapter of *Capital* had pointed toward the existence of a new dimension of signification, as had the space of incredible phenomenal intensity modeled by the Great Exhibition. Following Guy Debord, this sign system of commodities has been termed the "spectacle," that is, a state of signification in which much of society becomes a theater for the fictions it has created for its commodities. One can think of the spectacle as the ongoing oratorio of the commodity, what Debord calls a "monopoly of appearance" that "concentrates all gazing and all consciousness" by presenting itself "as something enormously positive, indisputable, and inaccessible."[65] But the spectacle does more than dress up commodities with charisma; this semiotic system not only appropriates but actually absorbs the raw materials it uses by turning them, too, into commodities.

One index of the transformative power of the spectacle can be found in advertising's reaction to the way Victoria's image had come unhinged. In 1876 Bagehot had voiced his opinion that the English people would soon forget the newly named Empress of India had ever been anything other than an Empress.[66] By the 1890's advertisers seemed to have forgotten that Victoria had ever been anything other than a commodity. In *The Art of Advertising* (1899) William Stead is quick to assert that "the Monarchy . . . advertises itself everywhere" and goes on to rave about all the "unlimited free advertisement from the cradle to the grave" that monarchy is heir to. The queen's movements are chronicled in *The Court Circular*. The royal standard, which announces the arrival of the queen, is "no bad substitute for the sandwich-man." The peerage pages of *Burke's* and *Debrett's* are "almost as essential to the maintenance of [the court's] position in the country and in society as advertisement is to the prosperity of Pears' Soap or Cadbury's Cocoa." All in all, "the Queen is probably the best-advertised person in the Three Kingdoms," benefitting from "a system of elaborately organized advertisement, which is none the less advertisement because in many cases it does not need to be paid for."[67] In Stead's book, signs as homely as coins, postage stamps, the royal arms, and the royal initials are all indices of advertisement. In his mind the elaborate spectacle of monarchy cannot be dissociated from the collateral spectacle of advertising; however one looks at it, the monarchy and the commodity are one and the same thing.

In such a state of affairs it becomes tremendously difficult to chart out what is usually called "commodification." In the society of the spectacle figured by the Jubilee image of Victoria, there is nothing left to commodify, nothing left in a pristine pre-capitalist state against which the commercialized artifact can be measured and judged. The Jubilee spectacle was the high water mark of commodity expansionism in late-Victorian England, the moment when the commodity's semiotic system was at its most expansive, the moment, as Debord has put it, when the commodity came close to attaining "the *total occupation* of social life." At such a moment, however provisional and however fleeting, the question of whether anything was once *not* a commodity becomes moot. Though Debord does not identify a particular historical moment when the commodity spectacle first achieved this charismatic dominance, the very term he uses to describe it points toward an event like the Jubilee. For hundreds of years, "spectacle" had denoted the ceremonial forms—the social illusions that Kantorowicz has aptly called "man-made irreality"—by which rulers took symbolic possession of their realm. Like the progresses of Elizabeth I or the *lits de justices* of Louis XIV, the 1887 Jubilee stamped a territory with manufactured signs of dominance. Only now, as Debord puts it succinctly, "things rule." [68]

Debord, however, does not work out the full implications of his analysis for the benefit of the cultural historian. When he turns to the role played by the spectacle in the nineteenth century, he confines himself to the blanket statement that "by means of a *ruse of commodity logic* . . . the commodity-form moves toward its absolute realization," reaching "its absolute fulfillment in the spectacle." [69] This is to conceive of the commodity as akin to a fully formed embryo, developed to near-perfection in the womb of the nineteenth century. In other words, Debord would see the commodity spectacle of Jubilee as somehow *inside* Victorian society, waiting to assume exactly the form it did. Though Debord, like so many theorists of advertising before him, describes the commodity as if it behaved exactly according to this inner logic, it would be more accurate to say that Jubilee commodities just happened to assume the form they did, and to admit that they could have assumed many others. The commodity had no teleology, no set trajectory; it did not have an underlying and universal form, the features of which, like a platonic master pattern, could be detected in all commodities regardless of the particular social circumstances in which they happened to have been embedded. What Marx calls the "commodity form" was not a *forma formata* but a *forma formans*. By separating image from text, text from context, and sign from referent, the advertising campaigns of Jubilee succeeded in establishing the malleable structure of the sign at the heart of commodity exchange. In this way the Jubilee campaigns temporarily succeeded in transforming the commodity into something that Marx had not foreseen, namely what Jean Baudrillard calls "a total *medium*, as a *system of communication* administering all social exchange."[70]

As a medium for signification, however, the commodity, like all signs, is an arbitrary convention. Nothing in nature decrees that a commodity should take on charisma, and certainly nothing decrees that charisma should become kitsch. Though Marx himself repeatedly calls attention to a charismatic aspect of the commodity—he calls it "something transcendent," something "mystical," something "abounding in metaphysical subtleties and theological niceties"—he uses this language of charisma merely as an analogy to underscore how the capitalist system of commodity exchange, like the products of the religious imagination, becomes a self-sufficient and self-validating system of representations, detached from its producers.[71] And though the images he uses to describe commodities in *Capital* uncannily summon up the iconography of kitsch—especially religious kitsch—nowhere does he specifically predict that commodities would necessarily manifest their powers by becoming, like gods, charismatic. Overwhelmed as we now are with the charisma of advertisements for automobiles that glow numinously, computers that speak with the voice of authority, and politicians that look forever young, it may indeed be difficult to imagine a time when these representations of commodity kitsch were not fixed. It is always hard to imagine a magician pulling anything other than a rabbit out of the hat, and even harder to imagine the old trick being pulled for the very first time. The campaigns of the 1887 Jubilee should not be treated as some manifestation of an already constituted system of advertised representations, but as evidence of its very process of constitution as part of a historical moment in which a heterogenous mass of competing commodities achieved temporary equipoise in a consolidated imagery of advertisement.

Though at the height of the Jubilee summer advertising looked like it would never let go of Victoria's image, that image was by no means a permanent blueprint to which it consciously adhered. The Jubilee advertisers took up Victoria's image for a shortsighted motive—namely, they wanted to turn an immediate profit. While the till remained full, they cared little to ask why it had become particularly and exclusively appropriate to their medium. Instead they ran it into the ground, repeating it over and over again like a potent magic formula they had happened to discover. Nevertheless, by increments and often by chance, late-Victorian advertising gradually defined a dominant semiotic system for a commodity culture. In the last years of the nineteenth century people like Gissing were still aware of its novelty; and yet during the Jubilee campaign, this semiotics of transcendent materiality—in a word, of kitsch—appeared so bound up with the animating centers of society that it relegated to obscurity all the other possibilities that nineteenth-century theorists of advertising had imagined.[72] During and after the Jubilee, the newly dominant system seemed to have no alternatives, as if it had been carried along by the very movement of history: as Luckworth Crewe remarks, "Till advertising sprang up, the world was barbarous. Do you suppose people kept themselves clean before they were reminded at every corner of the benefits of soap?"[73] Crewe's brand of advertising was now "natural"—just as natural and self-evident as the use of soap to promote hygiene had recently become. In fact, it soon became common for advertising handbooks to debunk the idea that "advertisements are of comparatively recent origin," thus carrying the new advertising back to a factitious point of origin in either "ancient" or "medieval" advertising.[74] Everywhere advertisers looked, they now saw the precursors of the 1887 Jubilee.

If for late-Victorian advertisers the past was prelude to the Jubilee, so was the future its postscript. For in the end, the most fitting sequel to the Jubilee was another Jubilee. The first Jubilee had been a domestic spectacle (even the cavalcade of princes had been a family affair), and it had transformed Victoria into a domestic article. What little charisma she possessed in 1887 she derived from the regard lavished on her by various institutions involved in using this unwilling center of attention to further their own interests. Many acknowledged the need for a more charismatic monarch—the overelaboration of the Jubilee events announced this need almost continuously—but in practice it was displaced onto a variety of commodities that staggered under the weight of the significance attributed to them. The image of Victoria in the year of the Golden Jubilee had been domestic kitsch; in the year of the Diamond Jubilee it became imperial kitsch. After ten years of empire building that had relentlessly laid claim to the heart of Africa (Gambia and Bechuanaland in 1888, Rhodesia in 1889, Uganda in 1890, Zanzibar and Nyasaland in 1891), the image of Victoria lost its home-and-hearth quality and became a transnational and transcendental absolute equivalent to that once projected by Judeo-Christian religion. The charismatic image of Victoria overwhelmed and finally obliterated the old image of the melancholy widowed queen.

At the very end, then, of a procession from Buckingham Palace to St. Paul's on June 21, 1897—ten years to the day after the first—rode Victoria, Regina et Imperatrix. Miles of the procession route in 1887 had been lined with red cloth, which had looked from end to end like a red carpet drawn across the streets of London. Now the organizers rolled out an imitation oriental rug in the form of a carefully contrived allegory of Empire that transformed its distant and often menacing otherness into the familiar sight of obedient ranks of soldiers under direct British military command. Riding high in the wake of hussars from Canada, carabiniers from Natal, camel troops from North Borneo, white-gaitered Jamaicans, Cypriots with fezzes, and Guiana police in peaked caps, the domesticated queen at last became the charismatic center of all the phantasmagoria of Empire, a symbolic exemplar of what the *Daily Mail*, in headlines of gold ink on June 21, 1897, called the "GREATNESS OF THE BRITISH RACE." Advertisers also paid homage to the new Victoria as, in campaigns that impressed her image on imported articles like tea as

FIG. 19. The 1897 Jubilee: Victoria, Regina et Imperatrix (*Graphic*, June 28, 1897).

well as domestic articles like soap, they respectfully deprived her of most of her portly body (Fig. 19).

It had taken ten years and two monster Jubilees, but Victoria's image had finally taken on all the charisma that Rider Haggard had once been able to imagine only as belonging to an Egyptian queen exiled for two thousand years to a fortress in central Africa. In the final analysis *She* must be seen as a novel of the first Jubilee, an extended fantasy about what the monarchy was and what it could become. At the beginning of the novel Haggard's Ayesha lives in a tomb and guards the memory of her long-dead consort. Like Victoria, her distinguishing feature is an excess of grief, and she lives the life of a recluse. Haggard's Ayesha is Victoria's Jubilee double, an emblem of the possibilities that commodity culture was beginning to discover in Britain's most ancient institution. As the novel proceeds she becomes everything that Jubilee kitsch tried to embody in old Queen Victoria: a queen presiding over a kingdom of dead matter; a ruler who breaks down historical time, bringing the past into the present and the present into the past; a monarch able to appear in different guises; a sign free at last from the grip of a living referent. Haggard's vision is exemplary because it displays the immaterial quality of charisma while preserving and even highlighting the material quality that made charisma into one of the great desiderata of advertising. An 1887 review in the *Athenaeum* commented that Haggard's novel tends to be "dragged down suddenly from the heights of the supernatural, the immortal and the divinely fair, by the sudden and superfluous mention of Gladstone bags, shooting boots, and Bryant & May's matches," all in all "a very good advertisement for the Army and Navy Store."[75] The reviewer is right to point to paradox but wrong to dismiss it as weakness. There is no better statement of the strong duality of charisma that made Jubilee kitsch what it was. The mixture of the immaterial and the material would remain a powerful ideological construction in commodity culture for years to come, and though Jubilee kitsch would soon pass into the marginal realm of junk, the commodity was now poised to enter a liminal realm where it would be able to perform spectacular feats it could perform nowhere else. Rider Haggard had the foresight to pinpoint the very territory—Africa—where a great imperial exhibition of things was about to begin.

Selling Darkest Africa

By all reports and by any reckoning late-Victorian England was a prodigiously abundant society. The Victorians invented the idea of a "standard of living," and by it they meant that life could be measured by counting the number of goods and articles that people consumed. Never before had a society succeeded in producing so much material evidence of its own prosperity. Studies proliferated showing that the English were eating more meat, building more houses, wearing more clothes, and drinking more alcohol than ever before.[1] In 1851 the Crystal Palace had crammed a vast array of manufactured objects into a cavernous interior space in which commodities appeared in the endless variety of forms that Darwin later saw in the natural world. It seemed only a matter of time until this superabundance of things colonized the country and made committed consumers out of every man, woman, and child in England.

Though the Crystal Palace and its publicists succeeded in making prosperity look like an accomplished fact, the extraordinary surplus of things which it assembled so spectacularly was, like mid-twentieth-century imaginings of the perfectly mechanized home, no more than an influential piece of wishful thinking. For the vast majority of spectators the objects it contained were unattainable and inimitable. Outside the confines of the Crystal Palace things quickly lost their euphoric character. Henry Mayhew's long descriptions of London streetsellers make it quite clear that the poverty of the seller still governed one's impression of whatever the seller happened to have for sale. In our time, historians like Eric Hobsbawm have been quick to point out that the sense of a surplus of consumer goods was actually created by exhibitions like the Crystal Palace and fostered by leading Victorian economists.[2] For a small minority of people, the middle and upper classes, abundance was a fact of life, but for the great majority it was a promise awaiting fulfillment. A spectacle like the Crystal Palace thus performed a dual ideological function: on the one hand it placed a limited number of objects within a confined space of exhibition, while on the other it made that confinement seem like an unparalleled surplus, the forerunner of a profusion of things that would soon overrun the country.

In the 1890's more and more people came to believe that this surplus served the specific interests of Empire and that it would, in time, overrun the world. As an island of prosperity in a less-than-prosperous world, the Crystal Palace bore the same relationship to London as, in late-Victorian theories of imperialism, England did to the rest of the world. Just as the Crystal Palace was the model for a consumer society that had not yet come into being in the rest of England, where a large number of people still lived in poverty, so too was the uncanny productivity of the English economy taken as the economic blueprint for the world at large. There is a historical fitness in the fact that Disraeli went to the Crystal Palace to give his famous speech calling for the expansion of England. For in the minds of many late-Victorian observers, the economic expansion of England was what Empire was all about, and almost everyone believed that that expansion would be spearheaded by consumer goods. It did not matter whether one was for or against Empire: it was an article of faith among jingoes and liberals and radicals alike that, in Marx's words, "it becomes necessary for capital progressively to dispose ever more fully of the whole globe . . . so as to find productive employment for the surplus value it has realized."[3]

This belief in the outward-bound movement of surplus capital and commodities finds its way into a great variety of narratives in the nineteenth century and culminates in one of the century's largest and most differentiated spectacles of commodity culture. In exploration narratives, political tracts, novels, short stories, and advertisements, the surplus commodity takes on a special role. It supplants capital and appears as the prime mover of imperial expansion. While it is true that the English were always looking for profitable new markets for articles of domestic manufacture, they were far more interested in looking for new commodities like raw materials and cash crops than in bringing along established ones to sell to colonial peoples. Nevertheless, the myth of surplus production continued to be of central importance in consolidating domestic support for imperial expansion. Throughout the 1890's and on into the twentieth century, a great number of narratives contributed in a great many ways to blinding the English public to the domestic costs of imperialism—among them burgeoning military and colonial administration budgets—by producing representations in which the sheer plenitude of English material wealth succeeded in creating an Empire the likes of which the world had never seen.

I

A Pears' Soap advertisement of August 27, 1887, set in northern Africa, enlists the commodity in the Empire's service and may be considered a sign of things to come (Fig. 20). It depicts a group of "dervishes" looking at a legend, "PEARS' SOAP IS THE BEST," chalked on a rock. Unlike modern advertisers, who attempt to create a global market by fostering dependence on Western commodities like baby formula or soft drinks, the Pears' Soap company had no intention of setting up shop in the Sudanese desert. This advertisement presents the "dervishes" as illiterate savages who cannot appreciate the value of things, so much so that the British do not even bother to make the inscription intelligible to them. The scene it pictures does not differ much from the scenes of Empire advertisers had been producing since the 1870's. What separates it from earlier advertisements of its kind is its claim, writ large above the scene, that the commodity offers "THE FORMULA OF BRITISH CONQUEST."

The real significance of this claim—perhaps the largest promise made by an advertisement in the nineteenth century—lies less in its practical application than in the fact that it was used by

THE FORMULA OF BRITISH CONQUEST

REG.D COPYRIGHT

PEARS' SOAP IN THE SOUDAN.

"Even if our invasion of the Soudan has done nothing else it has at any rate left the Arab something to puzzle his fuzzy head over, for the legend

PEARS' SOAP IS THE BEST,

inscribed in huge white characters on the rock which marks the farthest point of our advance towards Berber, will tax all the wits of the Dervishes of the Desert to translate."—Phil. Robinson, *War Correspondent (in the Soudan) of the Daily Telegraph in London*, 1884.

FIG. 20. "The Formula of British Conquest": the commodity (*Illustrated London News*, August 27, 1887).

English imperialists of the 1890's to represent commodities as a magic medium through which English power and influence could be enforced and enlarged in the colonial world. Back in the 1870's J. R. Seeley had said that the only way to keep the domestic market functioning smoothly was to keep opening new markets abroad for the surplus goods that a prosperous home economy was bound to produce.[4] Seeley and the first generation of imperialists, however, had all advocated exporting surplus commodities without trying to make them look like they could bring an empire into being all by themselves. It is precisely this grandiose claim that, in the spring of 1890, the explorer and journalist Henry Stanley advanced in a long travel book called *In Darkest Africa, or the Quest, Rescue, and Retreat of Emin Governor of Equatoria*.

Stanley's travels were not in themselves remarkable. He took a path across Africa very much like the one he had taken to rescue David Livingstone in 1871, and he ascribed his regular progress to having compelled his troops "to be guardians of peace and protectors of property, without which there can be no civilization."[5] What carries more weight is Stanley's conviction that he had a mission to civilize Africans by teaching them the value of commodities. In fact Stanley did not make a close study of the commodity form itself; he took more of an interest in championing it than in probing its workings. Nevertheless his rambling account is important because it reveals the major role that imperialists ascribed to the commodity in propelling and justifying the scramble for Africa. In the 1890's the main feature of Stanley's narrative—the harmony of interests it presumes between the commodity and the Empire—became one of the characteristic operations of advertising, reaching its high point during the Boer War, when products from all over the world were paraded forth as the crown's staunchest allies. Half consciously and hardly eloquently, Henry Stanley shared his conviction that the forms of commodity exchange that happened to structure economic life in England were not historical accidents but universal laws—laws so binding that the livelihood of the Empire depended on them.

The material world weighs heavily on Stanley's account of his "rescue" of Emin Pasha. In 1886 Stanley—veteran of the American Civil War, former correspondent for the *New York Herald*, and one of the founding fathers of the Congo Free State—had been dispatched to Africa by a coalition of businessmen with orders to assist a shadowy figure named Emin Pasha in consolidating British power in the East African interior and to return with a compensatory cargo of seventy-five tons of ivory. To this end—an end doubly sanctioned by the pressing Anglo-German rivalry in the region—almost any means could and did suffice. *In Darkest Africa* tells the story of how Stanley, like a nineteenth-century conquistador, resolutely cut his way across Africa at the head of a virtual slave army, leaving a wake of debris, death, and deforestation behind him. At no point, however, would Stanley have described his exploits so dashingly. As a writer no one could have been more careless. In the field Stanley jotted down conversations, things seen, descriptions of villages, notable geological formations—everything, in short, that could have been of use to him when he sat down to write for publication. On his return he strung this material together into a more or less connected narrative and made a book of it. Writing in the style of a quartermaster, Stanley almost always skips writing the long descriptive passages that were then a staple in travel writing, offering only the lame excuse that "I shall not delay the narration" (78). What we get instead are inventories, orders, letters, checklists, even menus—what Stanley calls "statements as to our forces and accoutrements" (111).

The mark of Stanley's narrative, then, is its fragmentation of all that he observes into little pieces so arranged that they can be picked out one at a time with the help of the appended charts, tables, and indexes. These pieces vary in length, subject, and mode of presentation; *In Darkest Africa* includes hundreds of passages that look like this one, which details the loss of some ammunition and other things:

A man of No. 3 Company dropped his box of ammunition into a deep affluent and lost it. Kageli stole a box of Winchester ammunition and absconded. Salim stole a case containing Emin Pasha's new boots and two pairs of mine, and deserted. Wadi Adam vanished with Surgeon Parke's entire kit. Swadi, of No. 1 Company, left his box on the road, and departed himself to parts unknown. Bull-necked Uchungu followed suit with a box of Remington cartridges. (227)

Though Stanley drops their names as if he knows them, none of these Africans appears elsewhere in his narrative. Indeed, Africans figure in Stanley's narrative primarily as carriers of Western goods. Nothing could be further from Stanley's mind than the spiritual welfare of his charges; in this he goes well beyond David Livingstone's missionary program to marry "Christianity and Commerce."[6] "When every grain of corn," writes Stanley, "and every fowl, goat, sheep, and cow which is necessary for the troops is paid for in sterling money or its equivalent in necessary goods, then civilization will become irresistable in its influence, and the Gospel even may be introduced" (9). For Stanley, establishing a stable medium of exchange precedes every other task. But to do so he must first drill the importance of exchange value into the hearts and minds of his three hundred or so carriers. He seeks to teach his carriers the basic elements of what Marx had outlined as the capitalist system of exchange, namely, "the fact that the *exchange-value* of the commodity assumes an independent existence," and that the person who possesses commodities "possesses social power in the form of a thing."[7] Much to his dismay, however, Stanley confronts tribal societies in which the producers of things do not divorce the things they manufacture from the uses to which they put them. As often as Stanley calls these products of indigenous manufacture art objects, souvenirs, or simply plunder, he cannot make his carriers understand that he endows both the African goods he collects and the Western goods they carry with an abstract exchange value. Not surprisingly, because these extraterritorial goods lack any concrete social role for them in the customs, directives, and taboos of their tribal lives, the carriers are forever dropping, discarding, misplacing, or walking away with them. Incensed, Stanley calls this theft. So committed is he to the spread of the market system that he executes three African carriers for stealing rifles even though he admits that the accused do not fully understand the principle for which they are being put to death.[8]

The obstacles in the way of the spread of the market system among the Africans were varied and numerous, as even Stanley acknowledges. But while the impediments were great—his African carriers resisted being turned into mere repositories for Western goods—his need to objectify his carriers was greater. Stanley is driven to deal with the inhabitants of the villages he passes through strictly on the basis of exchange. Upon entering a village he typically floods its market with Western textiles and trinkets, then sits back to observe with detached calm how confusedly the Africans squabble over their new property (*Darkest Africa*, 158–61). To Stanley's roving eye, not one African he meets belongs to an authentic community. Africans appear only as isolated interchangeable parts that drift in and out of his field of vision. To him they all look alike, act alike, even prattle alike.[9] Therefore Stanley can proceed to identify his carriers exclusively by the commodities they carry—by their Gladstone bags, Bryant and May matches, Remington cartridges—and can devote page after page to thanking the manufacturers of these articles for having donated them to such a worthy cause (38–39, 66). Stanley fails to see that the brand names by which he labels his carriers conceal a relation between human beings, a relation of social labor that he actively imposes, sanctions, and perpetuates. Instead he invests manufactured objects with phantasmagorical powers they do not in themselves have, as when he describes the expedition's Remington rifles as "our souls" (212). This love of gadgetry had been only a nervous tic in the adventure novels of H. Rider Haggard; Stanley elevates it to the *modus operandi* of Empire.[10] In his eyes commodities not only appear, as Marx had said, as "something transcendent," they appear as the self-validating vanguard of Empire, as the spearhead of English material culture in the campaign against the anarchy of the dark continent—as, finally, a means so powerful that it can realize itself in the absence of any end.[11] Indeed, as he writes, Stanley often jettisons all syntactical constraints governing the use of nouns, as if to admit that the manufactured objects those nouns name can exist without any human agency at all.

Though Stanley habitually venerates commodities in this somewhat abstract way, he does so for some very concrete reasons. In his effort to make commodities sound like they have replaced human beings, he also reduces human beings to economic ciphers. Britain had abolished slavery in 1834, and in the years after emancipation there were fewer and fewer people who thought of African blacks purely as objects of exchange. But most whites continued to read blacks economically. In 1840, at the same time as the abolitionist Thomas Fowell Buxton deplored the representation of "man as an object of merchandise," he advanced the idea that "the Government of this country [should] lend its powerful influence in organizing a commercial system of just, liberal, and comprehensive principles" in Africa. For a liberal abolitionist like Buxton, the root cause of slavery was legal and not economic; he not only exonerated the capitalist system for having created slavery but offered up "the extension of a legitimate commerce" as a remedy for "the nefarious traffic in human beings." Like most late-Victorian apologists for the extension of legitimate commerce, Henry Stanley does not preserve Buxton's high moral tone. But he preserves intact Buxton's habit of representing Africans primarily as producers of raw materials and consumers "desirous of possessing our manufactures." [12] In this sense, Stanley, like Buxton before him, does not so much do away with slavery as update it by encapsulating black Africans as subjects rather than objects of exchange.

Stanley would have been appalled at the suggestion that he went to Central Africa animated by the spirit of a slave trader, but he also would have had a hard time explaining just why it was he did go there. Like so many imperialist ventures in the late nineteenth century, the Emin Pasha Relief Expedition lacked any purpose that could be spelled out in plain English. In 1886, after letters from Emin appeared in the *Times* complaining that he was beleaguered by the same messianic movement that had overwhelmed General Gordon at Khartoum, the public had clamored for a last-ditch rescue attempt. Committees were formed, funds were subscribed, Stanley was hired—without the least indication from Emin that he wanted to be rescued (in fact, like Conrad's Kurtz, he did not). For its part, the East Africa Company's board of directors had subscribed funds in the forlorn hope that the great Stanley would single-handedly annex Uganda and so revive their flagging fortunes (he did not, and the company failed five years later). [13] The British government had refused to sanction the expedition because Germany, France, and Italy had all, at one time or another, laid their own claims to the area. Stanley's road to Africa, then, was paved with some very ambiguous intentions. In effect, he had been asked to expand the Empire without official sanction—to stake a claim without putting up a flag. Faced with this immense task, he improvised a rationale out of the material at hand: his roving store of English commodities. In the commodity Stanley sought and found a generalized power seeking a generalized embodiment. Nothing is so characteristic of Stanley's narrative as its movement from situated and calculable goals of national interest to the unregulated and uncontrollable expansionism of the commodity form, a fluid medium that could traverse the continent with no fixed national purpose and therefore with no insuperable impediment.

The commodity had never been given such latitude in England. There the production and distribution of commodities existed beside, and were regulated by, a variety of national institutions. The free market had never been allowed to create the war of all against all envisioned by Hobbes in *Leviathan*. In Africa, by contrast, the commodity became an instrument of unprecedented violence. In the last years of the nineteenth century, many traditional societies that had not earlier succeeded in adapting themselves to the market system and to the commodity form were washed away by a wave of things.[14] The introduction of money, and of goods whose value was regulated by money, disrupted the fragile economies of hundreds of villages that had formerly subsisted on barter and the rudiments of market exchange. This did not prove to be a promising way to advance international trade. In truth Stanley's activities, like the central African ivory trade managed by the Dutch and depicted by Conrad in *Heart of Darkness*, tended to wipe out native communities rather than to establish them as a permanent basis for a market economy. Even the geography of the place worked against its becoming a free field for the commodity. On the map central Africa was a collection of English place names tenuously strung together along dotted lines, which, more often than not, were little more than trails through a wasteland. As hard as

Stanley worked to turn these trails into a network of trade routes for commodities, the export of a functioning market system did not follow compliantly in the track of a few exported things. Indeed the real irony of the Emin Pasha Relief Expedition is that, despite its announced intentions, it did not pave the way for anything at all.

One cannot help observing, then, that Stanley takes commodities much more seriously in *In Darkest Africa* than the evidence he summons would seem to warrant doing. He pays heavy tribute to commodities by opening the floodgates of his narrative to them, summoning each article by its brand name and turning every laundry list into a product endorsement. Commodities appear everywhere in *In Darkest Africa*, but even more important are the extraordinary powers he attributes to them—echoing Marx's idea of commodity fetishism.[15] It is tempting to see Stanley as succumbing to the lure of an actual fetish. Perhaps, after putting hundreds, then thousands, of miles between himself and the nearest outpost of the British Empire, Stanley went native, reverting to the fetishes of primitive ritual by investing the commodities he carried with powers they did not in themselves have. Commodity fetishism, however, is only an analogy, and Marx does not mean to imply that people in market societies venerate objects in the same way that people once worshipped things as deities. The point is not that Stanley's commodities possess power inherently, but that they have derived their power from other sources. If Stanley thinks that commodities are all-powerful, it is because particular historical circumstances have made them appear that way to him.

The fact is that Stanley's vision of Africa subjugated by the commodity was not so much the product of his experiences in the wilderness as of the expectations instilled in him by domestic commodity culture. Elsewhere on the continent, as we shall see, the commodity became an enduring force, especially in South Africa, where beginning in 1887 European mines dug up the gold that set the standard for international exchange. But Stanley did not go to Africa because his imagination was fired by gold; he went to give his vision of the commodity a basis in reality. Extravagant as it seems today, that vision sprang from a broad and general consensus that the English were producing more commodities than had ever been made. In England this idea had been advanced with the utmost seriousness since the year of the Crystal Palace, when the Prince Consort spoke of abundance and English preeminence in manufacturing as accomplished facts.[16] Soon it became common for Victorians of all classes to stuff their houses with kitsch that reminded them daily of the extraordinary profusion of indigenous industry. This zeal for domestic productivity might have remained relatively harmless had it not been for the fact that it entered the national consciousness at the moment when Britain had initiated, and to a certain extent implemented, a new and aggressive foreign policy. The new imperialism adopted the idea that there was a direct correlation between commodity production and territorial expansion and so drove home the imperial importance of manufactured objects in a way that kitsch or the Prince Consort's speeches could never have done.[17] Thousands of cheering spectators roared approval at a music-hall song that, in a nutshell, offered a political philosophy of manufacture: "We don't want to fight / But, by Jingo, if we do, / We've got the men, / We've got the ships, / We've got the money too—."[18] The jingo's ability to harness the forces of the commodity—here, of what one Victorian observer called the song's "culminating stress upon the money-bags"—in the service of state policy inspired the English with awe, with an almost charismatic enthusiasm, which spread beyond the music halls of London and beyond the periodical press. In ways that surprised nearly everyone at the time, "jingoism" made the commodity a force to contend with in domestic political culture and contributed to transforming the commodity from a slight subject, hardly worth mentioning, into a spectacle, worthy of Henry Stanley's praise.

The word jingoism was recent, dating back a dozen years before Stanley published *In Darkest Africa*, when the hit song containing the phrase "by jingo" was first sung in a London music hall. Even before the advent of the new imperialism in the late nineteenth century, some people had been "jingoes" in the sense that they put devotion to country above all other concerns; but the phenomenon of jingoism involves much more than this.

The English became jingoes because they believed that overseas expansion was necessary for capitalism to survive in England. In the late nineteenth century they thought they had come up against national limitations to economic expansion, and because they believed that the hard and fast rule of the capitalist system was unceasing economic growth, they were forced to proclaim expansion to be a final goal of foreign policy. However little this goal may have been justified by economic realities, it required a special form of advocacy, for it could not be justified rationally under existing canons of law. The numerous treaties that held the European powers in a delicate balance throughout the nineteenth century did not permit, and indeed were intended to prevent, untrammeled expansionism.[19] Only by recourse to an extrarational discourse, to a form of patriotism heightened by the conditions of the music hall and amplified by the press, could these constraints be evaded and ultimately flaunted.[20] The strange growth of jingoism sprang up to fill the void left by the absence of a conventional political explanation for why the English were expanding blindly in every direction imaginable. That the explanation actually lay in a combination of business and political speculation was a fact that the jingoes, to their credit, never attempted to conceal. In truth, they were inclined to celebrate the circular logic of politico-economic expansionism, according to which expansion meant export and export meant expansion. In *In Darkest Africa* Henry Stanley merely pushes this logic to its breaking point, finding in the commodity not only an abiding instrument of trade but also a principal instrument of policy.

One of the most telling accounts of this transformation of the commodity from an instrument of trade to an instrument of policy is J. A. Hobson's *The Psychology of Jingoism* (1901). Hobson, for one, does not share Stanley's jingo enthusiasm for the commodity. In fact, precisely those spectacular qualities of the commodity that fascinate and charm Stanley repel Hobson, who tries to explain what happens to political life in a country where one interest group has succeeded in establishing political ascendancy by exploiting *commodity* culture. Throughout his study Hobson examines the mechanisms whereby the "quick carriage of persons, goods, and news" render people "habitually susceptible to the direct influence" of "a commercial clique or political party" (*Psychology*, 6, 10). Commercial cliques and political parties Hobson considers almost indistinguishable, and indeed he finds that the model the jingoes most often rely on to win support and influence opinion is "the trade advertisement, whereby one, who is known to be an interested party, recommends his own goods and, by continually repeated suggestions, produces a belief which induces the public to purchase his wares" (10). On one level Hobson comes right out and says that people have "precisely the same sort of evidence" for the claims jingoes make as for "the belief that Colman's is the best mustard, or Branson's extract of coffee is perfection" (28); on another, though, his point is that in jingoism, two formerly distinct realms of discourse—the commercial and the political—have merged. By relying on the medium of information established by advertisers to communicate messages about commodities, the jingoes both turn politics into a commodity and, just as importantly, turn commodities into the carriers of a political ideology. The commodity, of course, had always borne its share of ideological baggage. Among those who professed boundless admiration for the workings of the marketplace, the commodity was the subject of many an encomium in the eighteenth and nineteenth centuries.[21] The Great Exhibition was one long hymn of praise to things, and Jubilee kitsch made things look positively numinous. The difference is that now a specific political position inheres in the things themselves. In Hobson's analysis commodities are not simply goods destined for circulation and exchange in a market economy; they have become receptacles for containing, and vehicles for advancing, a specific political ideology.

In his little book Hobson does not give any examples of how this jingo ideology sought and found its material double; living as he did in a society where people lived under the perpetual rule of these cognate things, he must have assumed that his readers knew them well enough. In the late 1880's and early 1890's there seemed to be no limit to the number and variety of articles of jingo kitsch that enterprising manufacturers were capable of unloading on the public. Though jingoism began much earlier, most jingo kitsch came in the wake of Jubilee kitsch and relied on the same strategy of making individual articles bear the weight of immense social significance, here not of the monarchy but of the Empire at large. The roster of articles produced during this period reveals a salmagundi of kitsch charged with the task of legitimating the Empire. This was a large order, for the Empire was always expanding. But because recent innovations in print technology, notably the treadle and the jobbing platen, made possible large runs at low cost, entrepreneurs could now afford to keep pace with events. If an athlete swam the channel one week, he could well appear the next, as a Captain Webb did in 1895, on a matchbook label admonishing its readers to "ENCOURAGE HOME INDUSTRIES." Famous imperial personalities—nobility, high-ranking officers, decorated heroes, and athletes—soon came in all shapes and sizes, plastered over needle packets, feeding bottles, toothpaste pots, pencil boxes, varnish tins, cigarette containers, bale labels, sauce bottles, board games, sheet music, and paperweights.[22] One maker of cigarette cards, the Ogden tobacco company, set some kind of record by issuing no fewer than eight thousand separate picture cards which, taken together, offered "a panorama of the world at large." Far and away the most elaborate scheme was the glass slide system, which required a triple-lens projector to cast larger-than-life images on big standing screens. Sold in sets that each told a story, the slides seem to have been a better vehicle for out-and-out propaganda than any number of labels, cards, or matchboxes. Collections called "Celestials and Barbarians" and "Heroes and Fanatics of the Sudan" were evidently popular; one hand-colored set called "Soldiers of Britain" included action shots of troops bayoneting "fuzzy-wuzzies" in the Sudan. In all, these slideshow spectacles offer brutal confirmation for Hobson's idea that "the manufacture of Jingo spirit" was not carried out exclusively "amid the fumes of the music hall," but was "aided by many other instruments of information more reputable in appearance, and often more insidious in their appeal" (*Psychology*, 5).

Though late-Victorian consumers did not respond to this material onslaught of jingo kitsch in as clear-cut a way as Hobson says they did, he is right to call attention to how omnipresent it had become in domestic life. The purveyors of these allegorical articles made little attempt to sell them in any systematic way; still, one considerable advantage jingo kitsch had over more conventional propaganda was that people took these things home and used them on a daily basis. Whereas the jingo music shows were a passing holiday for most of their spectators, who could afford to go only once or at most twice a week, jingo kitsch like matchboxes and toiletries could be kept until the items wore out, or, as was more likely, until a new wave of kitsch appeared to replace them. To judge from the quick turnover, this happened every time new addition was made to the Empire. After almost every acquisition the manufacturers of jingo kitsch rushed in to reify history as it was being made. No sooner did England lay claim to fresh territory than jingo kitsch appeared as commemoratives enshrining a past that had only just taken place. These contrivances removed Empire from the domain of political struggle by moving it into the home, where, along with the samples from nature that Victorians loved to label and preserve under glass, it became an unthreatening decorative fixture. Paradoxically, as the Empire grew larger by millions of square miles, the spaces Victorians lived in became cramped with imperial allegories of kitsch.

The manufacturers of jingo kitsch could hardly have found a better medium for their message than the late-Victorian allegory. These allegories are rarely obscure, and one rarely has any trouble deciphering them. The ideas embodied in the colored lithograph of Queen Victoria in Richard Whiteing's novel *No. 5 John Street* are few and simple—the innate superiority of the English race, the heavy burden of Britain's God-given mission, the beneficence of the gifts the English bestow upon the world—and could have been found carved, etched, enameled, or inscribed on any number of public buildings. In many ways it is a typical allegorical scene: "The chief kneels on a loin-cloth of ostrich plumes. Ministers in the Windsor uniform hover in the background."[23] It would be a mistake to expect each of the elements in this scene to stand for a moral idea, a spiritual conception, or an ethical dilemma. Victorian public allegories only "stand for" something in the sense that a public official stands for a body of constituents. They are allegories of delegated authority in which the delegates of colonial lands are permitted to acquiesce in whatever the English have decided is best for them. Today we find it easy to dismiss these official metonymies as wooden and ineffective, but in Whiteing's novel the characters who examine them take them very seriously. The allegorical lithograph moves them to mull over the "evangelizing mission" of England and to hope that the English language, "if not exactly the sole language of heaven, is certainly the one most in use there" (*John Street*, 59, 60). It even leads one of them to suppose that since "His combined justice and mercy" are all "eminently British qualities," that is to say the qualities of a good administrator, the "Maker is at heart a Briton" (60–61). This interrogation of jingo allegories was repeated in homes, pubs, and workplaces all over the nation. Allegories were given as set texts for school examinations, presented to the queen on ceremonial occasions, posted as aids to recruitment, enshrined in public statues, and publicized by a flood of commodity kitsch. So crowded did life become with jingo allegories that the owner of the Victoria lithograph has trouble finding space for it on walls crowded with other prints which he also regards "with peculiar reverence" (61).

In many ways, then, jingoism was aimed at consolidating domestic support for imperialism; inward- rather than outward-directed, it was deeply and pervasively embedded in English commodity culture. Nobody knew better how to exploit this embeddedness than Henry Stanley. Unlike Queen Victoria, who did not have an appetite for celebrity, Stanley did not have to be lured onto center stage; he was hungry for publicity. From its inception, the Emin Pasha Relief Expedition was the most publicized of all African expeditions in the nineteenth century—an event that the major illustrated weeklies and their sponsors not only covered but, in a very real sense, created. Since the reports that trickled in from Stanley in Africa simply surveyed, in his usual telegraphic style, the status of his forces and the position of his supply train, the history of the expedition was largely written without him. Stanley soon became putty in the hands of the press, which reshaped the brash opportunist in the mold of a distinguished gentleman out to build an Empire. In much the same way did Stanley rely on a sedulously manufactured and impeccably timed publicity campaign to orchestrate his return. On his way home the explorer lingered for weeks in Belgium to dash off the two volumes of *In Darkest Africa*, duly released by Low, Marston, Searle & Rivington, Ltd. soon after his return. He also endorsed Victor Vaissier's "Congo" soap (Fig. 21), Keble's pipes, and Edgington tents. When Stanley's authorized biographer Frank Hird gushes that it became "Stanley" season in high society, he was not exaggerating. Preparations had been made for Stanley balls, receptions, banquets, lectures, parades—even for a Stanley medallion, struck in Welsh gold to highlight his Welsh heritage. *In Darkest Africa* was frequently translated and, according to one reviewer, "has been read more universally and with deeper interest than any other publication [of 1890]." In a letter to Ellen Terry, Bernard Shaw later complained that all society had succumbed to "Stanley worship." Well before Stanley set foot on English soil, then, his return had become the stuff of spectacle—the stuff of a jingo jubilee.[24]

Stanley's own efforts, however, did not define or exhaust the influence of the jingo spectacle during the spring of 1890. Indeed, in the advertising trade the Emin Pasha Relief Expedition soon acquired an eminence that temporarily outstripped even the popular royal family. Whatever else can be said about the expedition, it is clear that Stanley himself was mainly interested in using it to make himself more popular and, to some extent, to lay the groundwork for the annexation of Uganda. In a sense, the advertising industry took up where he left off. Together, advertisers drew on Stanley's vision of Africa overrun by the commodity, but they added a new and powerful dimension to it. At first glance it may seem otherwise, for the advertisements they produced appear to conceive of Stanley's Africa as a field of tourist attractions through which their products might pass, and pose for a snapshot, before being recycled back to England for the benefit of a domestic audience. United Kingdom Tea Company offers its version of the meeting of Stanley and Emin Pasha at Kavalli; Bovril depicts Stanley sipping bouillon in a rumpled safari jacket; Pears' shows a native inspecting the contents of a crate of soap. On closer examination, though, the paths commodities follow across Africa in these advertisements present

FIG. 21. The endorsing hero (*Illustrated London News*, August 8, 1891).

a more complex relationship between the Empire's center and its periphery. By introducing commodities into peripheral—indeed, liminal—areas, where, as even Stanley admits, they do not necessarily perform their usual functions, advertisers, in the words of anthropologist Victor Turner, negotiate the commodity's passage "from lower to higher status through a limbo of statuslessness." [25] In such a state as Stanley describes in *In Darkest Africa*, commodities are outside the positions assigned them by law, custom, and convention. To Africans they even appear valueless. But this devaluation is only temporary, and the commodity undergoes it only to return to England, having survived its ordeal by devaluation, to assert its authority more powerfully than ever before.

The story of the commodity's complex progress through liminal Africa comes out in bits and pieces in *The Graphic Stanley Number*, released in April 1890 to coincide with Stanley's return. With precious few facts available about the expedition, the periodical obviously gave its writers considerable poetic license, for both of its feature articles, "Stanley in Africa" and "The History of the Emin Pasha Relief Expedition," are murky and fictionalized. The periodical's illustrations and advertisements, however, tell a more interesting story. In *In Darkest Africa*, the commodity's procession through equatorial Africa was a clamorous and disorderly affair; here the same story has a rigorous order. It begins with the commodity's passage through Africa amidst stampeding elephants and marauding, invisible tribes.[26] Af-

FIG. 22. Stanley's African carriers (*Graphic Stanley Number*).

FIG. 23. At Kavalli (*Graphic Stanley Number*).

ricans predictably appear in their role as carriers, but, thanks to the process of monochromatic wood engraving, their dark skins merge into the general chiaroscuro of the forest, thus highlighting the white bundles of Western goods they carry on their heads (Fig. 22). It ends with the United Kingdom Tea Company's version of the meeting of Stanley and Emin Pasha at Kavalli (Fig. 23). Engravings in the illustrated weeklies had imagined this to be a polite occasion, the two men impeccably dressed, shaking hands at the head of a reception line of retainers. The tea ad improves on this: in a spacious tent amidst crates labeled "United Kingdom Tea Company's Teas—Used All Over the World," Stanley and Emin sip afternoon tea as smugly as a pair of gentlemen in a London club. The tent's curtains pull back to reveal a stage tableau in which the burning tropical sun of so many cautionary travel accounts has been replaced by the arcadian vacation sun.[27] So powerful is this commodity that it has made darkest Africa bright, comfortable, and domestic—so much so that in this ad a pair of complete strangers, one of them a German, greet one another in the old-boy language of the public schools.

While in the African interior, the commodity enters what Turner calls a "liminal" condition. In Turner's definition, a liminal condition is necessarily ambiguous, temporarily eluding or slipping through "the network of classifications that normally locate states and positions in cultural space."[28] One of the most eye-catching advertisements in *The Graphic Stanley Number* shows the commodity in this liminal state (Fig. 24). In full color, it depicts an inhabitant of equatorial Africa inspecting the contents of a soap crate that had chanced to wash ashore from a shipwreck. The African holds a bar of soap, which, though it was made to be exchanged as a commodity, is no longer a commodity for the simple reason that there are no white men around to teach him to impute exchange value to it. What is recorded in this advertisement, however, is not the demise of exchange value; as the Pears' copywriter correctly perceives, this moment is "THE BIRTH OF CIVILIZATION" in the sense that it expresses the developing movement of the commodity toward the colonial world. The clear implication is that the bar of soap will not remain in its liminal limbo forever, and that before long, Africans like this one will learn just what exchange value means. A hundred years earlier the ship offshore would have been preparing to enslave the African bodily as an object of exchange; here the object is rather to incorporate him into the orbit of capitalist exchange. In either case this liminal moment posits that capitalism is dependent on a noncapitalist world, for only by sending commodities into liminal areas where, presumably, their value will not be appreciated at first can the endemic overproduction characteristic of the capitalist system continue. As Rosa Luxemburg put it, the "historical process of the accumulation of capital depends in all its aspects upon the existence of noncapitalist social strata," so that "imperialism is the political expression of the accumulation of capital in its competition for the possession of the remainders of the noncapitalist world."[29] In its depiction of Africa as a safety valve for surplus manufactures, this Pears' advertisement recognizes the interdependence of imperial England and darkest Africa.

The image of darkest Africa had played a prominent role in imperial mythology from the beginning of the century.[30] By defi-

THE BIRTH OF CIVILIZATION— A MESSAGE FROM THE SEA ❄

"THE CONSUMPTION OF SOAP IS A MEASURE OF THE WEALTH, CIVILISATION,
HEALTH, AND PURITY OF THE PEOPLE." *LIEBIG.*
Specially drawn by H.S. MARKS, R.A. for the Proprietors of PEARS' SOAP.

FIG. 24. The liminal commodity (*Graphic Stanley Number*).

nition darkest Africa is the continent's most liminal region, a
place that civilization has not reached and may not reach for
quite a while. Throughout the nineteenth century travelers considered crossing it a rite of passage designed to test their mettle,
and many went there seeking what William Cornwallis Harris,
in *The Wild Sports of Southern Africa* (1847), called "romantic peril,
adventure, and discovery."[31] Henry Stanley had been to Africa many times before—by 1887 his writings on the subject
amounted to five stout volumes[32]—and he had often observed

this convention. In *In Darkest Africa*, it is no less conspicuous a convention as Stanley records a wide range of incidents that initiate his junior officers into the mysteries of the dark continent. The difference is that Africa has now become a proving ground primarily for the commodities he carries, and in *The Graphic Stanley Number*, where the explorers themselves appear as mere lackeys entrusted with the safekeeping of goods, the expedition becomes little more than an exercise in quality control. In *The Graphic* all the liminal forces that Africa can muster—darkness, wilderness, death, propertylessness—have been arreared against the combined forces of the commodity. Not for a moment is the outcome in doubt: without fail Stanley's provisions acquit themselves wonderfully, providing him with shelter, raiment, relaxation, even souvenirs—such that at journey's end he can strike a triumphant pose with a trophy, a cup of Bovril beef bouillon, in hand (Fig. 25). As if to underscore the commodity's new status, Bovril goes so far as to adopt the escutcheon of the late-Victorian church militant—the Salvation Army—and to affix it to a castle. In a periodical distinguished by the thickness of its advertising supplement, the commodity militant has triumphed, appearing everywhere as the expedition's spearhead, protector, justification, and reward.

The commodity's evangelical progress through liminal Africa in *The Graphic Stanley Number*, of course, corresponded no more precisely to the complex reality of commodity relations in central Africa than did Stanley's vision of commodities in *In Darkest Africa*; nor does *The Graphic Stanley Number* shed any new light on what actually happened during the expedition. Still, as tenuous a relationship as Stanley's advertised image bears to the full facts of Stanley's central African activities, it both met the needs of British national pride and succeeded in creating, on a large scale, a new and durable spectacle for commodity culture. For in the hands of 1890's advertisers the commodity was represented as the bulwark of Empire—as both a stabilizing influence and a major weapon in England's struggle against a bewildering variety of enemies. Shipped abroad, even the essential inertness of things—always the main barrier to attributing power to them—became a plus. As an inert object the commodity did not change

FIG. 25. The commodity militant (*Graphic Stanley Number*).

wherever it was taken, and whenever commodities were taken into the colonial world they asserted their "Englishness" as against everything irremediably foreign. Each commodity became a kind of portable Crystal Palace, exhibiting in miniature the superiority and surplus productivity of English industry. The truth, of course, was that only at so great a distance from England could a commodity be nothing but a self-sufficient manifestation of English manufacture. In a haphazard way advertisers exploited this, too, as year after year they pushed their wares closer and closer to the periphery of Empire, where each object could be depicted as an independent island of jingo material culture.

To this surge of interest in freestanding objects the illustrators and copywriters in the advertising industry responded predictably. All across the country it soon became the rage to show commodities deposited in any number of extraterritorial settings. Commodities turned up not only in Africa but in Ceylon, Java, Tibet, China, and India.[33] There did not have to be any causal connection between the setting the advertiser chose and the function the commodity served; Henry Stanley did not endorse a particular brand of pipe because he knew anything about pipes, and the African's discovery of a carton on a beach had nothing to do with the fact that it contained soap. But at the same time that late-nineteenth-century admen continued to exploit the old popular taste for spectacles of exotic origin, they placed additional emphasis on scenes whose attraction lay not in their oddity but in the homogeneity conferred on them by a form of exchange—the commodity—that was good anywhere in the world.

The unenviable position in which the homogenizing power of the commodity put indigenous peoples all over the world can be glimpsed in an advertisement for Liebig Beef Extract that appeared in the *Illustrated London News* on October 9, 1897 (Fig. 26). It shows four sandwich-board men at work on the Esplanade in Bombay. In England lines of sandwich-board men were a common enough sight on big-city streets, and over the years they moved many observers, from Henry Mayhew to James Joyce, to comment on the basic tension between the large promises made by the posters and the evident poverty of the men who carried them.[34] The advertising handbooks of the day attest that many advertisers felt the practice was outmoded but found it profitable and so chose to continue it while taking care to avoid picturing sandwich-board men in their printed matter.[35] The Liebig advertisement lives off this same tension between a glossy printed ad and its downtrodden carrier, but it uses it to serve a very different end. Here the carriers are Indian, and the advertisements they carry put them in their place and keep them there. The scenes the posters picture would not have been out of place in a middle-class English periodical like the *Illustrated London News*, but they serve no useful purpose in India. Indeed the ad implies that it is useless to promise these people anything. Not only does it make no effort to adjust its sales pitch to a foreign public, it offers to sell a product—beef extract—that seems calculated to offend the sensibilities of most Indians, whose religion prohibits

THE ESPLANADE, BOMBAY.

FIG. 26. The homogenizing commodity (*Illustrated London News*, October 9, 1897).

the slaughter of cattle. These sandwich-board men are not advertisers so much as they are prisoners on parade, able to view the world only through the small windows framed for them by English advertisements—windows as tiny as the air vents in Victorian model prisons. It would be hard to imagine a more humiliating tribute to the commodity's power, and yet such scenes were to become a staple item, appearing everywhere and undergoing many variations, in the advertising supplements of the 1890's.[36]

However powerful these later advertisements made the commodity out to be, they did not enshrine Henry Stanley's popularity as permanently as he had hoped. Stanley was essentially an adventurer, and adventures are by definition sensational and short-lived. The reason Stanley's popularity lasted as long as it did was because his foreign adventures diverted attention from the more pressing problem of what the English were doing in central Africa in the first place. Stanley had spent the better part of his career exploring the area and evading this question. In 1890, however, feasted by royalty and decked with honors,

Stanley's vision of a lasting English involvement in the region appeared to be shared by the nation as a whole. This bogus and momentary unanimity was chiefly responsible for prolonging English interest in a piece of Africa that many politicians in Westminster were eager to trade for a more profitable slice of the pie.[37] In Stanley's mind central Africa was a gold mine—but then Stanley was contemptuously indifferent to laying the groundwork necessary to turning his discoveries into long-term, profit-making enterprises. Though he succeeded in kindling a temporary popular enthusiasm for the region and though he succeeded in opening it up as a free field for advertised commodities, he had, in fact, staked his career on the wrong part of the continent. The real wealth lay elsewhere. True, for a few months during 1890 it appeared that Henry Stanley had convinced everybody that central Africa was a sound site for the play of English commodities, but those whom he had easily persuaded to stay were just as easily persuaded to go when gold, real gold, appeared on the horizon in the Transvaal.

II

No other commodity can rival the place that gold occupies in the Western material imagination. In and of itself, gold has few uses and makes up only a small fraction of the wealth of nations; rather, it is the oldest representation of the commodity. For centuries gold had an abiding relationship to the commodity, being sometimes actual currency and sometimes the guarantor of the value of currency. By the late nineteenth century gold currency had largely been replaced by paper money, and when it came to guaranteeing the legitimacy of exchange, the international monetary system depended on what was known as the "gold standard." Today what is best remembered about the gold standard is that it stood on the steady basis of a right to demand and receive gold for currency tendered, but the truth is that, then as now, a large part of the notes in circulation had no gold behind them. As J. A. Hobson pointed out in *Gold, Prices and Wages* (1913), "the influence of gold, either as coin or as a support of credit, is much smaller than has been represented."[38] What made gold influential was that it was a great leveler of markets. Under the gold standard, all markets, regardless of local conditions and complications, were ultimately homogenous because everything they could possibly produce could always be measured against a single yardstick. At a time when the African continent was yielding new raw materials at a rapid rate, gold gave these materials a place by assigning them a comparative value which, if arbitrary, at least conferred a sense of hierarchy on a market flooded with items of uncertain value. Though, as John Maynard Keynes later observed, "there is no historical warrant for expecting money to be represented even by a constant quantity of a particular metal," [39] late-nineteenth-century economists and investors chose to behave as if there were. In the heyday of the gold standard, gold appeared to possess absolute—inherent, not ascribed—economic value. In this situation, gold, formerly the province of marginal fortune-seekers, became one of the most legitimate commodities on earth.

If the gold standard brought a general change in the way people thought about gold, it also made them pay more attention to what was going on in South Africa, where most of the world's gold was being produced. Much to their chagrin, English investors found that they did not have a free hand to do as they liked in South Africa; they faced a determined group of white settlers known as the Boers. The Boer way of living put developers to task, for as primitive as they looked, they were shrewd businessmen who knew how to drive hard bargains. Much to everyone's surprise, the recalcitrant Boers proved to be a major obstacle in the commodity's predatory path through Africa. Elsewhere on the continent the commodity had never really faced an adversary. Recall that farther north, Henry Stanley had taken it as an article of faith that the commodity could surmount whatever barriers Africa threw up. All across the continent, in fact, the English were used to having things their way, taking what they wanted, ignoring what they did to indigenous peoples, and altering the economies through which they passed by manipulating a powerful form of exchange. Stanley steadfastly believed that his whole enterprise was essentially tied up with the commodity as a dynamic force, and it simply did not occur to him that it was also a destructive force that could conceivably encounter opposition or provoke resistance. For Stanley, as for many other late-nineteenth-century imperialists, the commodity had so frequently been represented as a conduit through which English power and influence were channeled into the colonial world that he did not stop to think that it had its limitations.

One limitation was that, despite all claims to the contrary, the commodity was never able to exist on its own for very long; like all forms of exchange, it required an economic structure to maintain it and a political structure to protect it. That the commodity was able to take root in South Africa as quickly as it did was due largely to the fact that a complex structure for exchanging manufactured articles already existed among the Boers. That just as quickly the commodity became the focal point for international controversy was due to the fact that the Boers were not interested in using their own political structure to further the economic interests of the English. To the contrary: they taxed them heavily, established a monopoly over dynamite, and slapped tolls on the roads connecting the mines to the cities. To English investors the Boers must have looked like trolls guarding treasure. It did not take long for them to decide that, as Arthur Conan Doyle put it in *The Great Boer War* (1900), the Boers were denying them "the freedom to which their home institutions had made them accustomed."[40] In truth, of course, it would be more accurate to say that what they were actually being denied was the complete freedom which the *absence* of their home institutions afforded them in Africa. Having grown accustomed to the wanton economic free-for-all of the African wilderness, the English were not prepared to have controls forced on them by anyone. By continually harassing them with what Conan Doyle felt to be "vexatious legislation,"[41] the Boers appeared to be dead set on holding the market, and with it the commodity, in captivity.

The most concentrated expression this sense of subjection ever found is contained in Rudyard Kipling's famous short story, "The Captive." Kipling wrote this story a year and a half after war broke out in 1899 and incorporated into it the same basic tensions that continued to aggravate the commodity in South

Africa and helped to foment war there. Though the British, and not the Boers, appear in this story as the captors, Kipling's choice of a captive makes the problem of the commodity's progress through Africa explicit: his captive is an advertiser. The advertiser's name is Laughton O. Zigler, and Kipling allows him to tell his story with very little interference from the third-person narrator who opens the story and supplements it with a few details from time to time. An inventor by trade, Zigler has come to South Africa from America to advertise and sell his contraptions to all comers. He offers two of them, "the Laughton-Zigler automatic two-inch field-gun, with self-feeding hopper, single oil-cylinder recoil, and ball-bearing gear," and "Laughtite, the new explosive." [42] As the story gets underway Zigler has come on hard times. He is being held captive by the British because he tried to sell his weapons to the Boers. Manifestly Zigler is indignant, but not because he was caught. He is indignant because, for what he considers some very poor reasons, the British, like the Boers before them, refused to buy anything from him. Zigler has no consciousness of wrongdoing and appears to consider his involvement with potential customers an involuntary response to the laws of supply and demand. Everyone seems to exist for him only as customers, and he does not much care who his customers are. When one of his English captors tries to explain to him that those who sell armaments are partly responsible for what their customers do with them, Zigler tells him he is wrong. Indeed the central feature of Zigler's character as Kipling has drawn it is his doggedness in arguing for the absolute freedom of commodity exchange.

Unlike the narrators of Kipling's other Boer War tales, Zigler has no hair-raising war stories to tell; instead the real interest of the story lies in the unconscious resilience he displays in defending the free market against a number of flabbergasted interlocutors, Briton and Boer. As a matter of fact the story reads like an encyclopedia of the ideas that, over a span of three centuries, the theorists of capitalism used to justify the practice of capitalism to the world at large. "The Captive" begins with a sweeping peroration as Zigler admits that he went to Africa to find the complete laissez-faire he thinks has been denied him in "two hemispheres and four continents" (51). Like Hobbes, he puts private before public interests and claims that he does not owe allegiance to any country in particular. "Have I gone gunning against the British?" the captive asks himself and answers "to a certain extent" without a trace of remorse. Like John Locke he views all human activity as paid wage-labor and surprises his captors by carrying this principle to its logical conclusion and offering to reimburse them for his "board" as a prisoner of war. And like Adam Smith, he holds that the wealthiest country in the world is not the one that amasses the most money but the one that produces the most goods. To the Boers he offers not a means for making money—they have plenty of that in the form of gold—but the means of producing consumable goods. Like a true disciple of Smith he proceeds to offer them his "gun-factory," and when they refuse to build it for him, he remarks, echoing Smith's famous description of a pin factory, that the Boers "don't amount to a row of pins" (33). No matter what kind of a fix Zigler finds himself in, he is ready to cite chapter and verse from the classical economists in order to steer his course through the free market, which he characteristically believes to be the best of all possible worlds.[43]

At first sight the arguments Zigler makes for the free market in "The Captive" appear to be the same as the arguments Henry Stanley makes for the market in *In Darkest Africa*. Both follow the call of the wild because they sense that there, in the absence of the regulated competition of the home market, they will be afforded the complete laissez-faire that they need to realize their aims; both, as a consequence, ignore the social character of all markets. If, however, we look at the story again, it becomes evident that Zigler strikes at the heart of Stanley's program for imperial expansion. For Stanley, the dictates of Empire and those of the absolutely free market are one; for Zigler they are at odds. Zigler's activities as an advertiser flatly contradict Stanley's claim that the commodity will, if it is given sufficient latitude, advance the imperial schemes of a particular nation. By selling to both sides, Zigler advances the simple proposition that the commodity is stateless. Trade had existed before in areas that were beyond the reach of Empire, but the assumption shared by people like Henry Stanley was that this was a temporary state of affairs pending the arrival of English law. What distinguishes Zigler from Stanley and the imperialists is that he regards the commodity as a permanently stateless institution that lives outside, and does not in fact require, any kind of legal protection. In his narrative Kipling's captive says in plain language what had only been implied in Stanley's narrative, namely, that it had become possible for commodities to be completely divorced from their origin, to the point where, as Marx had forecast, they had come to be "swept by universal commerce into the universal competitive struggle."[44]

Certainly the dangers of this development had been inherent in the structure of the commodity form since the beginning. In the mid-nineteenth century Marx saw it coming and devoted a large part of *Capital* to explaining what commodity exchange did to national identity. In Marx's account, whenever a product of human labor becomes a commodity, it loses its "specific social character."[45] Once a commodity enters the marketplace, it becomes a sort of free agent, and after it has changed hands a few times, it becomes very difficult to trace to its origin. In the narrowest technical sense of the term, the commodity form is simply a means for ensuring that exchange takes place on a common ground. Though, as even Marx admits, the creation of a common ground is bound to simplify exchange, it also takes from it the last semblance of its local character. The commodity form makes distribution placeless, for once the commodity has been established as the form of exchange, exchange can take place anywhere. Under the commodity form nationality hardly matters; as Marx perceived, this system of exchange "created everywhere the same relations . . . and thus destroyed the peculiar individuality of the various nationalities."[46] As with the splitting of the atom, once this destructive force has been unleashed there can be no guarantee that it will consistently be made to serve a single master. True, there can be no doubt that for a time it served the expansionist designs of late-nineteenth-century imperialists; because it did not respect national boundaries, the commodity form was a convenient vehicle for expanding the Empire's sphere of influence. But insofar as the commodity conveniently gave imperialists the Midas touch, it did so by turning whatever they touched into an object of exchange. Back in the 1870's the jingoes had the right idea when they tried to make the commodity look like a loyal servant to the crown, but no amount of wishful thinking could ultimately conceal the fact that the commodity was, in the end, nobody's lackey.

The matter would have been somewhat more serious if it had turned out exactly as Marx had predicted and the commodity had swept all human relations, including national loyalties, into a common basin of exchange. Marx clearly perceived a trend inherent in the market system, although he was wrong in assuming that this trend would assert itself by making nations obsolete. The hold nations continued to have over the marketplace may, in Marx's scheme of things, be somewhat of a paradox, but the fact is that even in a world more or less dominated by commodity relations, national loyalties persist. Whether he likes it or not, Laughton O. Zigler has to deal with a social order which, in time of war, has decreed that the Boers are the enemy and that trading with them constitutes a crime. By pursuing Boer customers, he has landed himself in a prison camp and has stopped the commodity's free progress through Africa dead in its tracks. Although Zigler claims that politics are none of his business and although he sees no reason why any impediment should exist between buyers and sellers, he is forced to recognize that impediments do exist and that when they do, they exist for political reasons. With all the clarity of hindsight Zigler sees that in South Africa "it was a condition and not a theory that confronted me" (34). He has to admit that his theory of free trade did not help him adjust to conditions there and that it may in fact have hindered any adjustment he wished to make by leading him to believe that the British and the Boers would, in the interest of maintaining free trade, not only allow him to move freely across the lines but also insure "free passage and freight" (33) for his wares. In South Africa he has come up against one of the central paradoxes of the capitalist marketplace, namely, that it establishes an international form of exchange while leaving intact the very national forms of government in whose interest it is to guard against unregulated international exchange ever taking place.

This paradox had never been quite understood by the armchair imperialists who were busy keeping the home reading public occupied with far-fetched tales of Empire. Sitting at home in a comfortable state of ignorance, many popular writers found it easy enough to make the commodity play a heroic role in winning the South African war. Had a novelist like G. A. Henty seen the commodity form in action the way Rudyard Kipling had in Africa and India, he might have been able to gauge correctly the limits of the free market as an instrument of imperial expansion. Nothing, however, could be further from what Henty did. A prolific writer of adolescent romances who typified so many attitudes of late-Victorian England, he embraced the commodity outright and put down his reasons in fictional form. Like so many of his novels, *With Roberts to Pretoria* (1902) makes it difficult to separate jingo ideology from fiction; on the whole Henty's South Africa does not resemble the real South Africa so much as it resembles his other novels, each of which, no matter where it is set, is like a single stage upon which the same props keep appearing in different guises in different productions. Here as elsewhere, Henty follows his usual practice of depositing his boy hero in one of the far-flung outposts of Empire in order to record how quickly he makes good. Nine times out of ten the boy, who makes up in pluck what he lacks in intelligence, manages to outfox the local inhabitants, who do not put up more than token resistance to him and who, in their heart of hearts, always seem to want the British to look after them. As in most of Henty's novels, it does not take long for the hero to make the locals conform to Henty's idea of what the British Empire should look like at whatever stage in the Empire's development he happens to be representing.

It required no great leap of the imagination for Henty to make his characters fulfill their historical mission yet still seem to have some say over the course their lives take; in *With Roberts to Pretoria* he gets around this problem by making his hero very lucky. The novel tells the story of a boy named Yorke Harburton, who attaches himself to Lord Roberts's army as it marches across the Transvaal to Pretoria in 1901. Along the way he meets Cecil Rhodes, who, impressed with the services Yorke has performed as a scout for Roberts's army, offers him a position that all but guarantees his success in postwar South Africa. As the story unfolds Yorke's every move is aided and abetted by the mysterious agency of the commodity, which always seems to be strewing his path with opportunity. Nobody compels this "specimen" of what Henty calls "the class by which Britain has been built up, her colonies formed, and her battle-fields won" to take advantage of his good fortune, and often when Henty lays it on too thick, he has his hero succumb to a fit of fairness and return some of the gold that comes his way to its original owners.[47] In this rather flat and predictable way the story manages to get its point across: that the commodity is a generally benevolent force, one which, if all goes well, acts as a kind of guardian angel watching over the interests of those who watch over the interests of Empire. So bound up are commodities with the fate of Empire that Henty goes so far as to attribute moral agency to them.

It certainly seems remarkable that anyone was ever capable of attributing moral agency to things, but it is all the more remarkable that G. A. Henty did not seem to have noticed what he was doing. By the turn of the century the assumption that the commodity had a manifest destiny whose aim and end was Empire had been so deeply ingrained in domestic commodity culture that it was possible for a writer like Henty to be completely unaware of the role it played in his work. As the novel draws to a close Henty lets pass without comment the glaring fact that Yorke resigns his commission on the eve of a major battle because, as he says, "I came out here to make my way in business . . . [and] should certainly have preferred to stay on until the end of the campaign, but the offer made me is so advantageous, that I am anxious to avail myself of it."[48] The decisive role that assumptions about the commodity played in South Africa were fully brought out only by Kipling, who knew too much about what the English were doing to the colonial world to let the commodity's role in it pass unexamined. In "The Captive" we watch Laughton O. Zigler from page to page thinking out ever new and ingenious expedients in order to resolve the dispute between the commodity and the state in favor of the commodity, but none of these expedients involves making things out to be the moral allies of the British crown. On that score Kipling had real doubts, and he became one of the first to break through the magic circle of the mutually reinforcing idea, first advanced haphazardly by jingoes and later maintained despite much evidence to the contrary by apologists like Henry Stanley and G. A. Henty, that the commodity and the state served each other well.

III

There could have been no easy way out of the dilemma posed by the coexistence of the commodity and the state; the fact of the matter was that, then as now, the relationship was subject to change and was always having to be renegotiated. Though in "The Captive" Kipling certainly makes it look as though the state is getting the better of Laughton O. Zigler and his commodities, it would be wrong to dismiss Zigler as an aberration. How pervasive Zigler's faith in the commodity was, and how uneasily that faith coexisted with strong national sentiments, came to light in the last year of the nineteenth century when, caught up in a whirlwind of jingo feeling after the outbreak of the Boer War, commodity culture tried its hand at propaganda.

To understand what happened when advertisers tried to sell the war to the public at large, it is important to remember that, until the war came, it had never occurred to anybody to think of the commodity as being anything other than a handmaiden to the state, let alone to imagine that it could conceivably pose a threat to it. Like the jingoes, whose every move they copied, advertisers in the 1890's were always willing to allow the commodity to run rampant in the colonial world so long as it served English interests; like the jingoes they stood for a version of free trade that asserted as an unalterable fact the primacy of national sentiments over international commodity exchange. Thus they were confronted with a dual task: they had to establish that the commodity was an unstoppable force, and they had, simultaneously, to prevent it from developing according to its own logic, eroding national distinction and with it the long-term prospect of world empire. The Stanley advertisements of 1890 held together as well as they did because in central Africa there appeared to be no national distinctions that needed to be eradicated; since the tribal nations Henry Stanley confronted had little or no legitimacy in his eyes, he was able to allow the commodity free reign without troubling to observe that what it was doing was bringing about the downfall of nations every bit as complex as his own. In due course advertisements registered Stanley's vested misperception by representing central Africa as an asocial vacuum on the periphery of Empire. As long as the commodity did not encounter any resistance more significant than what Conrad called the "incomprehensible frenzy" of colonial nations,[49] it seemed that no force on earth was capable of checking its momentum.

The chief value of the contribution advertising made to the war effort did not lie in its propaganda value for the state, but in its unequaled capacity to safeguard and perpetuate this fictitious alliance between the commodity and the state. In contrast to the actual relationship between the two, which was changing all the time, advertisers managed to elevate this fiction to the status of an entente cordiale. An advertisement for Pioneer Tobacco which appeared in *The Graphic* early in 1901 advances the alliance with a striking graphic and a memorable slogan: "ONE FLAG, ONE TOBACCO" (Fig. 27). The neat parallel structure of the phrase makes the commodity and the state look like they stand shoulder to shoulder, and the accompanying graphic goes so far as to merge the two by doubly superimposing the word "Pioneer" directly onto the Union Jack. Another cigarette, Ogden Guinea Golds, ran ads calling its product "a welcome comrade." With equally unwavering loyalty the makers of the "Tortoise-Shell Mixture" rushed to enlist their pipe-smoking icon, one Captain Kettle, in the 104th Transvaal Fusileers. In October 1900 Kettle appears in *The Graphic* dressed in full battle kit, calmly warding off enemy fire with a can of tobacco in his hand.[50] Whether they chose to depict the commodity as a comrade in arms or as a lucky charm, Boer War advertisers were to return time and again to the claim implicit in

FIG. 27. The war reified (*Graphic*, March 2, 1901).

each of these advertisements, namely, that a perfect harmony of interests exists between the commodity and the state.

Ironically enough, it is because advertising desired to serve the state that it began to concentrate all the state's military might in the form of the commodity. Balled up in the commodity, England's power appeared to be a single nucleus that could be directed with great force, and with devastating impact, against the enemy. How crucial to the war effort this nucleus of commodities became can be seen in those instances where, in one advertisement after another, the war has been transformed into a commodity crusade. Pioneer cigarettes shows Tommy Atkins sounding a "Joyful Voice from the Front" to celebrate the arrival of a "care package" full of cigarettes. Elsewhere a bugler sounds "the charge" for Pioneer (three shillings) while a competitor, Ogden, depicts the entire general staff smoking "Guinea-Gold" cigarettes. Cans of Aspinall's Enamel shield an officer from enemy fire. A row of blockhouses made of Lemco beef bouillon cans holds the fort (Fig. 28). An artillery battery blasts away as the caption of a cigar ad promises that "the BEST SMOKE in the WORLD is the Flor de Dindigul Cigar." A map traces the route Lord Roberts followed as he marched from Kimberley to Bloemfontein to demonstrate that he made "an indelible imprint of the word Bovril on the face of the Orange Free State." [51] It all adds up to a war in which the onus of battle has been assumed almost entirely by commodities; they have a hand in making and executing plans, sounding charges, displaying the colors—even in providing cover. Indeed, all these advertisements have one thing in common: the soldiers sealed off in them are treated as if they no longer matter, as if what happened to them hinged on the brand of tobacco they smoked, as if they were not active human agents but rather passive instruments of the goods they consumed. In the most basic ways it appears that the whole of the war has been thoroughly and systematically organized by, and even for, things.

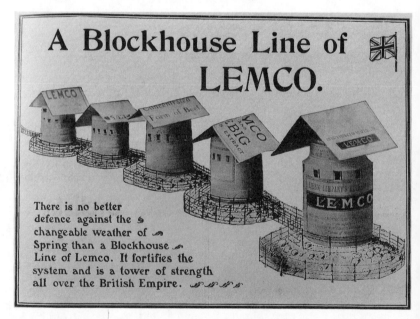

FIG. 28. The Lemco Line (*Illustrated London News*, April 5, 1902).

FIG. 29. The commodity vanguard (*Graphic*, May 12, 1900).

Once the commodity had become the most powerful weapon in the state's arsenal, it was in a position to pose a real threat to it. Though the above advertisements manage to make the alliance between the commodity and the state look like a perfectly normal measure, others depict it in terms that can only be described as mercenary. A remarkable cigarette advertisement that ran in *The Graphic* during 1900 puts advertisers in the difficult position of appearing to assist the enemy and returns us to Laughton O. Zigler's proposition that the commodity is stateless (Fig. 29). Here the commodity literally undermines the ground the English walk on. Above ground, a Boer surrenders his rifle to an English officer; below ground we can make out a keg of dynamite, a Maxim gun, and a box of Ogden Guinea Golds. The advertisement does not say how the Boer has managed to lay his hands on these goods; like so many other advertisements it is completely indifferent to the origin of the commodities it pictures. The point, rather, is that however the Boer got them, the goods appear to have arrived on the scene well before the

Englishman makes his appearance as conqueror. By the time the English officer arrives to assert his authority, the very ground on which he stands has been saturated with articles of European manufacture, and if he bothered to look around, he would find them directly underfoot. It may well be that he thinks a new world lies before him, but the truth is that whenever he ventures into fresh territory, he finds that the mercenary commodity has beaten the state to the punch. In this ad the conditions of commodity exchange, and the spread of those conditions into colonial countries, have led to a situation where the English, wherever they go, encounter unmistakable evidence that the market has been there first.

Though the threat the mercenary commodity poses to the state is very real here, it does not, on further evaluation, threaten it in any lasting way. The Boer's use of dynamite, Maxim guns, and Ogden cigarettes may benefit him in the short run, but in the long run it certainly serves the interests of English manufacturers, whose goods have sought and found a new market. It might require a war to consolidate the new market, but then most people at the time believed that the English won every war they fought and, having won, offered the loser generous terms and a place in the Empire. It had often worked out this way in the past, and on the whole this practice suited English business interests well. A beaten enemy was the ideal consumer, for he could be made to buy exactly what the victors chose to supply him with, exactly when they chose to supply it to him. Little wonder, then, that during the war advertisers conducted their business on the consistent assumption that they would eventually achieve this ultimate goal, and never lost sight of it no matter how remote it may have seemed or how decidedly its demands may have gone counter to the necessities of the moment. They therefore considered the Boers not as permanent enemies, but, on the contrary, as potential customers. Even at the height of the conflict Ogden cigarettes could look ahead to the day when a new market would open up by running an ad showing a captured Boer general smoking "Guinea-Golds" (Fig. 30). The cigarettes his captors have given him are, the caption tells us, "his only solace."

Cronje at St Helena

OGDEN'S
GUINEA-GOLD
ARE HIS ONLY SOLACE
Beware of Imitations

FIG. 30. The defeated consumer (*Graphic*, April 28, 1900).

We have little sense now of how incongruous the image of a
Boer consumer was in the early 1900's; the very idea must have
seemed like a contradiction in terms. Though, as we have seen,
the Boers had in fact developed a sophisticated market economy, throughout the world they were known for their complete
contempt for consumerism in any form. People assumed that
the Boers had feared the growing wealth and acquisitiveness
they saw rampant in industrial societies and, like the Mormons
in the United States, had fled to a place so desolate that they
could not imagine that anyone would ever take an interest in it.
Predictably, the foreigners who had come to South Africa had
been horrified when they saw how the Boers lived. "Disdaining
trade," wrote Sydney Brooks in 1899, "disdaining agriculture,
ignorant to an almost inconceivable degree of ignorance, without music, literature, or art, superstitious, grimly religious, they
are in all things, except courage and stubbornness, the very antithesis of the strangers scattered among them. The patriarch
Abraham in Wall Street would hardly make an odder con-

trast."[52] One account after another testifies that the Boers were, in Hannah Arendt's words, "the first European group to become alienated from the pride which western man felt in living in a world created and fabricated by himself."[53] As lords and masters of the Transvaal, the Boers conspicuously refused to consume things at the very moment in history when, as Thorstein Veblen saw clearly in 1899, the conspicuous consumption of things had become all-important.[54] To many onlookers the course of action the English needed to take was logical and unavoidable: the Boers had to be taught, against their will if necessary, to consume.

This course of action had long been clear to English advertisers. Even before the war began, advertising had marked out South Africa as the last pocket of conscious resistance to the commodity's inexorable progress across Africa. If all went according to plan, in time the Boer would see in commodities something more than consolation prizes; in them he would find enlightenment. A little advertising handbook called "In Brightest Africa" leaves no room for doubt about what the dark continent would look like in light of day.[55] The newly enlightened continent would be a utopia of manufactured goods and a monument to the English way of life. Not only would the Boer buy English furniture, upholstery, carpets, hardware, cycles, saddlery, harnesses, galvanized iron, cement, tiles, shop fittings, iron, steel, and in due time gas and electric light; he would take pride in displaying his wealth, thus paying belated tribute to what Veblen called the "ceremonial character" of the commodity.[56] Like all human beings he would continue to live in a world that had been created by human labor, but the labor that went into creating it would no longer be his own; it would be someone else's. "There is no limit to their demand," Thomas Fowell Buxton had predicted in 1840, "except their want of articles to give us in return."[57] The Boer would go on living in South Africa, but he would be living in a world in which, as a recent critic has put it, "the dictatorship of consumer goods has finally destroyed the barriers of blood, lineage, and race."[58]

To picture a South Africa in these terms is to imagine a society that never existed and never did develop—a society in which national identity has been liquidated among a colonial people. No one is about to deny the commodity the credit it deserves for helping to bring South Africa within the English sphere of influence; even before the war began South Africa was already a satellite market for English goods and was well on its way to becoming the first consumer society on the African continent. But it turned out to be no ordinary consumer society. In England the commodity had taken on the role of a great leveler. In department stores the consumer was queen and the queen was a consumer, and festivals like the Jubilees served to dramatize that monarch and commoner alike were equals in the eyes of the market. South Africa, however, became a consumer society without espousing this democratic ideal. The Boers were able to reap the benefits of a consumer society without acceding to its usual premise, namely, that quantitative values among things should take precedence over qualitative values among people. Instead of letting the market tell them what to put first, the Boers put race first and could discover no higher value than that which they conferred on the color of skin. Held back at first by the control the English exercised over the South African market, over time the Boers gradually turned the commodity into a more or less conscious instrument for dominating the black population. In this way they came very close to reviving the slave system. The blacks worked the mines, and the whites grew rich as the rest of the world looked on, appalled not so much by the suffering of a large number of human beings as by the incontrovertible fact that the market in general, and the commodity in particular, had not acted as agents of enlightenment.

The fact that the Boers used the commodity for their own purposes did not directly influence the course of events elsewhere in the world, but it had the force of example. In the late nineteenth century, economic expansion in the colonial world had been incomplete and haphazard at best, and—as Henry Stanley saw to his chagrin in central Africa—it had often been met with incomprehension and stymied by lack of cooperation. In the early twentieth century this latent opposition became manifest. With a twist of fate that would have surprised Marx had he lived to see it, the commodity became an instrument colonial peoples used to assert their national identity and to achieve their national independence. In India, for instance, those who worked for independence made the commodity the focal point of their struggle. There the British had flooded the market with so many cheap imports priced so far under local prices that it had become difficult for Indian manufacturers to compete with them, and by the turn of the century the mills of Manchester had become the clothiers of India. Three years after the war in South Africa ended, a struggle began for the right, as a character in Rabindranath Tagore's *The Home and the World* (1915) puts it, "to get the things required by our people produced in our own country." [59] This was a political struggle which was fought out quite deliberately on economic terrain: the adherents of the movement, called Swadeshi, boycotted British goods, encouraged indigenous industry, and held rallies at which they lit bonfires with British textiles. Though in 1905 Swadeshi did not manage to get any concessions out of the Raj, it pointed to what was essentially a shift of power in the British Empire. The thirty-year alliance between the commodity and the English state was coming to an end, and as Tagore understood, "no distinct vision" had developed for what sort of economy should take its place. [60] Only twenty-five years later, when Mohandas Gandhi marched to the sea to make salt in defiance of a British prohibition, did a large number of people affirm that they had a right to make their own goods in their own country. So open did resistance to British control of the means of production eventually become that a Swadeshi song composed to rally people around local products was proclaimed the Indian national anthem.

It was only in this later context that the commodity lost its sanctified association with the English state. At the turn of the century, however, England's reach had not yet exceeded its grasp, and the alliance between the two remained intact and inviolate, binding at home and abroad, praised by explorers, celebrated by jingoes, victorious in South Africa, and poised at the threshold of fresh territory. There was clearly some discord on the horizon, something which, in Boer War advertisements, prevented the commodity from being seen as the Empire's obedient servant. But by and large these advertisements, like the Stanley advertisements before them, held together well, and their popularity in the pages of the large dailies and illustrated weeklies leaves no doubt that they had struck a responsive chord in the reading public. For not only did the advertising industry's representation of British rule as an Empire of things have a solid basis in reality abroad, where there was considerable resistance to the commodity, it also had a solid basis in reality at home, where there was almost none. To picture Africa as a reified continent, as a free field for the commodity, as a locus of directed and supervised consumption, as a Crystal Palace in the making—these were not only representations of what was going on in Africa or India but also plain descriptions of what had happened to life in England when it had been fully colonized by the commodity. In the late nineteenth century the commodity had become a cultural force to be reckoned with, and people could no longer dismiss it, as Marx had said they were wont to do, as a "trivial thing."[61] Commodities now appeared to cement political coalitions, mobilize public opinion, make and break Empires. In 1851 the Crystal Palace had made a spectacle of things by placing them in a gigantic greenhouse. By the turn of the century that greenhouse had become a tropical hothouse as, in advertising and many other forms of narrative, the spectacle of commodities had become an imperial exhibition that encompassed the world.

The era of the great exhibitions of things, then, had not yet come to an end. There had been two Jubilees, the second of which, an imperial Jubilee, had traversed the full body of the earth. Around the turn of the century there were many grand imperial exhibitions that gave an architectural solidity to the evasive and ubiquitous spectacle of the commodity in the colonial world. Held in London nearly every year between 1895 and 1911, these exhibitions enveloped the world in the pervasive imagery of spectacle.[62] No jingo advertisement better embodied the spirit of commodity culture than these exhibitions, in which the semiotics of spectacle re-emerged in stark contemporary clarity. Largely ignored during the Great Exhibition, minerals and ores now became the chief icons of an expanding empire. In them consumers viewed not a replica of the colonial world, but the colonial world itself, in mass and in the raw. Thanks to refrigeration, even perishable commodities like fruit and vegetables now appeared as autonomous and indestructible icons. Any pretext of commemoration had disappeared; consumers no longer needed an excuse to go and see things. The sight of them now sufficed. Consumers mingled equally amid the spectacle of the fundamental inequality of the metropolitan and colonial worlds. The commodity looked like a dutiful civil servant of the Empire. Torn from the colonial world, abundance was everywhere; yet, by an astonishing reversal the English believed not that they had stolen the fruit of the earth from colonial countries but that, in taking it, they had bestowed it on them. In the late-nineteenth-century imperial exhibition, commodities were an arterial network of capitalist communication, a global system of domination and circulation analogous to what railroads had been for capitalism in the mid-nineteenth century. The spectacle of Victorian commodity culture had transformed the commodity into a technology of representation, a working model of the shape of things to come.

Like the organizers of imperial exhibitions, the jingo advertisers were mistaken in their glimpses of Africa's future, but they were not entirely wrong in their belief that the commodity would remake the world. The world it would remake, the society it would reshape, the material it would rework—all were English. General William Booth, founder of the Salvation Army, saw what was coming in the summer of 1890 when he brought out a companion volume to Stanley's *In Darkest Africa* and called it *In Darkest England*.[63] The details of Booth's program for social reform need not concern us here; the point is simply that Booth used Stanley's call for world empire to argue that the most promising terrain for exploration lay within England. Booth's call to examine England's dark core parallels the development of a specifically domestic extension of advertising during this most imperial of decades. It points to a massive internal expansion of the capitalist market into realms of life jingo advertising had left relatively untouched. For while jingo advertisers were putting forward a sweeping vision of the role the commodity played in the commonwealth at large, another kind of advertising was having a field day at home, where commodity culture was playing a much larger role on a much smaller scale. The commodity was coming to roost in everyday life. "It is ever present," wrote William Stead in *The Art of Advertising* (1899), "day after day, week after week, month after month. It reaches the consumer where he is most susceptible—his home. No other form of advertising has such opportunities of penetrating into the sanctum sanctorum of the consumer."[64] In the long run the commodity would invade and restructure whole areas of bodily upkeep, gender definition, and sexual practice. Uncelebrated, unheroic, and almost imperceptible, it would benefit not only from the authority gleaned from extraordinary events like the Emin Pasha Relief Expedition and the Boer War, but also from the continuity derived from ordinary activities that held dominion over every walk of life.

4

The Patent Medicine System

In the last years of the nineteenth century the new commodity culture appeared to be moving further and further away from the domain of everyday life. Queen Victoria invested ordinary domestic articles with a numinous aura that made them look extraordinary, and Henry Stanley packed them into some of the remotest areas of the earth. The events of the Boer War placed them in a positively world-historical context. Everywhere, on leaflets and hoardings, in illustrated weeklies and green advertising supplements, commodities had become larger than life, bigger than any continent, more powerful than any one country, until finally it seemed they had a life of their own. Late-Victorian commodity culture succeeded in presenting itself as an immense accumulation of spectacles unfolding in a world of goods. As models of socially dominant life and as instruments of legitimation, spectacles had been around for a long time. The Great Exhibition mobilized them on a grand scale. Parliament and the Royal Family depended on them. The difference was that now, through the medium of advertising, the immense powers of signification embodied in the spectacle had become separated from their institutional origins, harnessed to commodities, and displayed on a larger scale than ever before.

For all their grandeur, however, the advertised spectacles of Jubilee and Darkest Africa were limited in the extent to which they could invade and restructure social space. They could contribute to the formation of images of Monarchy and Empire, and in a very real sense they could supplant them. By representing

Victoria as a consumer queen and Africa as a repository for domestic articles, they could even make the commodity look like the great ordering agent of culture. In the hands of late-Victorian advertisers, the spectacle became, as Guy Debord has written, "the material reconstruction of the religious illusion," an aggregate of objects that presented itself "as something enormously positive, indisputable and inaccessible."[1] The sole drawback to this kind of spectacular affirmation was that while it elevated commodities to a new national prominence, it also removed them from everyday life. By consuming certain representative articles, Queen Victoria and Henry Stanley may have presided symbolically and macroscopically over a nation of consumers, but they did not, and could not, tell consumers how to go about making every little purchase. This task was reserved for another sort of advertiser, and it ultimately required the development of a new, microscopic form of commodity culture: the spectacle of the consumer's body.

The body of the Victorian consumer had long been a site of social controversy. Throughout the period relatively few critics rose in protest against the admen's collective defilement of the Monarchy and Empire. Instead they focused their attention on a more minute, more detailed, and in many ways more prevalent kind of advertising. During the Jubilee buy-all advertisers had found that they could use the image of the stout queen to sell all manner of common domestic articles, things like cloth, soap, cleanser, and chocolate. The imperial 1890's added the products of Empire to the list, and in due course the pitch artists were hawking rubber, silk, tea, and coffee. But as large as this horizon of activity was, it did not encompass the terrain that commodity culture was most eager to minister to, the government most anxious to control, and the consumer most hard-pressed to defend. This terrain was the human body and included all of its vital functions, the body when healthy or sick, perfumed or medicated, stretched or compressed. Almost every article of legislation that Parliament aimed at the advertising industry during the nineteenth century had been formulated with the human body expressly in mind and was intended to assert the government's hegemony over a site—the body and its manifold processes—

that many in power feared had long been forfeit to an under-world of advertisers.

I

This underworld was made up of quacks, and the quacks sold medicines of a very particular kind. Today when we think of quacks, we tend to conjure up images of catch-as-catch-can traveling salesmen standing on soap boxes or operating out of the backs of wagons, taking advantage of every opportunity to tout the virtues of some evil-smelling mixture to roadside passersby. These itinerant peddlers certainly existed—they inhabit Mayhew's London and roam Thomas Hardy's Wessex—but there were never enough of them to compel Parliament to act to suppress them.[2] Quacks, rather, offered their remedies to the nation at large. They advertised by every means imaginable—and then some. By hook or by crook they managed to infiltrate every layer of social life, and their products were in large use among every class of consumer. In spirit they were like a secret brotherhood of Freemasons, and by descent they were more closely related to alchemists and pharmacists than to doctors. They made pills, powders, lozenges, tinctures, potions, cordials, electuaries, plasters, unguents, salves, ointments, drops, lotions, oils, spirits, mouthwashes, medicated herbs, and healing waters. Because so many of the makers of this babel of articles applied for the protection of government patents to preserve their trade secrets, they were known as the "patent" medicine men.

From a distance of nearly one hundred years it is hard to understand why the patent medicine men had so many people in high places up in arms. Studies were continually being undertaken that proved to most everyone's satisfaction that most patent medicines were composed of little more than glycerine, sugar, sodium bicarbonate, gum, and starch. In the years between 1868 and 1909 Parliament passed no fewer than six acts designed to wipe them off the face of the earth—the Pharmacy Acts of 1868–69, the Sale of Food and Drugs Acts of 1875 and 1899, the Merchandise Marks Act of 1887, the Indecent Advertisements Act of 1889, and the Poisons and Pharmacy Act of

A Suggestion for the London Pageant
A splendid welcome would be assured to a trophy of the World's Favourite Dentifrice.

FIG. 31. The body's pageantry (*Graphic*, March 28, 1908).

1908.[3] The moralists and religionists of the realm rejoiced to find a common enemy in a trade that spent most of its energy flaunting the seventh commandment. All the available evidence—chemical, legal, and moral—seemed to indicate, in the words of a prominent member of the House of Commons, that "the public is spending its money on nothing really valid, but on a kind of neo-impressionism of journalism."[4]

But the patent medicine bubble of turn-of-the-century England was more than a lot of impressionistic hot air. An advertisement for Odol dentifrice that appeared in *The Graphic* in 1908 gives us a clearer idea both of what the patent medicine men were capable of and of why the authorities thought it was necessary to pay obsessive attention to them (Fig. 31). It shows a large crowd pressing in on a horse-drawn caisson. The caisson does not carry Queen Victoria to her final resting place in Westminster Abbey, nor does it form part of one of King Edward's processional trains. It does not accompany an imperial hero through the streets of the capital city of the British Empire. Instead the crowd has turned out to gawk at the triumphal pageant of a dentifrice. What the caption calls "A Suggestion for the London Pageant" effectively turns the logic of pageantry inside out. Instead of celebrating a showy exterior, the Odol pageant makes a spectacle out of a normally invisible interior—here, the inside of one's mouth. For hundreds of years people had been privately cleaning and perfuming their mouths, just as they had been privately plucking their eyebrows and shaving their armpits. Now these private rituals have become the stuff of public progresses, and the inside of the body appears as a field open to all comers. Products that minister to the body's hidden cavities have assumed Brobdingnagian proportions in a world where, as the caption promises, "a splendid welcome would be assured to a trophy of the World's Favourite Dentifrice."

It took sheer commercial hubris to magnify a dentifrice to these proportions, but it was hubris well earned. Patent medicine was big business. To get the word out the brotherhood of quacks spent two million pounds a year in advertising costs. In 1908 alone the government stuck patent medicine stamps on forty-one million articles, and the duties the public paid on them amounted to over three million pounds. By any reckoning the English public bought more potions than it did legitimate drugs, and more pills per capita than any other nation in Europe. The makers of Beecham's Pills sold a million pills a day. Only alcohol was more popular and more widely available—though not under such a variety of names. The quacks called themselves beauty doctors, fat curists, wrinkle eradicators, blood purifiers, sight restorers, flesh producers, hair renewers, rubber plasterists, ear drummers, and battery men. For the bedridden there were correspondence courses of treatment, for the rich there were "gold cures," and for the skeptical there were "Hygienic Institutes" offering testimonials and documentation. In the pharmacology of the time, a "drug" merely meant something that was dried to be kept for future use. Patent medicine labored under no such limitations, and the permutations were endless. Mechanical massage by air pressure was considered patent medicine. So were electric belts, artificial eardrums, and vacuum caps that fit over the head. So too was "gas pipe therapy," described as "a piece of tubing, which may have some charcoal or something else inside, to which two pipes are attached, and discs. You are supposed to put the piece of pipe in a bucket of water, and attach the discs to your ankle, and by this means your blood becomes oxygenated, and you are cured of anything that is the matter with you" (*Report*, 323). To people who willingly submitted to such treatments, Edwardian London must have looked something like the London that Defoe described in his *Journal of the Plague Year*—a city flooded with remedies, where the threat of incurable disease hung over everyone and cure-alls promised the only relief possible.

To Parliament and to the medical establishment it seemed abundantly clear that something needed to be done to stop this plague of patent medicines. On February 11, 1912, a Select Committee of the House of Commons was convened to consider what damage the manufacture, sale, and consumption of patent medicines had done to the public health of England. The hearings lasted two years and came close to arousing the kind of ongoing public interest the French displayed for the Dreyfus trials and the Americans for the trial of President McKinley's anarchist assassin, Czolgosz. The Select Committee held thirty-three public sittings and directed 14,000 questions at forty-two witnesses. Of these witnesses, eleven were physicians, five were chemists, four were wholesale or manufacturing druggists, and nine were quacks. This battery of witnesses represented the Customs and Excise Office, the Privy Council Office, the Home Office, the Local Government Board, the Director of Public Prosecutions, the Government Laboratory, the General Medical Council, the Royal Society of Medicine, the Royal College of Physicians, the British Medical Association, the Association of Medical Herbalists, and the White Cross League of the Church of England. While it sat, the Select Committee commissioned fourteen separate chemical analyses and read into the record the major published analyses of the past fifty years. The record of the hearings, plainly titled the *Report from the Select Committee on Patent Medicines*, ran to a thousand pages of tiny print, arranged in double columns. At no point, and by no standard of comprehensiveness, did the Select Committee's *Report* miss a beat.

Throughout the hearings the Select Committee expressed its alarm at the gravity of the problem in the most forceful of terms. As the evidence piled up, the committee members stopped talking about a glut of patent medicines and started referring to "this system of quackery" (336). The Select Committee's chairman came right out and said that "the vendors of patent and proprietary medicines can practically do what they like" (ix). When it came to the body and its functions, the patent medicine men seemed to be telling the world, as Humpty Dumpty told Alice, that "it means just what I choose it to mean." Indeed the hearings often proceeded in a Through-the-Looking-Glass manner, with none of the participants quite able to believe what they saw or heard. The chemists who compared the exuberant boasts of the vendors with the banal ingredients of their products were continually amazed that "the fancy is so free and the fact so simple" (vi). At other times the hearings were like a trial at which the defendant is never named, for had the committee members so much as mentioned a particular patent medicine their remarks would at once have been used for advertising purposes. The Select Committee considered itself forewarned by what had happened in 1909 to the British Medical Association soon after it released *Secret Remedies*, a long analysis of the chemical composition of various patent medicines.[5] Beset with similar difficulties, the Select Committee could not even keep track of its own adversaries. So protean were the quacks that they were liable at any time "to disappear and then to come up under another name with the same old remedies" (244).

Doubtless many remedies were hoary with age. In the sixteenth century Aqua Vitae was not taken as a beverage but sold by quacks as a secret remedy to prolong life and restore youth.[6] In the seventeenth century Autolycus had carried nostrums in his pack, and in the eighteenth Samuel Johnson had defined them as medicines "the composition of which has not been divulged to the public." By the mid-nineteenth century the situation had not changed appreciably. "Just as peasants in Germany go to be bled or cupped at certain seasons of the year," Friedrich

Engels wrote in 1844, "so the English workers now gulp down their patent medicines, injuring themselves while filling the pockets of the proprietors."[7] In 1855 the *Quarterly Review* commented that "it does indeed seem incredible that one [patent medicine man] should expend upon the mere advertising of quack pills a sum equal to the entire revenue of many a German principality."[8] To be sure, the government monitored the trade, but with so little interest that the laws were rarely enforced. When the Select Committee dredged up the Stamp Acts of 1804 and 1812, it found that the government's intention in taxing "medicaments for the prevention, cure, or relief of any disorder or complaint incident to or in any wise affecting the human body"[9] had primarily been to skim off revenues from a very profitable business. Over the years the government had, in effect, been pandering to the very patent medicine trade it was supposed to have been regulating. Stamping the products was tantamount to giving them the government's seal of approval, and the quacks responded by using the stamps as an advertising gimmick (*Report*, xxii). Little wonder, then, that to many observers the patent medicine men seemed to lead a saturnalian existence, reigning over a world where all laws were suspended in a permanent state of statutory neglect.

However unruly they may already have been, the patent medicine men became appreciably bolder in the late nineteenth century. As there were no laws on the books to regulate truth in advertising, there was no stopping them once they had gained access to the mass audience created and cultivated by the Victorian periodical press. The larger the audience, the more restive the quacks became. Lacking any precise notion of who it was they were addressing, they promised anything and everything to anyone and everyone, vying with one another to see who could produce the most comprehensive cure-all. Formerly the quack trade had been a rather specialized business, divided into small and established markets for such products as cough medicines, headache powders, hair restorers, consumption cures, and the like. But by the time the British Medical Association got around to cataloging the claims patent medicines made for themselves in 1909, these categories had become obsolete. Cough medicines cured headaches, headache powders soothed the nerves, nerve tonics ministered to the gout. It was now routine business to leave no absurd promise unmade; all cures had become cure-alls.

On nothing, then, did the Select Committee fix its attention so much as on what it called these "wild statements" (*Report*, 172). It did so like a diagnostician tantalized by an open sore. Some claims were vague: "it never fails," "surpasses anything ever discovered," "cures any old disease lurking about the system" (xlv). And some, like those printed on a circular wrapped around a box of Beecham's Pills, were more specific and promised to cure

Constipation, Headache, Dizziness or Swimming in the Head, Wind, Pain, and Spasms at the Stomach, Pains in the Back, Restlessness, Insomnia, Indigestion, Want of Appetite, Fullness after Meals, Vomitings, Sickness of the Stomach, Bilious or Liver Complaints, Sick Headaches, Cold Chills, Flushings of Heat, Lowness of Spirits, and all Nervous Affections, Scurvy and Scorbutic Affections, Pimples and Blotches on the Skin, Bad Legs, Ulcers, Wounds, Maladies of Indiscretion, Kidney and Urinary Disorders, and Menstrual Derangements.[10]

An even more daring offender was Bile Beans, a pill made of aloes, peppermint, and wheat flour, which claimed to cure no fewer than thirty-eight diseases; under the big "B" one read the latest additions to the epic list of ailments that these pills were said to cure.[11] The wiles of some vendors almost passed belief. "It is a common method among advertisers," one witness reported, "to pick out perfectly normal physiological phenomena and indicate to the person reading the advertisement that these normal phenomena are indications of incipient disease" (107). One quack went even further, adding insult to injury by palming off a pill containing a blue aniline dye and explaining that if one's urine turned blue it was a sure sign of kidney disease, which could only be cured by taking more of the same pills (xxii). To top it off, Elliman's Embrocations, a maker of veterinary preparations, took to selling its mixture under a different cover for use on humans. The outrageousness of these swindles prompted even such an impartial observer as Joseph Conrad, who weighed his words and did not take accusations of moral decrepitude lightly, to say that the "inventors of patent medicines" were

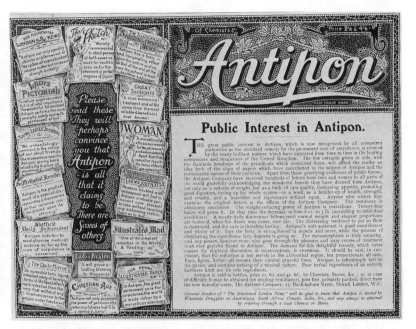

FIG. 32. Compounded interest in Antipon (*Illustrated London News*, April 28, 1906).

guilty of nothing less than "moral nihilism."[12] Robert Louis Stevenson exactly reflected the prevailing opinion when he went so far as to make his quack chemist, the genial Dr. Jekyll, double as the monstrous Mr. Hyde.

The Select Committee clearly had its work cut out for it, and it went about it as systematically as it could under the circumstances. But time after time the evidence it weighed widened rather than narrowed the scope of the problem. One problem was that, like pins in Adam Smith's pin factory, the patent medicine men were now multiplying faster than anyone could count them; even the official index on the subject said that the actual number of medicines sold was anybody's guess.[13] Another was that, like cigarette ads today, patent medicine ads actually underwrote a large number of British periodicals, which depended on them for income from advertising revenues. An ad for Antipon, "a tonic of rare quality," shows just how far the quacks had infiltrated the British press (Fig. 32). Here Antipon has compiled a little anthology of its various sales pitches, attributing each of them to the editors of a particular periodical. Of all the newspapers in England, only the *British Medical Journal*, the organ of the British Medical Association, made it a policy to refuse patent medicine advertisements. The rest justified accepting them by telling themselves, as one member of the Select Committee phrased it, "everybody else does it, and we will" (*Report*, 334).

The committee's biggest problem, though, was that patent medicine men were wizards when it came to staying one step ahead of the law. To some extent, on the one hand, the quacks regarded the lawmakers as partners in crime. On the other, they proved remarkably adept at outwitting their accomplices. Usually, as we have seen, the two lived together in a mutually profitable state of statutory neglect. This was not hard to do, for there were so many overlapping statutes on the books that it was difficult to arrive at a clear appreciation of how the law worked and almost impossible to administer it. The Stamp Acts of 1804 and 1812, the Arsenic Act of 1851, the Pharmacy Acts of 1868 and 1869, the Poisons and Pharmacy Act of 1908, the Merchandise Marks Act of 1887, and the Sale of Food and Drugs Acts of 1875 and 1899 all had something to say on the subject.[14] The resulting legal tangle was almost beyond repair, and it further emboldened the patent medicine men to keep on transgressing the already porous boundaries of the law. Even though prosecutions were few and far between, the patent medicine men took to tinkering with the one remaining form of government surveillance that posed any threat to them: chemical analysis.

The essence of every patent medicine's claim was that it, and it alone, possessed the one true remedy, the magic potion, the healing draught, the elixir of life. Chemical analysis posed a threat to this claim of uniqueness when it determined that the one-and-only was composed of ingredients available over the counter in any local chemist's shop. Safeguarding the secret formula thus became the order of the day. To keep the chemical analysts at bay, however, was easier said than done, for the quacks had to locate the loopholes in existing methods of chemical surveillance. The *British Medical Journal* had said that it was possible to know "the composition of all the preparations" but—and here comes the catch—"not necessarily to a grain" (*Report*, 165). In other words, chemical analysis then might be able to determine the ingredients but could not discover the precise recipe, especially if a large number of ingredients was involved. The difficulty of positive identification increased rapidly in proportion to the number of ingredients in a mixture, and if a quack kept stirring new things in, the likelihood was that he would multiply the number of ingredients beyond the range of accurate determination. Before the Select Committee one analytical chemist lamented that "a mixture of tinctures, infusions, decoctions or extracts of such familiar yet complex bodies as treacle, honey, aloes, cinnamon, liquorice, linseed, coltsfoot, cubebs, pepper, horehound, ginger, gentian, dandelion, rhubarb, saffron, etc., may defy all chemical, microscopic, spectroscopic, olfactory or physiological analysis" (xii). While such a mixture may have had no therapeutic value whatsoever, its complexity enabled the makers of Beecham's Pills to bite their thumbs at the medical authorities and say, with some truth, "the Government Laboratories have no great knowledge of handling drugs" (416).

In fact, the government laboratories had a copious knowledge of the preparation, use, and effect of hundreds of drugs; the real problem was that they had cribbed much of this knowledge from the patent medicine trade. When a government specialist sought to determine the contents of a given secret remedy, in all likelihood he would have reached for a copy of the *British Pharmacopoeia*, the standard reference work of the day. This tome classified remedies by weight, volume, temperature, properties, and doses. Today the *Pharmacopoeia* reads like a periodic table of the elements that has left out, say, every other element. At the turn of the century, however, it was considered an authoritative work and was compiled under the auspices of the General Medical Office. The medical profession hoped that the *Pharmacopoeia*, which it began to administer in 1858, would in time become a "national work," educating the public out of its quack-habit. If, the argument went, the public consulted the *Pharmacopoeia*, "they would get simpler, purer and cheaper remedies . . . than would be the case now" (*Report*, 345).

What they would have gotten, however, was the same old stuff. The *Pharmacopoeia* was riddled with recipes lifted from quackdom. The pig-Latin names which abound in the *Pharmacopoeia* should not fool us into believing that they were introduced in a way that the medical profession would have sanctioned. "Tinctura Sennae," a compound tincture of senna, began its life as "Daffy's Elixir." A witch hazel distillate called "Liquor Hamamelidis" started out as "Pond's Extract." "Pulvis Ipecacuanhae Compositus" was introduced as "Dover's Powder." "Matthew's Pills" made their way into the *Pharmacopoeia* as "Pilula Saponis Composita." In all, over thirty quack remedies were silently admitted to the *Pharmacopoeia* and listed as "official drugs."[15] Did the quack remedies have real medicinal value, or were the officially approved remedies devoid of it? Was it a case, as one Select Committee member thought, of "fiction founded on fact," or was it a case, as one witness asserted, of "fiction blended with fact in such a way that it is very difficult to say positively which is the fact" (*Report*, 210)? In many ways it appeared to be an open question whether the quacks were doctors, or the doctors quacks.

The real problem facing the Select Committee, then, was that there was still no definite line separating useful drugs from quack remedies. Pharmacology, even in legitimate incarnations, was still the provender of quacks. Turn-of-the-century doctors received very little education in *materia medica*, and in most cases they learned about drugs from traveling salesmen who represented the manufacturers of proprietary medicines.[16] To make matters worse, doctors, just like other consumers, developed brand loyalties over time. This meant that if a quack was able to keep a nostrum on the market for long enough, it tended to develop its own momentum and spawn its own cult of users. One Select Committee witness reported seeing a dozen or so of the most notorious nostrums in the business "in a very large number of doctors' surgeries" (*Report*, 598), and much to everyone's surprise, most of the doctor's testimonials that tagged patent medicines turned out to be unimpeachable. So for every government expert who proclaimed that secret remedies were base and valueless, the patent medicine industry could produce a counter-expert—just as for every accusation it could offer a convincing denial, and for every shred of evidence a smooth equivocation.

As the hearings moved into their second year, it became painfully obvious that the same porous line that separated useful drugs from quack remedies also separated the medical profession from the quacks themselves. Like medieval clerics allowing pardoners to sell indulgences so long as they did so in the name of the church, the English medical profession stood behind the quacks, and even conferred legitimacy on them, in a variety of ways. This relationship was productive and largely unspoken. Instead of conspiring to defraud the public, the doctors, like the government before them, simply entered into quiet economic collusion with the quacks. The collusion went in both directions. As we have seen, the doctors underwrote the quacks by buying their wares in bulk. But the quacks also helped the doctors do a brisk business simply by keeping patients from seeing them at the early stages of an illness. Undetected, serious illnesses could incubate unchecked. By the time a pill-eater got around to seeing a doctor, he or she was often in a sorry state and was subjected to a long and financially depleting course of treatment. This delay proved profitable for the medical establishment, and it made most doctors reluctant to criticize the quacks—a reluctance noted by the Select Committee when it observed that hardly any of the complaints filed against the patent medicine men came from doctors.[17]

Contemporaries had no difficulty in locating the source of this complicity between doctors and quacks, which even the medical profession acknowledged openly in its own textbooks. "The question is," wrote the author of *Medical Education and Medical Interests* (1868), "are we a profession or a trade?"[18] One of the loudest answers came from George Bernard Shaw, who regarded all professions as conspiracies against the laity and deplored what he called "a huge commercial system of quackery and poison." He wrote a long play, *The Doctor's Dilemma* (1906), and an even longer "Preface on Doctors," in which doctors are represented as little better than licensed butchers of human flesh. Directly or indirectly Shaw accuses the medical profession of paying unnecessary visits; writing absurd prescriptions; nursing imaginary maladies; exploiting hypochondriacs; effecting trumpery cures; manufacturing and prolonging lucrative illnesses; performing fashionable operations on tonsils, veriform appendixes, uvulas, and even ovaries. At times Shaw's doctors seem like stick figures malpracticing medicine in the great tradition running through Rabelais, Molière, and Sterne. Shaw's Dr. Ridgeon, however, is no ordinary trickster. He has a national reputation; he has been awarded a knighthood; he has been lionized for supposedly having made the most important discovery "since Harvey discovered the circulation of the blood." As Shaw sees clearly, the system of quackery has grown to such colossal proportions that it makes these earlier charlatans look like marginal grotesques. It has come to embody a consumerist ethic whereby "a demand . . . can be inculcated" and customers persuaded "to renew articles that are not worn out and to buy things they do not want." [19]

The Select Committee did not call Shaw to the witness stand; for all of its panicky pronouncements, it had decided to take a much narrower view of who qualified as card-carrying quacks. The legislators had begun the hearings by making the patent medicine men seem larger than life, but in the end they underestimated them. Essentially what the legislators were looking for was a place to draw the line between legitimate and illegitimate medicine. But when it came right down to it, as Shaw saw clearly enough, the line did not exist, and they were ill-equipped to cope with the conclusions that presented themselves before their very eyes. They knew that they were faced with a "system of quackery," but they failed to ask how that quackery was systematized and why that system appealed to such a large number of people. Why did quackery reign supreme? Various witnesses offered various answers, most of which scorned the evidence directly at hand—the representation of the body in the patent medicine advertisements of the time. True, everyone knew that patent medicine could not exist without advertising; after all, few pills or potions had any distinguishing features or palpable effects. People bought the stuff because advertisements made certain regular promises about what it would do to their bodies. But the legislators could not bring themselves to take these advertised promises seriously as a regulated *system* for representing the body, for turning it inside out and making it into a new kind of public spectacle and a new kind of therapeutic commodity. They habitually thought of advertisements as outrageous fictions and could imagine no reason for their popularity other than the weakness, gullibility, and ignorance of the populace. They did not stop for one moment to consider what sort of fictioneering they were up against.

The word that keeps cropping up again and again in the hearings to describe the activities of patent medicine advertisers is "fraud." A fraud is a deception deliberately practiced in order to secure unfair or unlawful gain. From the Select Committee's *Report* it would appear that the patent medicine men improvised whatever means were at hand to attain their desired end—a tidy profit. If we are to believe the *Report*, so completely did the end appear to have eclipsed the means that the nature of the deception itself would hardly seem to have mattered. But it did: the problem for the patent medicine men was not simply to defraud their customers but to create a therapeutic system by and through which English consumers might construe their bodies as a field for advertised commodities. They knew that they could not meet the medical profession on equal ground, so they took pains to rearrange the consumer's body and orient the commodity firmly within it. They took pains, in other words, to establish an alternative system of medicine. Yet as we shall see, the system the quacks created was not all that different from the system of capitalist medicine the doctors maintained, and in the final analysis it can be seen as an integral part of it.

II

The great paradox of the patent medicine system is that it existed both outside of and within mainstream medicine. In passing I have already characterized the quacks as carnivalesque, but the parallel deserves more than a passing mention. Certainly the quacks were an unruly bunch, but in a very real sense their unruliness was licensed and regulated by the medical profession. Patent medicine was a sanctioned inversion of the methods and materials of legitimate medicine, and the quacks must be seen as occupying a peripheral area of medical practice. Because this area was well outside the pale of the profession, it lacked the structure, definition, and hierarchy that convention customarily accorded to doctors. Even so, it contributed to the smooth functioning of the system of legitimate medicine in a great variety of ways. The quacks continually experimented with a variety of techniques that, as we have seen, often filtered into mainstream medicine. What is more, quacks showed how horrible life would be without doctors, and thus they acted as a spur to the "medicalization of life" so visible in the nineteenth century.[20] Every wild claim, every unlikely testimonial, every secret brew made the medical profession's shortcomings look positively insignificant. The louder the quacks raged outside the walls of the medical profession, the surer the refuge seemed within them.

The dual status of the quacks—as outsiders and insiders—made it very difficult for a government body like the Select Committee to make heads or tails of them. At one and the same time the quacks appeared to be a remnant and a vanguard; they were a repository for obsolete medical practices and the crucible for untested practices whose day had yet to come; they were the medical profession's greatest adversary and its greatest ally. More than any other turn-of-the-century document, the Select Committee's *Report* confronts this dual status without flinching. Faced with this fundamental confusion, however, most turn-of-the-century observers tended to emphasize the outsider status of the quacks. In *Tono-Bungay* (1909), H. G. Wells goes to great lengths to distinguish the quack-hero of his novel, Edward Ponderevo, from his nephew and partner, George, a scientist and aspiring technocrat. Written in the wake of much of his greatest science fiction, Wells's novel makes quacks seem like the exact opposite of everything rational and scientific. In line with the great romantic tradition of crazed chemists, Edward Ponderevo is a pharmacist who discovers the elixir of life, a placebo which he proceeds to offer to all comers. His story shows just how far outside of medical practice most people perceived the quacks to be, and it reads like a sustained argument for the obsolescence of patent medicine. Wells's quack sells out-of-date remedies that are completely unrelated to actual human ailments; he wantonly diagnoses diseases; he makes people sick; and he makes the workings of disease completely inscrutable. The way Wells tells the story, it would appear that the greatest obstacle to the consolidation of the medical profession in the twentieth century is not disease nor environment nor technology but quackery.

In Wells's book, Edwardian patent medicine advertising is a museum of the tricks of the Victorian patent medicine trade. Ponderevo writes some of his ads in the style of a catechism, with questions followed by immediate and unrelated answers. "Why does the hair fall out? Because the follicles are fagged." In others he adopts the bedside manner of the provincial physician, writing in what Wells calls a "let-me-just-tell-you-quite-soberly-something-you-ought-to-know" style. Sometimes, when he runs out of things to say, he simply capitalizes words like "HEALTH, BEAUTY, AND STRENGTH."[21] The ensuing success of these rhetorical strategies—long the staples of the trade—defies logical explanation, and his nephew can no more explain it than can the Select Committee. Even more puzzling, however, is the fact that this obsolete system of strategies seems to be quite popular with the customers. For a time Ponderevo's business is phenomenally successful, and it ultimately fails, not because someone else comes up with a better potion, but because he gets involved in some shady deals on the side. Like General Motors, which spends much of its energy devising ways to put the same old internal combustion engine in new-model bodies, Edward Ponderevo comes up with endless ways to market the old formula in new bottles. He proves frighteningly adept at modernizing an old appeal; Tono-Bungay metamorphoses into a whole line of products, each equally useless, each long familiar, each instantly successful at the moment when he introduces it. In rapid succession we get Tono-Bungay Hair Stimulant, Concentrated Tono-Bungay for the Eyes, Tono-Bungay Lozenges, Tono-Bungay Mouthwash, even Tono-Bungay Chocolate. In the story of this one quack, Wells seems intent on recapitulating the phylogeny of an entire species of advertisers. Though it is set in the present, the story of Ponderevo's rise and fall seems to belong to the past, and true to form, Wells calls him the "Napoleon of Commerce."[22]

Using every device at his disposal, Wells virtually hits his reader over the head with mounting evidence of the impending extinction of the patent medicine breed. His narrative is full of heavy intimations that Ponderevo will fail, is nearing failure, is about to fail, is failing, and has finally failed. Not for one moment can a reader of *Tono-Bungay* maintain the illusion that Ponderevo will become, like Sir Thomas Beecham of Beecham's Pills, a respected pillar of high society. Ponderevo does not stick to selling one pill; rather he embodies all pills and all pill-makers, balled up into one energetic figure. When Ponderevo's business empire goes out with a bang, his nephew, left to pick up the pieces, abandons the business and takes up a more scientific pursuit, designing destroyers. After his uncle's death as a bankrupt, young Ponderevo forswears the pandemonium of patent medicine advertising and becomes a kind of militarized Thomas Edison. In this replacement of a quack by a functionary, Wells sees a positivistic historical trajectory: rationality will out. His basic idea is that the quacks are vestiges of an irrational past order and that being of the past, they will sooner or later self-destruct. In *Tono-Bungay*, the future does not contain advertising (it ought to come as no surprise that Wells's sometime ally in Fabian Socialism, Sidney Webb, once wrote an article calling for the massive restructuring of the trade); it contains machines.[23] Set in the present, *Tono-Bungay* can best be understood as a prelude to science fiction. It clears the air of obsolete institutions like advertising and makes way for the technological society of the future.

What Wells and many others did not realize, however, was that patent medicine advertisers were willing and active participants in the effort to rationalize society in general, and the medical profession in particular. In *Tono-Bungay* Wells reproduces only a few of Ponderevo's advertisements, and they are pretty much of a mess.[24] The periodicals of Edwardian England tell a very different story. There patent medicines offer a series of sophisticated messages that can be seen as underwriting the very medical profession against which the quacks seem to be ar-

reared in pitched battle. The assumptions behind these advertisements are not so different from the basic tenets of the British
Medical Association. Like the doctors, the quacks assume that
all diseases can be cured; that cures will be technical in nature;
that disease is not to be blamed on circumstance, or more precisely, on the capitalist system; that symptoms of disease are
generally manifestations of individuality; that experts know
best; and that the body's needs can best be met by consuming
various kinds of therapeutic commodities. Like two corporations
competing for the same market, the doctors and the quacks took
care to develop and refine distinct versions of essentially the
same message. The result was a pseudo-choice: though in theory it looked like consumers were able to choose between two
entirely different systems of medical practice, they were in actu-
ality only being offered a choice between the complementary
parts of a single system of capitalist medicine.

The first thing that usually strikes one about patent medicine
advertising is its indefatigable optimism. No matter what is
wrong, it can be set right. Since the advertiser does not know
exactly what ails his readers, he makes an effort to canvass every
illness imaginable. The long lists of ills cured by pills were epic
inventories celebrating the powers of the Promethean pillmaker.
Included among these powers was not only the ability to eliminate disease but also the ability to invent it. Sometimes the invention of disease was a matter of pure fancy, as when a quack
named C. H. Stevens warned of a scourge called "germ disease"
and offered the healing energies of the "Umckaloabo root" to
combat it.[25] More often, the invention of disease was a matter of
autosuggestion. For most consumers, reading a patent medicine
ad was like reading a medical encyclopedia: people had no idea
that there were so many things that could go wrong with their
bodies. The great majority of patent medicine ads resorted to
scare tactics simultaneously to invent and eliminate precisely
the same diseases that occupied the waking energies of the
medical profession. Among these were all the great manufactured maladies of the late nineteenth century, especially nervous
ailments like neurasthenia, sick headache, and loss of vigor. In
an oblique way the quacks seemed to be aware that disease is a

socially created reality that can be produced and consumed in a great variety of ways. Like the doctors in Shaw's play, quacks engineered diseases and then sought to administer them under the guise of "curing" them.

In the main, the cures the quacks peddled did not differ much from the treatments the doctors prescribed: both claimed to be miracles of technology. Most people who study quacks wind up comparing them to faith healers, and sure enough, in *Tono-Bungay* Wells has Ponderevo compare himself to a Christian Scientist. But in the nineteenth century the most prominent faith healers were those who reposed their faith in the restorative powers of technology. Back in the 1840's Thomas Carlyle had perceived this conjuncture of cure-alls, and in *Past and Present* he transformed a quack's pill into an emblem of all easy solutions to persistent social problems. "I am weary of this sick croaking for a Morrison's-Pill religion," he says, and he proceeds to list any number of things that qualify as religion in his book. One of these is "the manufacture of liturgies that will never be alive," or more plainly, the manufacture of dead matter that appears to be alive.[26] This is the fetishism of commodities to which Marx later called attention in *Capital*, a process by which the products of human manufacture are animated with powers that they do not in themselves possess.[27] These products may be big factories or small pills, but for Carlyle, the act of investing them with lives of their own is exactly the same. At times the quack may speak like an old-time faith healer, offering to cure every disease under the sun, but what he is really offering is a new kind of faith. "The moment 'Antexema' touches the bad place, the irritation will immediately stop, and your cure will have commenced."[28] In patent medicine advertising, the pill is not a host that sanctifies the body but a switch that turns it on and off.

Though the quacks routinely claimed that diseases could be cured through social intervention, they carefully avoided any implication that any existing social structure was to blame for disease in the first place. In other words, they neatly separated the effects from the causes of disease. Disease has not been socially constituted; it is simply part of the order of things. Nowhere in patent medicine advertising does one find the remotest suggestion that society at large is to blame for the social reality of sickness. Illness in England is neither endemic to the capitalist system nor historically determined. In adhering to this principle the quacks sometimes out-doctor the doctors. At about the time Wells was writing *Tono-Bungay*, one manufacturer of baby food ran a series of ads extolling "the body-building powers of Mellin's Food." One of these ads (Fig. 33) reproduces three photographs. The baby in the top photograph is a classic case of malnutrition and could represent any of the thousands of poorly fed children who died every year in the tenements and slums of Edwardian England. In this ad, however, the little girl simply wastes away of her own accord, and blame is shifted from the slum system to the mother, who has "tried several different foods," presumably Brand-X concoctions, without hitting on the right one. The second photograph looks more like a typical child, but just in case the reader has one of these, the ad warns her that this healthy-looking child is merely "progressing well." The third photograph shows a fatted calf, the force-fed child of Edwardian children's books. She lies still and assumes the prone posture of an artist's model, looking at the camera like a contented bourgeoise-in-the-making. The three photographs progress from contraction to composure, from lower-class poverty to middle-class satisfaction, and the clear implication—an implication about which I will have much to say later in this and the next chapter—is that Mellin's Food has not only saved the child's life but has invested it with the attributes of affluence and has contributed materially to the formation of its identity. The origin and etiology of the actual disease in question hardly enter into the picture.

To the degree that patent medicine investigates the origins of diseases at all, it tends to regard them purely as manifestations of individuality. Even though everyone succumbs to the same basic diseases, and even though everyone is being asked to ingest the same basic remedies, the assumption is that since disease has no discernible social cause, each individual must be suffering from a unique ailment and must therefore require a course of treatment tailored precisely to his or her needs. Certainly there may be an element of commonality to these dis-

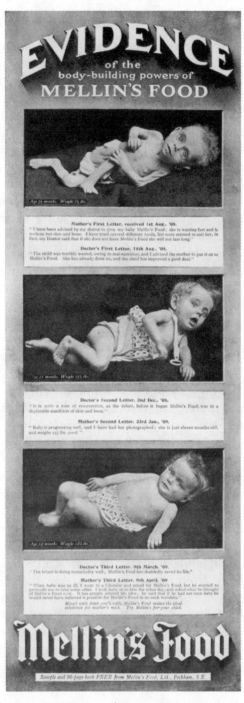

FIG. 33. The body-building commodity (*Illustrated London News*, November 6, 1909).

eases, but insofar as possible, quacks seek to reduce the social component of diseases to a minimum by *customizing* them. In Edwardian England quacks customized illnesses the way today's drivers customize cars, and for much the same reason: to project a uniform image of unique personality. The usual figure for this customized sickness in turn-of-the-century patent medicine ads was the common celebrity—someone famous but not too famous; unique, but never singular (as Queen Victoria was). An Odol ad from 1907 features a collage of these peculiar characters (Fig. 34). Notice how difficult it is to make out most of the faces (a lot of these ads go so far as to show only the facial features undergoing treatment); the ad further claims that these celebrities are only "a small proportion of the many hundreds of celebrated personages who constantly use this celebrated preparation." In Edwardian patent medicine ads celebrities rarely appear alone; as unique individuals they apparently crave anonymity. If all celebrities are so anonymous, the parallel implication seems to be that every anonymous consumer is really a celebrity. Odol thus performs quite a balancing act: it is simultaneously "the world's dentifrice" and the dentifrice of the individual. The catch here is that the only way the individual consumer can manifest his or her individuality is to buy a mass-produced commodity. Here as elsewhere in late-Victorian advertising, the advertised commodity both upholds and undercuts the privileged individuality of the statistical consumer.

Though the British Medical Association went on record disapproving celebrity testimonials, it would have wholeheartedly endorsed a sentiment that animates nearly every patent medicine advertisement in the late nineteenth and early twentieth centuries: that experts know best.[29] What experts generally know best is that they know best. The Odol ad puts this bluntly right on the bottle: "By the authorities of Modern Science ODOL has been proved the best for cleansing Mouth and Teeth." The ad does not appeal to any authority in particular; it appeals to the authority of authority, and it relies on the presumed unanimity of all those set in authority. No matter how exaggerated the claims a patent medicine makes for itself, it persists in summoning up the Sanhedrin. In fact, the more fraudulent the product,

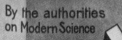

FIG. 34. The common celebrity (*Graphic*, March 2, 1907).

the more strident is the appeal it makes to authority. The worst of the patent medicine advertisers—the cure-all hawkers—were the ones who relied the most on the detailed testimonials of royalty, nobility, generals, lawyers, even doctors. Yet for all the variety of authorities to which they had recourse, far and away the favorite form of authority among quacks was the faceless authority of literary convention. The quack columns teem with literary quotations taken out of context. "I say, is there any black lead in Pepys?" Ponderevo asks his nephew. "You know—black lead—for grates! *Or does he pass it over as a matter of course?*"[30] Even if Pepys passed over black lead, Ponderevo and his brethren would take to imitating him using a form that can be called mock-quotation. A mock-quotation has all the weighty pretentiousness of authority without the inconvenience of an actual author. A cure-all called Eno's Fruit Salts built a little empire of pills on ads that appealed to the form of authority while divesting it of any real content. Among quacks, the ideal authority is one that speaks with a disembodied voice proclaiming what Eno's Fruit Salts calls "THE GREAT AND FUNDAMENTAL TRUTHS OF NATURE."[31]

The greatest and most fundamental truth of them all—the prime directive of the fraternity of quacks—was that the body's needs could best be met by consuming commodities. As if with one voice all the experts agreed that the body had an insatiable need for commodities. Roughly half the patent medicines on the market in 1909 called themselves food or drink, and the Select Committee often found it difficult to track quacks down because, for one reason or another, the government had decided to license them as victuallers. The quacks devoted most of their waking energies to convincing the public that the public needed them, and in so doing they contributed to breaking down the already eroded barrier dividing wants from needs. As witness after witness told the Committee, it now happened that people who were quite well sought out quacks, not because the quacks had convinced them that they were sick, but because patent medicine led the way in developing preventative medicine. In *Medical Nemesis*, Ivan Illich points out that by the turn of the century the doctors had already perfected what he calls diagnostic imperialism, a method of examination built around the minute and detailed scrutiny of the patient's body by the doctor.[32] The term implies that the closer the doctor looks, the more diseases there are to be found. The quacks, however, pioneered a complementary medical technique that proved useful in snaring customers who as yet showed no sign of sickness. This technique can be called therapeutic imperialism, for it colonized the body, not with diseases, but with remedies, which were invariably commodities. Doctors, of course, had long practiced therapeutic imperialism after they diagnosed illnesses. The simple innovation of quackery was to practice it beforehand. Therapeutic imperialism was concerned with the daily maintenance of the healthy body, and it relied on regimen. The advertising supplements were full of diets, methods, measures, regimes, exercises, and other forms of what was called health "culture."[33] A product called Harlene Hair Drill speaks for the clan when, after the usual litany of dread diseases, it announces that "the foregoing diseases and others are easily preventable by proper culture."[34] Here culture is no longer the product of human work and thought characteristic of a community or population; it has become a euphemism for the therapeutic powers of the commodity.

The invention of a specifically therapeutic form for the commodity had far-reaching consequences both for quacks and for commodity culture at large. With each passing year patent medicine moved closer and closer to legitimate medicine until finally it was very difficult to tell them apart. Aspirin was introduced as a patent medicine in 1899, and it soon became the most popular drug in England. In 1915 an American came up with the brand name "Vitamin" to distinguish a new pill from dozens of more or less identical pills on the market, and in so doing conferred a new legitimacy on pill popping. Drugs were no longer "drugs on the market" but mainstays of a modern consumer economy massively mobilized to address the individual self. Commodity culture now seemed to address each individual personally in a way that it had never done before. Hitherto the imperatives of consumerism had been embodied in aloof figures like Queen Victoria and distant places like Darkest Africa. As powerful as these images were, and as materially as they contributed to the formation of late-Victorian commodity culture, they addressed the consumer indirectly at best and existed at great remove from everyday life. By contrast, patent medicine was radically transitive. Patent medicine ads were like recruiting posters: they were generic forms of address that attempted to single out individual readers, and they had that "Hey, you there!" form of address that Louis Althusser later saw everywhere in twentieth-century mass culture.[35] By addressing one of the most basic experiences of individuality—pain—patent medicine advertisers established a beachhead within the self and opened the way for a full-scale invasion of selfhood by commodity culture.[36] The therapeutic commodity was the first in a long line of advertised encroachments upon the self that eventually culminated, as we shall see in the next chapter, in the circumscription of sexuality by desires sanctioned by the capitalist system. For the aim of patent medicine advertising was not only directly to address the consumer's self but in a very real sense to transform it, in its entirety, into a spectacular commodity.

III

The medium that transformed the self into a commodity was the same medium that had already transformed so much of culture into a commodity: spectacle. As defined, spectacle was a reorientation of representation around the fundamental economic dictates of capitalism. At the most basic level, capitalism had always turned everything it touched into a commodity, into an object of exchange. Spectacle was simply a set of aesthetic procedures for magnifying the importance of the most basic element of exchange, the commodity. By the turn of the century the commodity spectacle was well on its way to becoming the dominant form of capitalist representation. The commodity had been exhibited in a vast hall; it had gone on a royal progress around London; it had colonized Africa. Much of social life now appeared to be a vast collection of exchangeable artifacts displayed prominently for all to see. The unseen areas of life, however, still beckoned. In 1897, at the time of Victoria's second Jubilee, the commodity was arguably the dominant form of signification in England, but as yet it was not signification itself. What Jean Baudrillard calls "the political economy of the sign," or the absolute equivalence of signification with commodity exchange, was still in the future.[37] Too many areas of social life remained unoccupied by the commodity, and by its now coterminous vehicle, spectacle. The self, traditionally represented as distinct and inviolable, remained intact as the last bastion of resistance to the burgeoning commodity culture of high capitalist England.

The invention of the therapeutic commodity changed all that. Patent medicine advertising laid the self completely open to commercial assault. It eroded the boundaries of the self by opening it up to various kinds of therapeutic intervention. Simultaneously it fragmented the self by reducing selfhood to a series of acts of consumption, and it told consumers that the only way they could sustain a secure sense of selfhood was to consume more and more commodities.[38] In the patent medicine system the quacks constituted the human body as a new kind of commodity spectacle, thus moving the private world of the consumer into alignment with the public world of exhibitions, jubilees, and imperial conquests undertaken for the greater glory of commodity culture. The basic elements of spectacle remained the same, but they changed shape and took on new meaning in the context of the therapeutic commodity. The placebo-drug became the ultimate icon of consumer capitalism; its use and appeal cut across class lines and created the illusion of a consumer democracy; it transformed the body first into a field for advertised commodities, and later into an entity so dependent on them that it had become one in its own right; it reorganized the myth of the consuming subject around the ingestion of quick-fix remedies; and it equated abundance with the easy availability of self-transforming substances. In many ways, as we shall see, the spectacle of the therapeutic commodity holds a mirror up to the present, when no industry is closer to the violent free-for-all of the classic capitalist economy than that underground cartel concerned with the production, distribution, and consumption of mind-altering drugs.

In the patent medicine system, the placebo-drug is the ultimate commodity: it has no intrinsic value; it has no use; it has no origin; yet it is so tangible, so palpable, so material, that one can hold it in the palm of one's hand. The placebo is the commodity writ both small and large, for the smaller it shrinks in reality, the greater the number of attributes that can be attached to it. "The Thing" becomes, as Thomas Carlyle saw in *Past and Present*, "a no-Thing."[39] In a series of ads that appeared from 1906 until 1909 a bottle of Odol mouthwash takes on a variety of iconic postures in which it is simultaneously something, nothing, and everything. In some ads an Odol bottle is being squirted into a glass. Though the caption promises that the mouthwash will kill millions of "microbes and bacteria," what the ad actually shows us is not the liquid but the container (which resembles a squirt gun) in action. Here the action of Odol is represented metonymically, not as the action of the product but as the action of its package. At one and the same time Odol acts, does not act, and acts on everything (for the simple reason that it opposes germs, which, after all, are everywhere). This same diffuseness appears in a later ad that depicts "The Odol Museum of Shams." The ad shows an enlarged Odol bottle casting its shadow over dozens of tiny Odol bottles, most of which have captions in languages other than English. Here Odol is queen bee in a hive of imitations: as a commodity Odol is simultaneously something (because it is imitated), nothing (because it is imitated), and everything (because it is imitated). In few patent medicine ads is the twisted logic of the autonomous commodity made so obvious.[40]

Many patent medicine advertisements amplify the omnipresence of the autonomous commodity and take it to its logical conclusion: if the commodity is everywhere, it belongs to everyone, equally. It must therefore speak to as many people as possible, cutting across class lines to create the illusion of equality among users. This commodity Bill of Rights, however, has only one provision: all people are equal only when they consume the same products. The only assemblies permitted are those in which consumers join together in anonymity to pay obeisance to the one and only thing they have in common, namely, the commodity. In a 1908 ad for Harlene Hair Drill the commodity upstages its balding communicants, who look like they are raising their hands to touch their heads in a parlor game of "Simon

Says" (Fig. 35). Other contemporary ads have more disturbing implications. An Odol ad shows a hard-faced demagogue addressing a crowd beside an enlarged Odol bottle that serves as his rostrum.[41] In an unusual ploy for turn-of-the-century advertising, the ad eliminates the caption; the message seems to be that the commodity does his speaking for him, and as if to steady himself, he rests his left hand on the neck of the bottle. As a later Odol ad makes clear, the man's presence as speaker was an unnecessary adjunct to the commodity, which, it turns out, can stand alone and speak for itself (Fig. 36). In 1906 the speaker still dwarfs the commodity; in 1908 it stands taller than any dignitary and dictates policy to the assembled crowd. The caption says, "A Thing of Universal Utility cannot be too Widely Promulgated," and the accompanying photograph bears an eerie resemblance to those taken of eager crowds awaiting the

"HARLENE HAIR DRILL"

Read this article for detailed information how to grow a luxuriant crop of beautiful hair. Full instructions are contained in the new booklet included with the sample bottle offered free to our readers.

FIG. 35. Hair-drilling (*Graphic*, May 23, 1908).

A PUBLIC PROCLAMATION.
A Thing of Universal Utility cannot be too Widely Promulgated. The Hygienic Benefits of Odol, the World's Dentifrice, are Proclaimed Everywhere.

FIG. 36. The freestanding object (*Illustrated London News*, April 25, 1908).

news of war in August 1914. As dictator and perhaps as warlord, the commodity now has it in its power to issue "A Public Proclamation." It no longer needs a Crystal Palace to make it spectacular; it has become a spectacle in its own right.

By far the greatest number of proclamations that the therapeutic commodity makes, however, have to do not with the well-being of the body politic but with the maintenance of the body. Maintaining the body means transforming it into a field for advertised commodities, but it also means making the body into an entity indistinguishable from the action of commodities. The two states—the body as container for commodities and the body as commodity—are hard to tell apart, and in many ads the status of the body seesaws between them. A case in point is a series of ads for Allcock's Plasters that appeared between 1906 and 1909. In some of these ads the consumers are shown partially clothed, and the implication is that the therapeutic commodity is an unsightly appurtenance that must be veiled by many layers of clothing.[42] Here the body is a strictly private site for consuming therapeutic commodities. In other Allcock ads, however, the commodity appears as a badge of fashion worn by a well-coiffured woman in a ruffled strapless top (Fig. 37). She seems unperturbed at displaying this brand, and sure enough, the Allcock company ran a number of similar ads showing her posing in different positions like a model striking different postures at a fashion show.[43] This series of ads treats the plaster as an integral part of her body; at one and the same time it is a tattoo, etched permanently onto her skin, and a birthmark, a

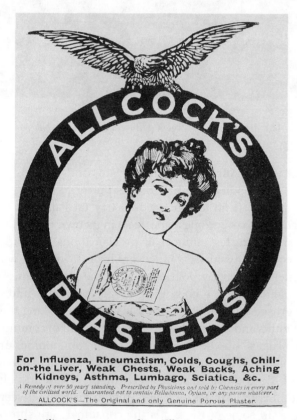

FIG. 37. Unveiling the commodity (*Illustrated London News*, January 19, 1909).

product of nature there for all to see. Like the hide of an animal, good skin has become a specialty item, and skin products were now among the most widely advertised in the industry.

If the patent medicine men set out with the limited aim of making the commodity palatable to their customers, they accomplished much more than they ever dreamed of. For they succeeded in producing a great number of advertisements in which swallowing remedies becomes a figure for constituting the self. In the patent medicine system, the human subject develops only in relation, indeed in response, to the manufactured objects that it ingests. More plainly, you are what you swallow, and what you swallow determines who you are and what you can become. When in the "Lestrygonians" chapter of Joyce's *Ulysses* Bloom goes into a pub and watches its patrons wolf down lunch, he in some measure sees them as being shaped by what they eat.[44] In much the same way the patent medicine system equates the making of the self with the consumption, not of food (though as we have seen it very well might be called that), but of commodities. From birth the self takes its cues from commodities, and one of the most virulent strains of patent medicine advertising consists of ads that, like Pavlov's experiments, train us to respond to a made thing rather than human contact. An ad for Mennen's Toilet Powder begins the work of interposing commodities between mothers and children, a work that would in another fifty years culminate in the unscrupulous export of baby formula to women in third-world countries (Fig. 38). Another ad in six frames shows stages of progress over five years (it looks like an expanded version of Fig. 33). Here three children have been "reared, almost from birth, on Mellin's Food." The children in the ad are little more than "living evidence" marking the progress the commodity makes as it develops within them. In a very real sense these ads rewrite Lacan's notion of the mirror stage of human development, for in them the human subject recognizes in the mirror, not itself, but a commodity in which it is taught to see itself and through which it can remain forever young.[45]

In the image of the consumer addicted from birth to a variety of drug-commodities, we can see the degree to which the myth

FIG. 38. The mothering object (*Illustrated London News*, May 22, 1909).

of the abundant society, so visible in all the advertised spectacles of late-nineteenth-century England, placed consumers in a relation of dependency. Pills had been mass produced since before the advent of mass production, and in the age of mass production they were the most widely available commodity in Britain, bar none. Very early on, the quacks showed the advertising industry how important it was to instill in consumers a renewable craving for more and more standardized objects. They discovered that advertising, far from creating false needs, must be grounded in real ones.[46] The aim of patent medicine advertising was not to create needs out of thin air, but to locate quite legitimate needs—in this case, the care of the body—and redefine them. Instead of trying to bring extraordinary events like Exhibitions and Jubilees down to earth, they bored down deep into everyday life and invested the quotidian with the panache of the extraordinary. Their genius was that they taught consumers to become dependent on things they actually needed, all the while extending the boundaries of those needs to encompass more and more things. Though they began by assuming that necessity is the mother of invention, they ultimately recognized that invention can become the mother of necessity. That they were in the vanguard of commodity culture soon became clear, for as we have seen, the major enterprises of late-nineteenth-century advertising took as their base of operations such staples as soap and cloth, moving from there into cash crops like coffee and tea, and from there into various "foods," gadgets, and other contrivances. Like the capitalist economy itself, the patent medicine system offered its consumers immediate gratification followed by a desire for more immediate gratification. In doing so, as has already been noted, they have bequeathed to us a lasting emblem of an abundant society that has not yet come to terms with the limits to material satisfaction: drugs.[47]

Patent medicine, then, began the drugging of England. In the Crystal Palace drugs had figured prominently in several exhibits, intended to illustrate what one lecturer called "the progress of pharmaceutical chemistry."[48] There were dried medicinal plants, mineral preparations such as ultramarine, and oils derived from flowers. These drugs, however, were primarily a matter of scientific interest and had been sanctioned by the medical establishment. By contrast, patent medicine located consumption outside of the enshrined order of conventional values. Though, as we have seen, the postulates of the patent medicine system actually differed little from those of established medicine, the quacks succeeded in making all social space, legal or illegal, approved or disapproved, moral or immoral, into a fertile field for the manufacture, distribution, and production of commodities. A 1910 book called *Popular Drugs: Their Use and Abuse* actually lumps patent medicines together with Indian hemp, mescal, and cocaine.[49] The lure of patent medicine was that it allowed consumers to reverse socially accepted values—to consume drugs with exotic and illegal-sounding names like "Tono-Bungay"—while at the same time upholding them. "Tono-Bungay" itself figures this process, for it both sounds vaguely foreign and is derived from some very mundane associations, "tono" being short for "tonic" and "Bungay" being a city in Suffolk. In patent medicine, all of society becomes part of a single symbiotic system of therapeutic commodities. Formerly "a drug on the market" meant something that did not sell; now everything that sold had to be a drug, offering to intervene in the daily lives of consumers, to shape their minds, to alter their consciousnesses, and ultimately, as we shall see, to circumscribe their most guarded lives—their sexual lives—in such a way that the most private cells of life became a repository, and finally a bastion, of commodity culture.

5

Those Lovely Seaside Girls

In the world of patent medicines the too-solid flesh of the Victorian consumer was beginning to yield to the ministrations of commodity culture. The quacks set to work on an ever-increasing number of areas of the body, laboring to expose them to an ever-increasing number of therapeutic commodities. Every minute region of the body was now exposed to the etiology of the commodity. Whether visible like hair and skin, partly visible like nose and throat, or invisible like blood and lungs, the quacks multiplied the parts of the body accessible to marketing. They delivered up a large drama on a small scale, transforming the body from an off-limits zone into a site of voluble speech and the privileged seat of spectacle. In patent medicine all the processes of the body—in sickness and in health—were coordinated with the action of commodities. After the First World War patent medicine died out when chemistry, which had lagged behind the other sciences in the nineteenth century, caught up with them and devised antibiotics. But by then the quacks had already dug the pincers of the marketplace deeply into the flesh of the consumer. The body had become the prevailing icon of commodity culture, and there was no turning back.

The quacks set up a particular trap for consumers, and we will never know how many of them actually fell into it. In patent medicine as in all other types of late-Victorian advertising, the voice of the consumer is silenced. The voice that speaks in the pages of the advertising supplements is the voice of the generic advertiser addressing the statistical consumer. One thing is certain, however: the quacks were men who sought out a large and diverse audience of women. Like male ministers in nineteenth-century churches who tailored their sermons to a female clientele and propounded a gendered vision of Christianity, the quacks adapted their message to a female audience and advanced a gendered vision of consumption.[1] "Women are more imposed upon by quacks than men are," announced one authority in *The British Medical Journal*. He then proceeded to list five reasons that pinpoint and define the characteristic consuming subject of late-Victorian advertising: "Women are by their nature more confiding and less wary than most men"; "many women are specially prone to functional nervous disorders"; "women in many cases have a natural desire to keep their ailments secret"; "women are very anxious to preserve a good personal appearance"; "women will rush to quack remedies for the cure of what are called 'female irregularities.'"[2] In the late nineteenth century this neurosis-racked woman became the prototypical consumer, and her traditionally feminine attributes were translated into a psychology of consumption and preyed upon by a new "science," the psychology of advertising. The quacks set into motion the use of women as icons of consumption and began to transform the female body into a specific site of advertised spectacle.

Advertising managed to establish a female model for consumption without ceding the activity entirely to women. Advertisers defined consumption as an extension of the sexual division of labor enshrined in the Victorian household. Shopping was an errand to be run rather than a choice to be made, and advertising was eager to avoid identifying itself too closely with the needs and desires of women. So consumption became something that women undertook on behalf of men. An illustration in an 1886 advertising handbook, *Successful Advertising*, makes it clear that women consumers acted in a subordinate capacity (Fig. 39). For nineteen frames the ad acts more or less exclusively upon the male consumer. Only in the last frame does he call on his wife to fetch what he has decided to buy. Here the woman does not consume commodities in her own right; she operates as an extension of the male. Clearly advertisers saw women as go-betweens between men and their commodities.

What this sequence of events also reveals, however, is the extent to which the male consumer acts in complete accordance with the feminine psychology of advertising supposedly reserved for his wife. He hesitates, hedges, hems and haws. As a consumer he has been feminized unawares. As we shall see, the model of consumption that advertisers established with women in mind did not remain confined for long within the boundaries of a single gender. The gendering of consumption worked both ways.

This calculated sequence of events, then, does not adequately portray the impact of advertising on Victorian women. Because advertisers assumed that women acted as consumers only on the explicit instructions of men, they were not alert to the many ways in which advertising spoke with a female voice and contributed to the formation of a specifically female consuming subjectivity. As usual, few accounts of this consumerist subjectivity survive, and these show women consuming under strict male supervision. In Gissing's *In the Year of Jubilee* (1894), Nancy Lord marvels passively at the fecundity of advertiser Luckworth Crewe's imagination. So does Carrie Meacham in Dreiser's *Sister Carrie* (1900) when she passes through a department store run by a crack team of male managers. The most detailed and variegated picture of a female consumer we have comes much later, in Joyce's *Ulysses* (1922). Like so many modernist writers, Joyce sought to explore the furthest reaches of human consciousness in all its manifestations. Commodity culture figures largely in this scheme. For the first time a writer confronted the lived reality of the advertised spectacle—not just as a social space for displaying commodities but as a coercive agent for invading and structuring human consciousness. The "Nausicaa" chapter of *Ulysses* defines the impact of all this calculated consumption on a single consumer, Gerty MacDowell. In 1902 Walter Dill Scott published *The Psychology of Advertising*, which made grandiose claims about what entrepreneurs could do to the human mind; Joyce set his novel in 1904. In Gerty's narrative the advertising industry becomes a consciousness industry and moves at last onto the familiar terrain of the twentieth century.

To explore the mind-set of an early-twentieth-century consumer requires a different method than that used in the previous

"The first time a man
looks at an advertisement
he does not see it."

"The second time he does
not notice it."

The third time he is con-
scious of its existence."

"The fourth time he
faintly remembers having
seen it before."

"The fifth time he
reads it."

"The sixth time he turns
up his nose at it."

"The seventh time he
reads it through and says,
'Oh! bother!'"

"The eighth time he says,
'Here's that confounded
thing again!'"

"The ninth time he
wonders 'if it amounts to
anything.'"

"The tenth time he
thinks he will ask his neigh-
bour if he has tried it."

FIG. 39. The female consumer as go-between (Smith, *Successful Advertising*).

"The eleventh time he
wonders how the advertiser
makes it pay."

"The twelfth time he
thinks perhaps it may be
worth something."

"The thirteenth time
he thinks it must be a good
thing."

"The fourteenth time he
remembers that he has
wanted such a thing for
a long time."

"The fifteenth time
he thinks he will buy it
some day."

"The sixteenth time
he makes a memorandum
of it."

"The seventeenth time
he is tantalised because he
cannot afford to buy it."

'The eighteenth time he
swears at his poverty."

"The nineteenth time
he counts his money care-
fully."

"The twentieth time he sees
it he buys the article, or
instructs his wife to do
so. — Moral: Advertise
steady and regularly."

four chapters. The commodity culture of the Great Exhibition, the 1887 Jubilee, the Africa campaigns, and even patent medicine can be pinned down in time with some exactness. But the more diffuse and localized spectacle becomes, the more difficult it is to trace its movement across social practice and assess its impact on human consciousness. It is a pity that Freud did not take up the study of advertising, which Leo Lowenthal later called "psychoanalysis in reverse."[3] For better or worse Freud's sense of the social life of objects was restricted to the etiology of the fetishist, a person fixated metonymically on an object or body part as a surrogate for sexual desire. Freud considered these substitutes flatly "unsuitable" and left it at that. Had he not shared the late-nineteenth-century disinterest in advertising as a field meriting serious study, Freud might have found that advertising had come to play an important tactical role in shaping desire, articulating consciousness, in fact performing much of what he termed "the dream work"—"a work of condensation on a large scale."[4] In the early twentieth century advertising became a primary vehicle for condensing the detritus of consciousness into a commodity language. Advertisers now became specialists not only in constituting discourse but in constituting selves—especially female selves—to take up positions within commodity culture.

A full account of how this process worked will always elude our grasp, for conditions never have and never will exist for the unmediated scrutiny of human subjects. Nevertheless partial accounts survive, and the narrative of Gerty MacDowell—a fragment of a chapter which is itself a fragment of a much larger narrative—is the first text in literary or cultural history to register in great detail the impact of advertising on consciousness. In cultural history Joyce's narrative of Gerty MacDowell ought to occupy a position similar to Freud's narrative of Dora, for in very different ways both examine the sexual basis underlying modern paternal authority. Freud published his account of Dora in 1905. Joyce wrote "Nausicaa" in 1917, set it in 1904, and summoned up a world of advertising that would have been current in England and Ireland in the early 1890's—about the time when he himself, like Gerty MacDowell, was an impressionable adolescent reading advertisements on the walls of Dublin. Freud's Dora wanted to sleep with her father; a detailed examination of the thirteenth chapter of *Ulysses* will show that Joyce's Nausicaa also nurses forbidden desires—desires aroused and arrested, prescribed and proscribed, sanctioned and prohibited by a new mutation of commodity culture.

I

Gerty MacDowell does not cast a long shadow over *Ulysses*. Apart from "Nausicaa" and several brief appearances in other chapters, we know next to nothing of her. Seaside girl, child of Mary, window shopper, scamp, seducer, and importunate victim, Gerty is largely sealed off from the epidemic of disappearances and reappearances that touches every major character in the novel. Joyce goes out of his way to contain her in one voice and to mark off that voice from the enigmatic forces that break Bloom into anagrams in Nighttown and tear Stephen between roaring worlds in the National Library. A line of explicit integrity divides Gerty MacDowell from these myriad forms of Stephen and Bloom.[5] Gerty lives on not so much for her puzzling idiom or for her participation in eccentric events that must be carefully collected and reconstructed, but because she is an encompassing experiential record of a turn-of-the-century Irish common reader. She is part of Joyce's recognition, developed during the writing of *Ulysses*, that common readers, so far as they are shaped by the developing forms of commodity culture, have acclimated themselves to the world of goods to such an extent that they have become generalized and impoverished. Joyce made Gerty MacDowell one-dimensional. Descended from the beleaguered virgins and routine spinsters who troop through the nineteenth-century domestic novel, figures like Gerty had by 1900 become a shopworn fixture of pulp fiction and penny dreadfuls; as the prop of billboards and postcards, her facsimile surfeited the public with snug seaside settings and cheap tableaux. No other character in *Ulysses* can be so summarily pigeonholed; yet no other's discourse in *Ulysses* is so much the product, not of an exclusive persona, but of the collective pressure of the customs and ideology of a burgeoning commodity culture.

In Joyce criticism, the case of "Nausicaa" is not typical. For many readers, "Nausicaa" yields its meaning more easily than any other chapter in *Ulysses*. Experiencing the chapter as an oasis after 350 pages of urgently difficult prose, readers are relieved to find more normative forms of representation, such as they are used to in the realist novel. Clearly "Nausicaa" uses stock ways of articulating the world. But in reading "Nausicaa" we must not see this use of established forms of intelligibility as treating—as it often did in the realist novel—language and society as a passive framework within which individuals move. Joyce, it will be argued, stresses not only Gerty's immersion in a prefabricated language but the ability of that language to fulfill diverse and even contradictory social and psychological needs. But to see how this works we first have to undo the relationship between the integrity of Gerty's realism and its underlying narrative and ideological plurality. Despite the chapter's habitual method, which is to present characters and scenes that are conspicuously conventional, the reader of "Nausicaa" faces a document that must be pieced together at every turn. An immediate way in which the reader is led to do so is through its status as a palimpsest, a new story superimposed on the world of Maria Cummins's *The Lamplighter* (1854), the novel from which Joyce draws Gerty's name and many of her attributes. Working from *The Lamplighter* we can begin to isolate narrative currents that often pass unnoticed through the novel's flood tide of voices.

Because of the complexity of its transformation, it is easy to overlook the presence of *The Lamplighter* in "Nausicaa." Like many novels of the school of domestic realism, *The Lamplighter* sanctions a staid set of mid-nineteenth-century values we do not readily associate with Gerty MacDowell: unremitting labor, obsessive frugality, public-spiritedness, and an unyielding ethic of continence and renunciation. With a predictability equaled in fiction only by the didactic stories in the Sunday School chapbooks of the period, Cummins casts each of her heroes and heroines to fit this moral mold: Trueman Flint, lighter of lamps who adopts Gerty, works evenings, pinches pennies, patrols the streets at night, and abstains from any leisured pursuit save regular reading of the Bible. The sensational appeal of the novel comes when Cummins recasts her less virtuous characters to fit the mold of Trueman Flint. The few who resist are nearly suffocated by the officious moral instruction both of the righteous and of the attending novelist who, never dropping her mantle of piety, consistently places them within spiritually exemplary scenes of nature. When Gerty Flint goes on a tour of upstate New York with the spiritually recidivist Mr. Phillips, Cummins snares her unbeliever in a sentimentally spiritualized landscape in which "a mountain-top was rejoicing in an unusually brilliant and glorious dawn," and in which "a fairy bark might have floated upon the undulating waves which glistened in the sunshine like new-fallen snow, and which, contrasted with the clear blue sky above, formed a picture of singular grandeur."[6] Joyce carries forward this spiritual connoisseurship of the natural landscape in the famous first paragraph of "Nausicaa," which calls attention both to the stylistic form of *The Lamplighter* and to its explicitly moral standards of value. As readers we register Joyce's adaptation of the domestic novel, which continues until the catechistic paragraph "But who was Gerty?"—a question which characteristically, in a foretaste of the mechanistic method of "Ithaca," triggers a rush of response.

The first sentence in which we detect a shift in voice stands as a model for others that follow: "Her figure was slight and graceful, inclining even to fragility but those iron jelloids she had been taking of late had done her a world of good much better than the Widow Welch's female pills and she was much better of those discharges she used to get and that tired feeling" (*Ulysses*, 348). Until the conjunction "but" we could be reading *The Lamplighter*. After the "but" the haze lens of calculated vagueness has been dropped, revealing a muddle of interchangeable slogans, products, and brand names that evoke a standard more economic than moral. From fragile beauty we proceed to its material maintenance; today, of course, the two are integrally associated, with a magazine like *Cosmopolitan* beginning on its cover with an idealized beauty and coming to earth by degrees until on its final pages we find girdles for cellulite and devices for the removal of warts. At the turn of the century magazines were just beginning to explore the possibility of reaching women, who (it was assumed) would prove especially vulnerable to emotional appeals in the tonic tones of the domestic novel. As collections of sensational "inside" stories with a moral twist, which proved as popular in Ireland as in England, *The Lady's Pictorial* and *Pearson's Magazine* (founded in 1881 and 1896 respectively) worked from the assumption that only with an array of sanctioned consumer goods could one lead a full life. By 1901 fully one-third of a typical number of *Pearson's Magazine* contained advertisements for such gimmicks as get-rich-quick schemes and patent medicines; in Gerty, a confessed reader of both *The Lady's Pictorial* and *Pearson's Magazine*, we begin to observe the impact of this commodity culture. For her emphasis on the comparative virtues of pills entails a significant departure from the expected style of sentimental domestic fiction, and in more ways than through its simple litany of commodities: in the above passage, the lack of grammatical linkage and the use of the gratuitous "and" signal, as they commonly do in modernist fiction, entry into a character's interior monologue. Moreover, following the lead of advertisers, who as we have noted had, as early as the Great Exhibition, seen grammar as an impediment to establishing a bond between consumer and commodity, Gerty's narrative allows commodities to hover free from the logical constraints imposed by syntax. The presence of brand names and slogans assimilated through advertising (for eighty years the phrase "that tired feeling" has been the mainstay of the makers of pills) characterizes this voice, which clearly has displaced that of the domestic novelist.

In the next sentence we can no longer be sure who speaks: "The waxen pallor of her face was almost spiritual in its ivorylike purity though her rosebud mouth was a genuine Cupid's bow, Greekly perfect. Her hands were of a finely veined alabaster with tapering fingers and as white as lemon juice and queen of ointments could make them though it was not true that she used to wear kid gloves in bed or take a milk footbath either" (348). Earlier in the day, while skimming *Titbits* in the outhouse, Bloom considers trying to write a prize *Titbits* story. He never does, but

Gerty's narrative picks up the mawkish tone of both his aspiration and its probable product. Gerty's syntax, however, is her own: presumably Bloom would not construct a sentence in which alabaster has fingers, "queen of ointments" has no article, "though" introduces a non sequitur, and "either" is left dangling. After "tapering fingers" the narrative clearly lapses from the voice of the domestic novelist into the idiom of Gerty, which we recognize both by the breakdown of syntax and the presence of objects and slogans. The grammar runs amok in describing Gerty's altercation with Bertha Supple, returning to a more syntactically sound idiom, more elevated in diction, to describe the "languid queenly *hauteur*" about Gerty that "was unmistakably evidenced in her delicate hands and higharched instep" (348).

This pairing—hands and instep—is in many ways exemplary. For several pages the narrative couples physical attributes with material objects until one feature of the style finally overwhelms the reader: the sheer abundance of manufactured objects present in her voice. Multiplied examples soon convince us that Gerty understands her world as a consumer not only of novels like *The Lamplighter* but of magazines like *Pearson's*, which consistently link the moral style of the domestic storyteller with a variety of commodities presented in advertisements between the same covers. The superabundance and specificity of these commodities are striking. In one paragraph we find a blouse of electric blue, dolly dyes, perfumed cottonwood, a hat of wideleaved "nigger straw," a butterfly bow, patent toecaps, ribbonslotted underwear, wide garter tops, high spliced heels—a full ensemble from the pages of *The Lady's Pictorial*. Even when the objects are less specialized, they are treated in a department store idiom: "navy threequarter skirt cut to the stride," "*petite*" (in the sense of a dress size), shoes as "the newest thing in footwear."

A neat blouse of electric blue, selftinted by dolly dyes (because it was expected in *The Lady's Pictorial* that electric blue would be worn), with a smart vee opening down to the division and kerchief pocket (in which she always kept a piece of cottonwood scented with her favorite perfume because the handkerchief spoiled the sit) and a navy threequarter skirt cut to the stride showed off her slim graceful figure to perfection. (350)

In this sentence, and in many that follow in this crucial paragraph, the idiom of the domestic novelist is steeped in a commodity language that we had formerly associated only with the narrative voice of Gerty's interior monologue. It is the hallmark of her narrative, which both calls up droves of commodities by naming them and alters language, making it into a commodity. In the first case Gerty's language, though lexically imprecise, powerfully depicts the persistence of commodities and their allied argot in the mind of a consumer; we have already seen this abridged language at work in the 1851 Exhibition *Catalogue* and in the narrative of Stanley's *In Darkest Africa*. In the second, language itself becomes a reenactment within the mind of a consumer of relationships between commodities formed within commodity culture. In the above passage Joyce uses certain formulations current in Gerty's time that reveal this bivalent influence of manufactured objects on language: "electric blue," "fingers" (used as a monetary measurement), "blued" (that is, the use of any of various coloring agents to counteract the yellowing of laundered fabrics), "footwear" (a term popularized by department stores as a division of space on the display floor), "extra" (its position in the sentence implies here that "extra" means not "more than normal" but "something for which an additional charge is made"), and "ribbon-slotted underwear" (the only kind of underwear available to Gerty at that time for those prices was made of artificial silk). At other moments in the paragraph the narrative uses terms of manufacture as attributes rather than as extrinsic qualities. Gerty says that her hat will "take the shine out of some people," as if people were lustrous objects which could be polished and defaced. Gerty's "higharched instep" describes simultaneously the arched medial position of the foot and the part of the shoe covering it. "Wellturned ankle" can mean "well-displayed," "misshapen," and, significantly, "skillfully turned or grounded" (as on a lathe). Following this, "spliced heels" can refer both to shoe and to foot. Finally, one of the few punctuated appositives in the chapter names Gerty by an extrinsic quality, her shoe size: "but she never had a foot like Gerty MacDowell, a five, and never would."[7]

It is not the actual list of these occurrences that matters. Anyone can add to or take away from it under the impulse of his or her own recognition. What does matter is what these examples have in common: the filtration into language of the commodity in its ubiquitous and liquid modern form, and in a broader sense the experimentation with a new syntax by which to convey a new order of *things* through an old order of words. Without being aware of it, texts like the Exhibition *Catalogue* and *In Darkest Africa* had contributed to the formation of this new speech. Joyce, however, was aware of what he had done. In a letter to Frank Budgen, he remarks: "*Nausikaa* is written in a namby-pamby jammy marmalady drawersy (alto la!) style with effects of incense, mariolotry, masturbation, stewed cockles, painter's palette, chitchat, circumlocutions, etc etc."[8] The two et ceteras are important here. The narrative geometry of "Nausicaa" is not static. The chapter frequently lacks coherent syntax; by leaving out conjunctions (or by using the wrong ones), the narrative tends to place juxtaposed elements in suspension. Against the background of what is often hastily called a unitary narrative, manufactured objects—pills, cosmetics, and clothing—hover free, mediating Gerty's relationship to her world via a veil of commodities with which she finally lives in symbiosis. Absolved from the shifts in narrative voice that so frequently depend on and are signaled by syntax, the narrative becomes a climatized display of the docile coexistence of commodities which Gerty has invested with human energy. As on the floor of a turn-of-the-century department store, contradictions—like the ostentatious display of articles of clothing that could not be worn in public—are not realized but left suspended in smooth abeyance.

In this fluidity of relations among commodities in "Nausicaa" we find a miniature version of a new interconnectedness of commodity with human culture operative in Irish society in Joyce's time. In bringing the novelist of *The Lamplighter* and the romances of popular magazines within the expanding universe of commodity culture, "Nausicaa" marks the capacity of manufactured objects to become dominant images for the self, to take on, as we say, "personality." This bringing together of the linguistic components of the commodity creates a web of connection from which Gerty MacDowell cannot be freed. As Cocteau writes: "Decorative style has never existed. Style is the soul, and unfortunately with us the soul assumes the form of the body."[9] As we know, Joyce wanted to embody Dublin with such exactitude that if it were to disappear tomorrow from the face of the earth, his novel would suffice to reconstruct it, down to its last habit of mind. Gerty's cognate style is not simply a parody of entrepreneurial jargon, but just such a panoramic view of Irish commodity culture from within language. What we find in "Nausicaa" is not simply commodification—a process by which commodities suddenly appear where they have not been before—but a thoroughgoing psychological assimilation of the practices, methods, aims, and spirit of commodity culture in its Irish form.

The architecture of adaptation in "Nausicaa" gives us some idea as to how this ponderous materiality of language and culture has come about. In "Nausicaa" the idealist spirituality present in "Telemachus," and in *The Lamplighter*, has been assimilated into and transformed by a materialist spirituality, a reverence for objects we have already seen at work in the transcendent materiality of Jubilee kitsch. The resulting mesh of styles documents at close range the appearance and articulation of a new way of seeing the world peculiar to the felt presence of the commodity. Remembering an experience in the confessional, Gerty characteristically begins to weigh the merits of various gifts she could buy for her confessor (359). Neatly following Marx's account of the fetishism of commodities in the first volume of *Capital*, Gerty exhibits the tendency of failing to see that she is dealing with a social relation among human beings and has supposed instead that she is dealing with a relation between things.[10] She operates, Georg Lukács might say, with a notion of facts instead of a notion of processes.[11] This is a far cry from the mnemonic status of objects (here keepsakes once owned by Stephen Dedalus's mother) in "Telemachus": "Her secrets: old feather fans, tasselled dancecords, powdered with musk, a gaud of amber beads in her locked drawer. A birdcage hung in the sunny window of her house when she was a girl. . . . Phantasmal mirth, folded away: muskperfumed" (9–10).

Crucial to this passage is an understanding of the history of the keepsake. In the early nineteenth century a keepsake was a literary annual, usually a collection of verse, prose, and illustrations. Given as gifts, keepsakes were kept for the sake of the remembrance of shared experiences. With Stephen's mother these remembrances are not evoked by the written word, but through objects; these objects have not been circulated or exchanged but simply retained as private remembrances kept locked in a drawer. This condition of keepsakes bears comparison with Gerty Flint's experience of keepsakes in *The Lamplighter*:

Each article was endeared to her by the charm of old association, and many a tear had the little maiden shed over her stock of valuables. There was the figure of the Samuel, Uncle True's first gift, now defaced by time and accident. As she surveyed a severe contusion on the back of the head, the effect of an inadvertant knock given it by True himself, and remembered how patiently the dear old man had labored to repair the injury, she felt that she would not part with the much-valued memento for the world. There, too, were his pipes, of common clay, and dark with smoke and age; but, as she thought how much comfort they had been to him, she felt that the possession of them was a consolation to her. She had brought away too his lantern, for she had not forgotten its pleasant light, the first that ever fell upon the darkness of her life; nor could she leave behind an old fur cap, beneath which she had often sought a kindly smile, and, never having sought in vain, could hardly realize that there was no one for her still hidden beneath its crown. There were some toys too, and picture-books, gifts from Willie, a little basket he had carved for her from a nut, and a few other trifles.[12]

When her maid accidentally throws away this stuff it is too much for Gerty to bear. She becomes disconsolate and collapses in bed. Giving way to tears for one page and vowing revenge for another, she gradually works her way from her bed to a windowsill, where Cummins has laid out for her a natural scene which she does not fail to construe as an exemplum:

The window was open; the shower was over, and the smiles of the refreshed and beautiful earth were reflected in a glowing rainbow, that spanned the eastern horizon. A little bird came, and perched on a branch of a tree close to the window, and shouted forth a *Te Deum*. A Persian lilac-bush in full bloom sent up a delicious fragrance. A wonderful composure stole into Gertrude's heart, and, ere she had sat there many minutes, she felt "the grace that brings peace succeed to the passions that produce trouble." She had conquered; she had achieved the greatest of life's victories, a victory over herself. . . . This was the first instance of complete self-control in Gerty, and the last we shall have occasion to dwell upon.[13]

The key moment in Gerty Flint's education comes when she masters the temptation of keepsakes. For Stephen's mother and for Gerty Flint, the keepsake is a means of evoking the past through objects. It embodies a complex of values—of memories, of psychological safeguards against the passage of time, and of a sentimentalized valediction of a lost landscape—to which both are ready adherents. Objects have always borne a problematic relation to experience: what should we do with the material remnants of the past? The evangelist Maria Cummins dramatizes a rigid Christian determination to be created anew by showing Gerty in the act of cutting ties with her material past. There is a crushing finality to this scene, for it violates our notion (itself an endless source of narrative complication) of the continuity of human beings in time. Scarcely one hundred pages into the novel, Gerty Flint hesitates for the last time. To highlight Gerty's triumph in attaining this "first instance of complete self-control," the narrative includes a parody of Portable Property (and of the sartorial bulk so fashionable in the 1850's) in the person of Patty Pace, possessor of "the most remarkable toilet [Gerty] had ever witnessed,"[14] a wardrobe that includes green string, a multicolored reticule, a black lace cap, feather fans, and a black silk shawl and gloves. Having withstood the further temptation of keepsakes embodied in Patty Pace, Gerty suffers no further internal struggles. Ultimately, however, this sudden shift in character reveals just how dependent Gerty was on objects to evoke memories; once her keepsakes disappear, so, for the most part, does her past. Clearly Cummins senses something opposed to the dictates of Christianity in the sentimental spiritualization of objects as keepsakes. Yet the virtual disappearance of Gerty's past after the immolation of its objects manifests not only her renunciation of, but her radical dependence on, the keepsake.

In Gerty MacDowell this struggle against the weight of objects vanishes:

For Gerty had her dreams that no-one knew of. She loved to read poetry and when she got a keepsake from Bertha Supple of that lovely confession album with the coral-pink cover to write her thoughts in she laid it in the drawer of her toilettable which, though it did not err on the side of luxury, was scrupulously neat and clean. It was there that she kept her girlish treasures trove, the tortoiseshell combs, her child of Mary badge, the whiterose scent, the eyebrowleine, her alabaster pouncetbox and the ribbons to change when her things came home from the wash and there were some beautiful thoughts written in it in violet ink that she bought at Hely's of Dame Street for she felt that she too could write poetry if only she could express herself like that poem that appealed to her so deeply that she had copied out of the newspaper she found one evening around the potherbs. (363–64)

Upon receipt, Gerty's keepsake album is blank. With its coral-pink cover, it is a manufactured object designed for consumption and replacement. Except for her child of Mary badge, Gerty purchased all the objects in her "girlish treasures trove." The paraphernalia of the writing desk figures importantly in this trove. A pouncetbox, once used to sprinkle sand or pounce on writing paper to dry the ink, is now a box for her perfumes. Her ink is from Hely's. The poem she admires was printed in a newspaper: even though such jingles were expressly designed for the forgetful, she remembers only traces. Even her recollection of *The Lamplighter* merges with that of Reggy Wylie on his bicycle: "Reggy Wylie used to turn his freewheel like she read in that book *The Lamplighter* by Miss Cummins" (363). The literal implication of the syntax is that the scene with the boy on the freewheel bicycle is in *The Lamplighter*. Unwittingly Gerty places contemporary technology—a 1904 invention, a bicycle equipped with a clutch that would disengage the rear wheel—in the past and almost out of time. As much a reader of billboards, throwaways, and leaflets as of novels, her tendency is to wander; she has an attention span of about thirty seconds. In all probability her notion of a literary experience consists simply of reading a magazine or newspaper and throwing it away. In doing so she reflects the experience of many turn-of-the-century common readers. For by 1895, according to the *OED*, the word "literature" itself had come to encompass "brochure" or "printed matter." In a commodity culture, Marx has argued, "*all* the physical and spiritual senses" give way to "the sense of *having*." [15] In Gerty's transitory consumption of the written word, the sense of having is whittled down to a moment of possession followed by instant obsolescence. The phantasmal mirth of the keepsake had become the cheap phantasmagoria of the commodity.

II

This haphazard life of commodities in Gerty's narrative partially derives its significance from the manner in which an Irish common reader of the early twentieth century experienced material objects in their most hyperbolically available form: through advertisements. Her narrative coincides historically with the transformation of the sale of common objects such as soap, shoes, and stockings into advertised spectacles on an unheard-of scale. Surveying the most successful advertisements of the previous twenty years, an advertising primer of 1925 advises its readers to "go on a Gulliver tour, pictorially," enlarging products to "heroic size" in order to "loom large on the horizon of the vision and of the mind." [16] In *Ulysses* just such an aggressive world of advertisements clogs the horizon. Joyce does not overlook even the lowliest of ads, granting even a humble throwaway a heroic progress through Dublin. Wisdom Hely Ltd., Manufacturing Stationers of Dame Street, advertises ostentatiously with an animated street parade of five sandwich-board men spelling out "H. E. L. Y.' S." [17] Bloom himself, who plies the trade of advertising canvasser and worked in advertising for Hely's on and off between 1888 and 1895, imagines that he can improve the firm's campaign by filling a mobile float with pretty secretaries in the act of using products from Hely's. On the floors of a Hely's or Cleary's, great interior horizons of appealing merchandise opened up to a consumer like Gerty, brimming with objects her mid-nineteenth-century counterpart had never thought of seeing in such numbers, except in the specialized haven of the Crystal Palace. For in the world of Gerty Flint and May Dedalus material objects more closely resembled keepsakes, one-of-a-kinds. In the world of Gerty MacDowell, on the contrary, the unique object stands as an oddity; only branded objects, packaged in new forms and distributed in new locations, possess any appeal for her. On Dame and Grafton streets she could inspect ongoing expositions in display windows in which goods advertised themselves. In department stores Gerty places her loyalty less in the immediate testimony of her fellow consumers and more than ever in the advertised promises and familiar packages of distant merchandisers.

Tied to other Irish consumers by a thin web of shared loyalties to things, Gerty does not notice that the advertisements she has assimilated also function as a stay on her social autonomy. In "The Work of Art in the Age of Mechanical Reproduction," Walter Benjamin has shown how technological reproduction for prolific display deprives a work of art of its unrepeatable uniqueness, its aura of authenticity. [18] For Benjamin a reproduced work successfully accomplishes the occultation of its origin; the human and time-bound circumstances of its creation effectively disappear behind a protective veil of technology. Faced with an advertisement, therefore, the consumer confronts the reproduced commodity in a vacuum as an object without cause, with the appearance of a phenomenon so natural and necessary that it could not be justified except as a pure and simple fact. By affecting neutrality and naturalness, each advertisement makes a silent claim of contingent necessity for itself, a claim of emancipation from the capitalist fiat that advertising purvey goods for monetary exchange in the marketplace. In an advertised reproduction a consumer neither sees traces of the fabrication of the commodity nor places himself or herself in any critical historical relation to that commodity. In "Nausicaa" Gerty does not see that a slogan like "Queen of Ointments" (used in ads for Beetham's "Larola") masks, in the form of a complex aura of connotation, the correlation of a dermatological cure-all with an urgent sales pitch. Such apparent connotation further weakens Gerty's understanding of her place in a real historical world—

the Dublin of 1904—because, to paraphrase Roland Barthes, the advertisements she consumes habitually assume a panache of connotation while remaining doggedly denotative. Barthes thinks that collectively this orbit of connotations works denotatively to trip off the buying impulse in the mind of the consumer. As he writes in *The Fashion System*, "in order to blunt the buyer's calculating consciousness, a veil must be drawn around the object."[19]

This statement of Barthes's belies a belief in the close and circumscribed manipulation of reader by advertisement. Like so many others, he studies advertisements as if they worked automatically; moreover, Barthes often treats the audience for advertisements as if they responded instrumentally and instantaneously to the most rigorous semiotic laws. But the veil drawn around a product by its advertisement does not blunt the calculating consciousness of a consumer to the point of paralysis. Although an advertisement like the "Queen of Ointments" exercises unprecedented influence over Gerty, it does not do so in a vacuum but remains subject to her varying needs and capacities. Gerty may experience severe financial and physical strictures on her participation in the confusion between needs and wants that advertising strives to create. Of necessity she must often contemplate rather than consummate consumption. What is more important, she participates in the creation and maintenance of that veil around objects that Barthes describes. Well-dressed and annealed with the latest ointments for protection from the seaside sun, Gerty is not only an object of advertising but its carrier and practitioner.

Even in the simple "Queen of Ointments" we can plot the variables of Gerty's behavior as a consumer. In the ease with which Beetham's Larola converges agrammatically with lemon juice and kid gloves in the passage cited above, we see precisely how susceptible Gerty has become to a central tenet of twentieth-century marketing theory and practice: the liquidation of the customary material and social borders defining the individuality of commodities. Now a commodity like the "Queen of Ointments" aspires to the plurality of the ensemble. Part of Gerty's attraction to the comparative study of ointments is that it helps her to add to an ensemble of toiletries that she has come to think necessary to a life of domestic bliss: "She would care for him with creature comforts too for Gerty was womanly wise and knew that a mere man liked that feeling of hominess" (352).

As we have seen, of course, a life of such open-ended demand remains impracticable for her. By weighing the ability of a given good to add or detract from this ensemble, Gerty manages to reduce her appetite for all manner of effluvia to a finite choice. While it is tempting to treat this restricted ensemble of commodities as a persisting nucleus created by Gerty, the case is somewhat more complex. Many commodities have the appearance of floating benignly in and out of the foreground of Gerty's narrative. Under scrutiny, however, the membership of the "Queen of Ointments" in allied orbits of connotation grows both more intensive and more extensive. In remembering the slogan Gerty undoubtedly rehearses her experience of possessing and using the commodity; but she also remembers it because it recapitulates the Litany of Our Lady, which she repeats later in the chapter and which reads in part: "Queen of angels, Queen of patriarchs, Queen of prophets, Queen of apostles, Queen of martyrs, Queen of confessors, Queen of virgins . . ." Queen of Ointments: if for Gerty this advertisement evokes and satisfies a religious impulse, in its dependence on a litany it also takes on an implied anaphoric repetition through which it becomes a jingle. Just as importantly, it promises her a more earthly satisfaction in a simulacrum of both the white skin and the "languid queenly *hauteur*" of sheltered royalty. In each of these ways Gerty's body has itself become a field for advertisements. Indeed her fetish for personal hygiene rarely ventures beyond a more detailed definition of hygiene than that held up by a widely advertised slogan for another Beetham's product: "IT HAS NO EQUAL FOR KEEPING THE SKIN SOFT AND SMOOTH . . . IT ENTIRELY REMOVES AND PREVENTS ALL REDNESS, ROUGHNESS, IRRITATION, TAN, &c." (Fig. 40).[20]

To shrug off such slogans as ephemera is to neglect the powers at play in the constitution of an advertisement. In "Nausicaa" not only the foreground but the background of Gerty's narrative draws on a particular run of advertisements. During

FIG. 40. The queen of ointments (*Illustrated London News*, October 12, 1895).

the 1880's and 1890's M. Beetham & Son, Cheltenham, marketed a line of ointments, lotions, and salves by framing their campaign around a proven formula: the seaside girl.

The "seaside girl" was a catch phrase popularized by a hit song in the late nineteenth century. Snatches from this music-hall favorite drift through Blazes Boylan's mind as he goes about his business in Joyce's Dublin:

> All dimpled cheeks and curls,
> Your head it simply swirls.
>
> Those girls, those girls,
> Those lovely seaside girls.[21]

Habitat of the seaside girl, the seaside resort was an extension of nineteenth-century urban life. Railways made excursions to the seashore possible, and the mass migration to the Great Exhibition showed that leisure was profitable. The new work week and Bank Holidays provided the necessary free time. The hotel-lined colonies at Brighton, Scarborough, Hastings, Blackpool, and Southport sprang up to fill the leisure void. In the 1850's and 1860's the seaside studies of Kingsley, Gosse, and Lewes became best-sellers as people discovered the genteel science of marine biology. Domestic aquariums became fashionable fixtures in the Victorian home and shell collecting became so popular that it damaged the coastline. The annual stampede to the sea had begun.[22]

The seaside resort was a site of fantasy and a primary locus of Victorian sexual politics. Sick people came to soak in the waters of spas, inlets, tidal pools; Freud's case studies testify that, more often than not, miracle cures took place while his patients were vacationing at the seashore.[23] Healthy people came to see and be seen. The sight of men and women bathing together at the seashore is enough to make Blazes Boylan's eyes pop out of his head: "Your head it simply swirls." The sexual density of what was called "mixed bathing" was quite unlike the repression we customarily associate with Victorian sexual practices. At the seashore in June 1874, the Rev. Francis Kilvert confided to his diary:

One beautiful girl stood entirely naked in the sand, and there as she sat, half reclined sideways, leaning upon her elbow with her knee bent and her legs and feet partly drawn back and up, she was a model for a sculptor, there was a supple slender waist, the gentle dawn and tender swell of the bosom and the budding breasts, the graceful rounding of the delicately beautiful limbs and above all the soft exquisite curves of the rosy dimpled bottom and broad white thighs.[24]

Kilvert may or may not actually have seen this girl, but she could only have appeared to him at a seaside resort. Just as old houses were places likely to be frequented by ghosts, seaside resorts encouraged the apparition of naked Gerty MacDowells. The seaside resort not only promoted the diversification of sexual practices such as nude bathing, but it also refined the forms that sexual desire and gratification took. At a seaside resort it was now possible for a minister to rely on the style of domestic realism to articulate his sexual longings. At the Great Exhibition the display of the female body had been restricted to a few statues like Hiram Powers's "The Greek Slave"; at the beach the body of the adolescent or prepubescent girl became a cultural ideal even for clergy like Kilvert. The sumptuous seaside resorts of Victorian England had become Crystal Palaces for the libido, places where the male consumer could become, like Nabokov's Humbert Humbert, a connoisseur of nymphets. The space of leisure had been sexualized.

In a great variety of ways, then, seaside resorts successfully integrated sexual practice into the practice of consumption. They pioneered a volatile mixture: material comfort, sexual excitation, and hard selling. At some resorts, such as Brighton and Bournemouth, the advertisers virtually outnumbered the bathers. A progressive advertiser like Gissing's Luckworth Crewe dreams of defacing seaside resorts with pier-to-pier billboards. Sometimes advertisers went so far as to invest in resorts so that they

FIG. 41. The cheesecake pose (Hindley and Hindley, *Advertising in Victorian England*).

FIG. 42. The seaside girl (*Illustrated London News*, July 9, 1887).

could have a say about where their posters would be placed. But their real contribution was a new formula for commodity culture: the seaside girl. According to the formula, the common use of which can be traced back to the 1870's and the new emphasis on outdoor physical fitness for women, a girl—alone or in a *petite bande*—strolls, sleeps, or swims along the seashore. If sitting, she strikes, in a swimsuit with low bodice and exposed legs, a cheesecake pose (Fig. 41); if strolling, she reaches out in the conventional posture of Eve (Fig. 42); if swimming, she floats ex-

THE SEA MAIDEN.
DECORATIVE PANEL.

HAL HURST

FIG. 43. The decorative template (*Poster* 3.18, 1900).

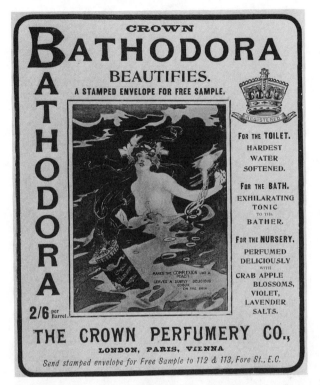

FIG. 44. Instant advertising (*Illustrated London News*, March 29, 1902).

posed to the waist under the scrutiny of bobbing male heads.[25] Depicted in detailed monochromatic wood engravings, these advertisements approached the intricacy of the lithograph and included cloud formations, sunsets, and horizons. By the turn of the century this image had proven so popular, carrying off two prizes in the Scarborough Poster Design Contest of 1899, that it now became possible to buy a template or "decorative panel" of a seaside girl which left a large blank space for inserting the brand name and slogan of the product of the buyer's choice (Fig. 43). The result was instant advertising (Fig. 44).

Only rarely does the image of the commodity advertised intrude into the scene of the seaside girl; the irreferentiality of the image is nearly complete. Instead a slogan appropriates the seaside girl. "WHAT ARE THE WILD WAVES SAYING?" asks one adver-

FIG. 45. The irreferential image (*Illustrated London News*, July 23, 1887).

tisement: "TRY BEECHAM'S PILLS," comes the response (Fig. 45).
Other products of the period advertised using the seaside girl
include Edwards's Harlene for the Hair, Clearer's Terebene
Soap, Cadbury's Cocoa, Chicester Brand Potted Meats, Y&N Di-
agonal Seam Corsets, and, more to the point, Beetham's ointments. A typical Beetham's advertisement of the 1890's shows
two girls resting near the hulking form of a pier (Fig. 46). Sitting
straight up and wearing a hat, one girl admires the striated rays
of the sun. The other has fallen asleep, one hand pulling up her
dress to reveal a crumpled segment of underwear. With her hat

thrust aside, the sun's rays shine ominously across one side of her face in such a way—stark white on a dark woodcut—as to convey an impression of glare. Under such conditions, however, we need no longer fear, "For BEETHAM puts her all to rights / with GLYC'RINE & CUCUMBER."[26] In this situation an immediate need of material life may well include a preparation against the sun. When, however, the advertisement shows the sun setting and its rays partially obscured by clouds, it becomes clear that Beetham's has sacrificed plausibility for a strident dose of the picturesque. Having framed the display so as to enclose the con-

FIG. 46. Mock-up of incongruities (*Graphic*, July 21, 1888).

sumer in as wide an orbit of connotations—day and night, calm and storm, waking and sleep—as possible, the marketers are really asking their hypothetical consumer to participate in a precarious mockup of incongruities.

Only the familiar image of the seaside girl promises a fix on this whirligig of contexts. The seaside girl displays an all-purpose allegiance that accommodates a violation of a sexual taboo just as easily as it promotes a white skin befitting the modest and the chaste. Here Gerty and the seaside girl meet. For the contradictions folded into the seaside girl are, in the final analysis, virtually identical with those of the world disclosed in the narrative of Gerty MacDowell, a world constructed by and for commodity culture, a world in which language exists only to advertise. It is an imagined world—in part because commodities had become not so much material objects as their fantastic representations—but one in which the imagination has been appropriated to a new end. When in *A Portrait* Stephen Dedalus sees a girl strolling along the seashore, he experiences a tremor of sexual shock for, as he observes, "her thighs, fuller and softhued as ivory, were bared almost to the hips where the white fringes of her drawers were like featherings of soft white down."[27] Transfixed like Rev. Kilvert, Stephen has caught a glimpse of a bared thigh during a decade when women's bathing costumes included skirts to mid-calf and opaque stockings. Gerty begins where Stephen's passing fancy leaves off. What was once the distanced reciprocity of the observer and the observed now yields to the "wonderous revealment half offered . . . before gentlemen looking" (366), an unflinching imitation of the magic appeal of the advertised self-exposure of the seaside girl. We can no longer see her as straying unexpectedly across the field of vision of a lonely man; now Gerty is herself the seaside girl, looking at passersby from within the frame of an advertised fiction by which she is wholly circumscribed, looking out at a scene over which she reigns as the queen of ointments.

In this hegemony of the advertised image of the seaside girl the values sanctioned by advertising begin to coalesce. In the holiday world of the seaside setting, filled with required accessories and permeated by a narcotic peace, the hallmarks of com-

BOVRIL

FOR

HEALTH & BEAUTY.

The Bovril sold on a single day recently was sufficient to provide a brimming hot cupful for 7,000,000 beautiful women.

Bovril repels Influenza and keeps one fit in all weathers and circumstances.

FIG. 47. Statistical consumers (*Illustrated London News*, January 26, 1907).

modity culture appear: as in the pages of *Pearson's* or *The Lady's Pictorial*, the stress falls on leisure time, impulse buying, nonpartisan quiescence, and a therapeutic ethos of individual fulfillment through a manufactured utopia of commodities. For all its specificity Gerty's narrative reflects this common lot of consumers in the early twentieth century. In the nineteenth century, Walter Benjamin has written, the crowd became a customer: behind Gerty we can imagine lives with shared attitudes and aspirations that would crave representation in similar statistical terms (Fig. 47). Available to millions, the seaside girl and the allied "queen of ointments" have been directed at private but tacitly collective acts of statistical consumption. So while stamping the world of a market society with a constantly festive and euphoric mark, the seaside girl exists firmly within it. For Gerty the lines of consumption are drawn. In her mind she can only see reflected the changing glare of commercialized signs, all in a jumble like a page of rotogravure. In the volatile world noted so eloquently by Marx in the *Communist Manifesto*—"all that is solid," he wrote, "melts into air"—the best that Gerty can do is to find in the advertised image of the seaside girl, which is fundamentally a tool for the transmission of the urge to consume, a prescription for living.

That Gerty cannot get the prescription straight, that without hesitation she buys into the advertised confusion between needs and wants, both comprises the sadness of her historical situation and, more especially, accurately represents an ideological process. Louis Althusser has called this meeting of social consciousness and economic activity a "practical" ideology. His definition suggests connections between ways of appropriating the world and ways of seeing or sensing it: "ideology is the 'lived' relation between men and their world, or a reflected form of this unconscious relation."[28] This relation does not represent "the system of real relations which govern the existence of individuals, but the imaginary relation of these individuals to the real relations in which they live."[29] The integrity of "Nausicaa" is that it comprises just such a practical—and by implication, usually unexamined and imperceptible—ideology, of which the multivalent stylistic surface of the chapter is an accurate mirror. Note that a practical ideology is invariably an inward and often contradictory process of cultural practice. Importantly, Joyce does not let Gerty's voice stand unmediated, as a continuous and authoritative illustration of a commodity language in "Nausicaa." Faithful to the practical ideology of her day, Gerty's absorption in commodities is swallowed up by the whole body of discourse about keepsakes which it appears to have displaced. By finally conflating Gerty's understanding of language via the commodity with the idiom of Victorian domestic fiction, Joyce summons the popular literary tradition of the sentimental object, or keepsake, through the very materiality of the commodity that displaces that tradition. Joyce puts expressly the problem, as Derrida formulates it, of "the status of a discourse which borrows from a heritage the resources necessary for the deconstruction of that heritage itself."[30] This problem, inescapable in this chapter, marks "Nausicaa" as a text which continually puts its own status into question. The ground upon which Gerty places a well-turned ankle turns out to be a remarkably unsettling strand.

It may well be more unsettling for us than for Gerty. For to admit that we can discover no key to the exact content of the narrative voices that constitute "Nausicaa" is to nullify the attribute of narrative voice as the identifiable property of a particular individual. Instead, narrative voices such as domestic realism become attributes temporarily allied with the names of commodities available on the marketplace. At the disposal of advertisers the single and distinct voice is altered to multiple, interchangeable, and increasingly irreferential voices. These infinitely divisible narrative voices allow us to see Gerty both as an innocent consumer of language and as language: Bloom says it himself, "Still it was a kind of language between us" (372), a language standing at the intersection of any number of social and historical voices, none of which is objective. The old categories for understanding language no longer work here—referential and emotive, denotative and connotative, even ordinary and literary language are displaced and redistributed by "Nausicaa." Instead, each of the oscillating voices in Gerty's narrative emerges in all its implications as a specific milieu of linguistic productivity, practice, and transformation. It is not possible for a reader of "Nausicaa" to remain, like Gerty, an unconscious consumer of language. For Gerty language is an instrument; for us it cannot help but appear as the powerful and unstable agent for a regime of reading and understanding produced and disseminated by commodity culture.

This treatment of "Nausicaa" at the level of large economic forces exposes both the genius and the danger of reading "Nausicaa" as a key document in commodity aesthetics. Implicit in Gerty's idiom is a phenomenology of consumption, a study of subjective response called into life by commodities. Of course

Joyce's imagination has selected and retained the most telling patterns in the language of advertising and has rearranged them into a more concentrated commodity language than could have been observed on the open marketplace of language. He intensifies into sequences of associations patterns that in everyday systems of speech would seem very submerged indeed. Joyce does not give us a glimpse of the process by which habitual representations such as the seaside girl become entangled with commodities, resulting in habits of mind such as we observe in Gerty; instead he shows several reified forms of language tangled up with one another. Joyce has not confined his inquiry in "Nausicaa" to social class and the relations of exchange, but to the broader question of the shifting economic relationship of human beings to language. It is not economic but linguistic determinism that captivates Joyce. Seeing in Gerty's voice the substance and temporal solidity of a predetermined—indeed, overdetermined—language, we can affirm the limitation of what can appear an endless process of narrative causality.

We have seen that Joyce locates with great insight the cause of Gerty's sadness in the fact that as a turn-of-the-century Irish common reader, she is a figment of representations produced and offered to her by commodity culture. But the side effects of this insight can be severe; it is tempting to treat Gerty as a lapidary creation, a static exposition of a rigid economic identity. She is not: the wonder of "Nausicaa" is that in Gerty Joyce has managed to convey the immediacy of a thoroughly reified response to life. In Gerty's prevailing need to behave and consume in accordance with advertisements, we see the euphoric unhappiness that results when people begin to recognize themselves in their commodities. In no sense, however, is Gerty aware of her own alienation. As readers we come to see Gerty's onedimensionality through the second leaf of this diptych: Bloom. Only under Bloom's watchful eye do we fully recognize Gerty as a preconditioned receptacle of false needs. The counterpart to Gerty's unconscious absorption in commodity culture is Bloom's cheerful and conscious creation and acceptance of that culture. Although Bloom's consciousness has undeniably been invaded and whittled down by the technology of advertisement, he remains able to articulate Gerty's lameness in the face of the over-whelmingly elliptical avoidance of that fact by Gerty's narrative.

So crammed with piety, romance, and sentiment, so over-burdened with material detail, her narrative cannot finally be considered an exhaustive representation of life as it was lived among Catholic schoolchildren in Dublin in 1904. It is, rather, an abridgement of that reality in fixed images, a picture of the arrested development of a consumer in the grips of the self-validating formulas of commodity culture. Although Joyce tren-chantly renders the power of that culture over her, a full picture of the workaday life of Gerty MacDowell might conceivably require as much narrative variety and ingenuity as Bloom's. Despite its multivalency, however, Gerty's narrative nowhere presents her with the tragic historical clarity of Stephen Dedalus's vision of the "high shoulders and shabby dress" (243) of his sister Dilly, in age and class Gerty's nearest rival in *Ulysses*. In one page of terse dialogue in "Wandering Rocks" we see Dilly drowning in the squalor of daily life with her father, yet buying a primer for a penny in a bookcart in the forlorn hope of learning French. In contrast, Gerty's narrative—in which Gerty speaks directly only twice—stands as a common ideological imposition upon that life, a mass-produced product of a historical moment that Gerty both approximates and appropriates.

So there can be no doubt that Joyce's representation of Gerty MacDowell leaves her off balance and curiously vulnerable. De-spite her aspirations Gerty cannot become the seaside girl of Vic-torian and Edwardian advertisements. If we consider that she lived in a country in which there were no seaside resorts on the scale of Hastings or Brighton or Bournemouth; that billboards had not yet invaded every available wall in Dublin; that its shop-ping centers operated on a scale comparable to those of a suburb of contemporary London; that it remained, moreover, the only great European city to undergo a decline in population during a decade of stifling European expansion; then we recognize that in Dublin life remained much more provincial, much more old-fashioned, much less contemporary than in the Paris of Zola or the London of Gissing. No wonder that Irish writers took so long to discover the commodity. Even after 1904 a consciousness of modern life was slow in awakening, especially after the lack of interest manifested by Celtic revivalists in the conditions and constitution of their material world. In his grasp of the extent to which Ireland had become so materially modern while remaining immersed in traditional attitudes and institutions, Joyce stands alone in Irish literary history. His emphasis, that common readers in the twentieth century are somehow anchored to and expressed by their material world, was not new. In his own time Joyce could hear the cries of Irish nationalists, with their dreams of an agrarian, deindustrialized Ireland. But more often, the figures of protest were more cautious, pointing darkly to a deeper enmity between human beings and their materially acculturated world. In rebuttal, and with a leap of insight, Joyce united the two and made his Nausicaa lame.

III

The seaside girl was the most modern form of spectacle devised by late-Victorian commodity culture, and it has proved to be the most lasting. Most of the other spectacles of Victorian advertising had a very short life span; they came and went like brush fires. The Great Exhibition had synthesized all the elements of a specifically capitalist form of representation, but only in 1851 did an exhibition of things merit the prefix "great"; no other exhibition held in Britain ever equaled it. For all the energy expended in celebrating them, Victoria's two Jubilees left remarkably few traces in historical memory. In any event she died in 1901, and her son Edward did not reign long enough to become a stable fixture in commodity culture. The same is true for Henry Stanley, who in the early 1890's exercised a fascination for which allegedly no precedent existed and who fell from fashion so quickly that by 1895 his magnum opus, *In Darkest Africa*, had been out of print for three years. The quacks basked in Wagnerian twilight; under siege by the medical profession, their days were clearly numbered. As influential as each of these spectacles was in shaping the characteristic topoi of twentieth-century advertising, the shape of things to come had not yet assumed permanent form. The perdurable spectacles of modern commodity culture—that culture which, as Roland Barthes later saw, traffics in images "of consumption alone"—were as yet adumbrated only in the battle figurine of the seaside girl.[31]

That the vast resources of representation placed at the disposal of turn-of-the-century advertising should have been mobilized around such a slight subject may at first seem paradoxical. When Proust's Marcel first meets Albertine at the seashore, she evokes for him nothing more than the frivolity and caprice of the first flush of youth. But the image of the seaside girl was equal to the demands advertisers placed on it. Its appeal was both general and specific. It spoke to consumers exclusively as an image—so much so, as we have seen, that it circulated among advertisers as a template and made the cover of the house organ of turn-of-the-century advertising, *The Poster*. More specifically, it carried consumption to a segment of the population whose purchasing power was only then beginning to be recognized. The seaside girl eulogized adolescence and signaled the formation of what we now call "youth culture." At one and the same time she marked off the adolescent female body as an object of commodity culture and changed the shape of women's anatomy by making that body normative and compulsory. In compact form she realized what must have been every patent medicine advertiser's dream: every act of consumption now became an act of rejuvenation.

Commodity culture had taken a long time to cordon off adolescence as the time of life ripest for consumption. "It is hardly credible," wrote advertiser William Smith in 1862, "what wonderful advertising mediums children are."[32] He goes on to imagine using children as cheap labor carrying sandwich boards and distributing leaflets, but he does not imagine directing advertising at them. The only reason he is interested in children is because they are likely to appeal to adults. As Dickens had recognized in his *Christmas Books*, children were effective ploys for getting the public's attention. But they could consume only by proxy. They had no purchasing power, and they often provoked the protective intervention of parents and courts. Magazines published for children carried few advertisements, and even the makers of toys tried to appeal to adults. Over time advertising

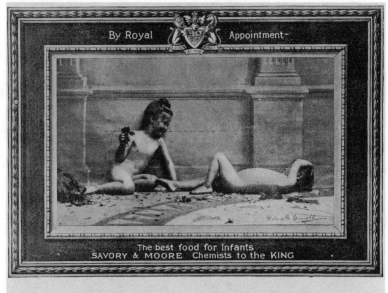

FIG. 48. Inventing adolescence (*Graphic*, December 19, 1903).

remained fixated on childhood, but in such a way that it accorded less and less importance to it. At about the same time as Freud published *Three Essays on the Theory of Sexuality* (1905), a baby-food advertiser manifested a telling interest in infant sexuality (Fig. 48). This ad places a pair of naked children in sexually suggestive postures reminiscent of the odalisque. Freud had characterized infant sexuality as predominantly self-directed and auto-erotic, but here one girl fixes her attention on the other's body. In Freud's scheme these are no longer children. Because they have discovered each other as sexual objects they have entered puberty.[33] Though this advertisement seems to be about childhood (the caption speaks of Savory & Moore as "the best food for infants"), it actually replaces the diffuse and objectless sexuality of childhood with the directed and differentiated sexuality of puberty. Adolescence has encroached upon childhood as the prime territory and primary medium of commodity culture.

The introduction of adolescence into commodity culture did

not break up the market into segments segregated by age, as some have suggested. For adolescence was in the process of becoming something more than a stage of life through which everyone passed. In his monumental *Adolescence* (1904), G. Stanley Hall went so far as to claim that adolescence is the single most formative stage of life. Hall's rendering of adolescence reads like an extended account of the modern consuming subject. As someone young enough not to work but old enough to consume, the adolescent lives in a state of pure leisure. Family ties dwindle as "the child develops a life of its own outside the home circle." The child becomes an autonomous consumer whose "character and personality are taking form, but everything is plastic." This adolescent self is protean but not too protean; it can be shaped without getting out of hand: "Never again will there be such susceptibility to drill and discipline, such plasticity to habituation, or such ready adjustment to new conditions." Whatever it is faced with, the adolescent's putty-like self remains in a continual state of distraction, seeking out new and changing objects of sense perception, manifesting a "general craving" to amass what Hall calls "sense capital." Far and away the most acquisitive stage of life, the adolescent regards youth as a prized possession: "He would touch it at every point, explore its every possibility, receive everything it has to give, and revel in it to intoxication." "Thus," Hall concludes, drawing on a metaphor from interior decoration, "the soul is furnished."[34]

The seaside girl replicates in every way possible Hall's vision of consumer adolescence. Gerty MacDowell is full of general cravings and unsatisfied longings, and her insecure sense of selfhood finds refuge in the sensory capital which manufactured objects supply for her. Like a typical adolescent, too, she is oblivious to the social forces that shape her. Though she cannot live without things, she remains unaware of the ties that bind her to them. It used to be that consumers experienced craving for commodities as a response to external stimuli such as the Crystal Palace; now the need for commodities arises in response to internal stimuli originating within the consumer's body. The phenomenology of consumption has become grounded in human biology, for adolescence now provides a biological basis for consumption by coordinating it with physiological changes that issue from the consumer's body. Gerty's blemishes cry out for Beetham's Larola; when she menstruates she reaches for Widow Welch's Female Pills. During adolescence, as Hall observes, "the functions of every sense undergo reconstruction,"[35] but only to be strung around the helix of the commodity.

But commodity culture took Hall's conclusions even further. Whereas Hall was interested in how people passed through adolescence, advertisers were interested in adolescence as an end in itself. Gerty's narrative makes her out to be an impressionable teenager, but at twenty-two she no longer qualifies—not even under Hall's blanket definition, which extended adolescence from eight to eighteen. Many seaside girls were in fact seaside women. A 1928 advertising handbook called *Advertising for Women* makes it clear that what mattered was not actual youth but the appearance of what was uniformly called "youthfulness," defined as the "desire to remain attractive—young—in the eyes of man."[36] Quite a few advertisements showed grown women trooping along the beach among the seaside girls, and by the turn of the century, mothers with children began to appear regularly (Fig. 49). Though their age is evident and advertisers make no attempt to conceal it, they have been made to conform to a paradigm contained in the immature bodies of thirteen-year-old girls. The ideal type of womanhood has become prolonged girlhood. As yet this type went against the grain of fashion, which at the turn of the century called for sharply accentuated curves and concealed limbs. The slender and visibly hairless body would have to wait until the 1920's to become fashionably tyrannical. By then advertised adolescence had long been a permanent condition, the privileged domain of modern commodity culture. The cult of adolescence had become a standing culture of youth.

For all its familiarity, however, the commodity culture of youth embodied in the figure of the seaside girl had not yet coalesced into what we now call youth culture. The youthfulness of the seaside girl remained oriented around a manufactured commodity culture and had not evolved into a discrete subculture capable of creating a different way of life out of the artifacts of commodity

HITCHINGS' GOLD MEDAL BABY STORES.

Under Royal Patronage. The Emporium of Baby Carriages an Baby Cars *par excellence.*

LONDON { 198, Oxford Street, W.
29, Ludgate Hill, E.C.
28, St. George's Place
(Hyde Park Corner).

Bankers { CITY BANK, LTD.
CAPITAL & COUNTIES BANK.

LIVERPOOL : 74, Bold Street.

Works { Duke Street, Liverpool.
Ludgate Square, London.

HITCHINGS' NEW OSTEND BABY CAR.

HITCHINGS Limited are the Premier Manufacturers of HIGH - GRADE BABY CARRIAGES in the WORLD

Latest Inventions. Newest Models. The Perfection of Style, Workmanship and Finish.

Pictorial List and Particulars Free by Post. Prices from 2 to 20 Guineas.

HITCHINGS' RENOWNED BABY CARRIAGES ARE THE COMBINATION OF EASE, ELEGANCE, AND STRENGTH.

FIG. 49. The seaside woman (*Graphic*, August 6, 1898).

culture. Though as an Irishwoman Gerty consumes the seaside girl in her own sad way, she does not look for others who have invested themselves in the same image. Altogether her narrative omits the key element of modern youth culture: juvenile delinquency. Wherever they go, seaside girls always chaperone and are chaperoned. Gerty's little performance for Bloom takes place while she is babysitting Edy Boardman's baby brother, and the watchful presence of the Roman Catholic Church is never very far from her mind. Though her family, in particular her parents, do not figure at all in her narrative, she is far from rejecting the social order which they represent. The only norms she violates are sexual, and from the ease with which that violation has been contained within a narrative as conventional as domestic realism, we can infer that it represents no significant challenge to the established order. Gerty has nothing of what Hall calls the adolescent's "reckless carelessness."[37] She does not cultivate an image, a demeanor, an argot that places her within an alternative form of social reality.[38] If anything the reverse is true: she is a conformist without a cause, for she belongs to a subculture not of persons but of things.

A differentiated form of consumption may not yet have existed for Gerty within an oppositional youth culture, but this does not mean that Victorian and Edwardian consumers all related to the seaside girl in the same way. Women and men had different domains of response mapped out for them. Women were taught to identify with the seaside girl image while men were encouraged to desire it.[39] These gendered variants are illustrated simply and directly in "Nausicaa," where Gerty consumes the seaside girl while Bloom consumes Gerty. These two labors are interdependent and unequal. Male identity exists prior to and during the act of consumption; female identity gets effaced in the process. Bloom remains Bloom, but Gerty must become the seaside girl. Gerty's labor is self-directed and passive; Bloom, who sees Gerty for what she actually is, is other-directed and active. Moreover, in a very real sense the male consumer sets up the whole scenario to which both male and female consumers conform. In early-twentieth-century advertising parlance, an "advertising man" was someone who created advertisements, while an "advertising woman" was someone who consumed them.[40] In our example Bloom is an advertiser, a member of the clan that invented the seaside girl. So the equation can be altered to read: Bloom produces the seaside girl, Gerty identifies with it, and Bloom consumes the product of that identification. A 1906 advertisement makes this connection between male production and female consumption utterly explicit: "WOMEN can't do without MENnen [Toilet Powder]."[41] The female labor of consumption remains bracketed within male production and consumption as women become the go-betweens mediating men and their particular desires. The gendering of consumption thus works exclusively to masculine advantage, freezing women in postures prescribed by the watchful gaze of the male. Gerty does not stop Bloom dead in his tracks. The medusan glance of "Nausicaa" belongs not to her but to Bloom.

The seaside girl was a major breakthrough for commodity culture. Quite apart from its psychological significance, its semiotic implications were far-reaching. The seaside girl catapulted the consumer into a social space not only wholly dominated by capitalist representation but wholly created by it. The monarchy, the empire, and the medical profession had existed prior to and alongside advertised efforts to appropriate them, but the seaside girl came into being solely to sell. Coordinating advertising with these institutions was a tricky and speculative business; even an advertiser as progressive as Gissing's Luckworth Crewe could not see the Jubilee boom coming, and he spends most of the lucrative Jubilee summer cursing his lack of foresight. Advertisers who relied on the image of the seaside girl were far less likely to discover consumers slipping through their nets. For the seaside girl did not just personalize and customize the spectacular representation of the commodity: she removed from the spectacle all soiling trace of historical origin and went about it with such brio that the resulting lack of specificity seemed timely and contemporary; she replaced political with sexual overtones; she phased out the written word and replaced it with the printed image; she crossed national boundaries (into Ireland and America) and artistic barriers (into Pre-Raphaelite and art nouveau styles and, later, into photography). What is more, she integrated all the advertised spectacles of the past twenty years into a single dense locus of commodity culture. Simultaneously, a seaside girl like Gerty MacDowell is the "Queen of Ointments," a third-world consumer gravitating in the orbit of first-world manufacture, a walking receptacle for patent medicines, a traveling exhibition of the world's manufactures. No previous campaign had done so many things at once. The net that linked the consumer to the commodity was visibly tightening.

Few Victorians saw it happening, though. In the vast majority of cases the long-term significance of commodity culture was lost on late-Victorian observers. The essential modernity of the seaside girl struck modernists like Joyce and Proust twenty or thirty years later, just as it strikes us today. The reason for this lag is quite simple: the basic images of consumerism came into being well before the consumer economy did. In the late nineteenth century the consumer economy had advanced into the middle class but had stopped short of colonizing the working class; a novel of working-class life like George Moore's *Esther Waters* (1894) finds few signs of the consumer revolution in working-class homes. Thirty-five years later the same sort of homes display a different aspect. When George Orwell barges into working-class lodgings in *The Road to Wigan Pier* (1931), he marvels at the signs of abundance he finds even amidst the squalor and privation brought on by the Depression. Those intervening years had extended the consumer economy into realms of life that late-Victorian economists had only dreamed of. We can only suppose that when commodities at last reached these consumers, it must have been after they had anticipated their arrival for many years. The people of England had been bombarded with large promises for a long time, through two Jubilees, through the rise and fall of an Empire, through holiday and through business as usual, through peace and finally through war; and over time they must have become inured to them. In any case they would soon experience the disappointment of consummated consumption. Never were the promises of commodity culture larger and more spectacular than in the years before the consumer economy started fulfilling them, the years in which a new breed of advertisers stocked bright Crystal Palaces with the things to come.

Conclusion

Few observers in 1851 could have predicted what the new com-modity culture would look like in 1914, on the eve of war. The political and ideological demands of monarchy, empire, medi-cine, and psychology that had been realized over sixty years gradually unfolded within, were advanced by, and ultimately became the servants of a diverse and competitive cohort of ad-vertisers. In 1851 advertisers had not been invited to participate in the Great Exhibition. By 1914 advertisers and their entrepre-neurial allies organized most of the commercial exhibitions held in Great Britain, including the only moderately successful Dub-lin Exhibition of 1907, which had failed to convince Dubliners that their city was in the process of becoming a utopia stocked with manufactured objects. The business of advertising had be-come the business of presenting and re-presenting commodity culture to the English and, increasingly, to the Irish and the In-dians and the South Africans. Its influence was felt in every sphere of life. "We live in an age of advertisement, the age of Holloway's Pills, of Colman's Mustard, and of Horniman's pure tea," said Lord Randolph Churchill.[1] Writ small or large, the na-tionally advertised commodity was a proud product of late-Victorian England. Advertisers may not have rushed out to de-face the cliffs of Dover, a traditional symbol of defiant British sovereignty, with slogans touting soap, but by 1897 they imag-ined they could (Fig. 50). As the self-appointed guardians of commodity culture they assumed the role of a commercial avant-garde, and in due course they won the respect of the artistic

FIG. 50. Rewriting Dover (*Illustrated London News*, October 29, 1887).

avant-garde, which took to imitating their typefaces and integrating their icons into the collages of high-modernist art.

The advertising manuals liked to talk about the great diversity of the industry in the nineteenth century, and a number of historians have taken them at their word. But competition and specialization among advertisers did not breed diversity; to the contrary, they enforced likeness and consolidated a dominant machinery of specifically capitalist representation, which has been called "spectacle." Spectacle entailed the autonomous iconography of the manufactured object, the replacement of history by commemoration, the invention of a democratic ethos for consumerism, the constitution of a manageable consuming subject, a reshaping of language, a mythology of abundance. These elements of spectacle wrought a cultural revolution that altered the very fabric of life in Britain. The final unification of the capitalist system had required the creation of a compatible cultural form—a theater through which it might reproduce its fundamental imperatives in a striking and memorable way. The commodity culture pioneered by the Great Exhibition and later translated successfully into the discourse of advertisers provided a semiotic base from which to manage the difficult process of a controlled broadening of the capitalist system within England. Great advertised exhibitions of things celebrated unrestrained capitalist development and lowered the pressure of mass discontent. Never before had capitalism succeeded in translating its fundamental dictates into a popular culture of its own. In the first half of the nineteenth century popular culture had been an explosive mixture of regional elements and class rivalries. In the second half spectacle defused it for a time and in the process created mass advertising and, for the first time, a truly national commodity culture.

This nationalization of culture had many parallels in Europe throughout the nineteenth century, though none of them exact. National culture took on a cultic status in countries undergoing rapid unification, like Germany and Italy, or rapid expansion, like the United States. In a country like Britain, which had been federated in 1707, this process took on a different cast. The new commodity culture of Britain came into being without official sanction and operated in a diffuse and decentralized manner. Its major exponents—advertisers—were not interested in taking up specific political positions, and its basic medium—spectacle— sidestepped politics whenever possible. The spectacles of Victorian advertising may have been effective capitalist propaganda, but their makers were not propagandists in the sense in which we now understand the word. They made no attempt to advance a specific political agenda or alter an existing political opinion; politics was present only to the degree to which it could be taken for granted. Even during the Boer War advertisers had no very precise notion of what the politicians wanted to carry out in South Africa, to say nothing of a well-defined purpose that would even remotely suggest a specific political intent. To the contrary, they used images of authority not so much to ally themselves with any specific authority as to identify themselves with bourgeois authority as such. If for a brief time the Boer War appealed to advertisers, it was because it had emerged as the one issue which it was possible to count on for an almost undivided attention and a nearly unanimous opinion. The new national culture was a culture of the lowest common denominator, and under capitalism the lowest common denominator of all was the commodity.

The consolidation of a commodity culture in and through advertising came to a temporary halt during the First World War. The persistence of the new spectacular culture would not have been a safe bet in prewar years, and its staying power was not generally recognized until after the war had ended. Though in the long run the war increased the productive capacity of domestic industry, in the short run it cut off the supply of consumer goods and curtailed the demand for them. Its bloodletting also made the one and only subject of advertising, the commodity, completely marginal. Robert Graves relates the experience of repeating a jingle to himself over and over again in the trenches during a shelling. Peter Weir's film *Gallipoli* (1981) makes a mockery of advertising when, just before the climax of the final slaughter, it shows a soldier madly fingering a box of Eno's Fruit Salts. At home, the new commodity culture went to war and won a new legitimacy for itself. Lecturing at the London School of Economics in 1919, the economist Thomas Russell declared that during the war "advertising has come into its own. We have lived to see governments soliciting its aid, war waged with this weapon, and the sinews of war collected through advertisements."[2] Russell was right to say that advertisers played a crucial role in disseminating propaganda but wrong to say that this experience brought advertising into its own. We have seen that advertising came into its own in the years before the First World War. After 1914 most of the images associated with commodity culture during the preceding quarter-century were simply put to new uses. With the coming of war, images formed in the crucible of the commodity were pressed into national service. In propaganda posters, many of which were donated by London advertisers, the monarch stepped back into the limelight to call for recruits, the empire mobilized its colonial subjects to serve king and country, patent medicines scoured the bodies of soldiers, and the seaside girl donned a sailor's outfit to keep a vigilant coastal watch.[3] While people like Russell credited this wartime propaganda for making modern advertising possible, it would be more accurate to say that modern advertising made wartime propaganda possible.

By modern standards the number, role, and function of Victorian and Edwardian advertisers remained modest enough. They did not yet possess the resources to create advertising campaigns out of thin air. Turn-of-the-century advertising handbooks were full of wild claims like "this is the golden age of trademarks, a time when almost any maker of a worthy product can lay down the lines of a demand that will not only grow with years beyond anything that has ever been known before, but it will become to some degree a monopoly."[4] So many advertisers made these claims, and so many people believed them, that for many years even the severest critics of advertising were likely to confer on advertisers magical powers they could not possibly possess. In fact their power was of a completely different order. They could not take a commodity and stimulate demand for it more or less at will. Their function was purely parasitical, though over time they became very engorged parasites and overwhelmed their hosts. Victorian and Edwardian advertisers worked within the dominant institutions of the age and adapted them to their own ends. And they had no reason not to: the public they addressed reposed its confidence in the monarchy, empire, and professional elites in a way that no advertiser could take for granted after the First World War. After 1918 advertisers sought to remove all soiling traces of history from their euphoric productions. Monarchy became a thin veneer of nobility, Rolls-Royce style; empire became florid exoticism; patent medicine died out and was replaced by the great pharmaceutical monopolies, most of which date from the 1920's. Only the seaside girl lived on intact, becoming so prevalent that Roland Barthes recognized her throughout France's fashion system in 1957.[5]

The technology of the time also placed certain limitations on the activities of late-Victorian advertisers, which, try as they might, they were not able easily to overcome. These impediments can be glimpsed in the above Pears' advertisement on the cliffs of Dover. Here is an enormous project undertaken with the simplest of tools—rope, ladders, brushes, paint. The painters dangle by a slender thread. No machines invented in the nineteenth century assist in the task; the men at the edge of the cliffs do not rely on iron winches or elaborate scaffolding such as helped erect the Crystal Palace. Everything is done by hand in the face of nearly insuperable obstacles posed by the natural world. Here advertising is not a form of communication in its own right but an extension of the massive public works projects that punctuated the nineteenth century. The Victorian material imagination liked to think in terms of shifting earth, splitting rock, and scaling cliffs; its characteristic achievements were the Thames Embankment and the London Tube. Victorian advertisers also thought big, but the kind of technology available to them was better suited to move mountains than to convey information. Faster printing presses arrived in the 1840's; the Crystal Palace decade gave advertisers the cultural form of spectacle, but to begin to exploit it they would have to wait until the 1880's, when print technology began its own industrial revolution.[6] The nineteenth century had witnessed an astonishing transportation revolution, but apart from the invention of the telegraph, which did not assist advertisers in any way, for the most part it still transported its information using the printing press. Advertising did its best to follow in the wake of new technologies, defacing train station after train station, but its long day in the sun awaited the commercial development of sympathetic technologies such as radio and television.

Nevertheless, what Victorian advertisers did with the resources available to them would strongly affect what later advertisers would consider doing with the resources available to them. They created the mold from which most of the familiar images of modern commodity culture were cast. That staple of twentieth-century advertising, the appliance, had not yet made its appearance on the scene, but when it did so in the 1920's, it was supported by all the topoi of late-nineteenth-century advertising. When the automobile became the quintessential icon of commodity culture it did so by mobilizing and refining all the existing clichés of advertising. To an unprecedented extent the spectacle of advertising became a stable reality of the modern capitalist world, a form of representation that, for all its variations, centered on a single theme. People began to feel lost without it, as travelers in underdeveloped and Eastern bloc countries started to testify.[7] People began, too, to take advertising for granted. In the nineteenth century observers had been shocked to see capitalism creating an image after its own world; in different ways the writings of Carlyle, Ruskin, Morris, and Wells registered and resisted the invasive aesthetics of advertised spectacle. In the twentieth century, critics have called attention to a far more disturbing phenomenon, for capitalism had begun to create a world after its own image.

The spectacle these later critics saw differed in many ways from the spectacle of late-Victorian advertising. Though late-Victorian advertisers successfully synthesized the cultural form of spectacle, they did not, and could not, bring into being what Guy Debord later called "the society of the spectacle." The distinction is crucial. Late-Victorian advertisers created a dominant form of specifically capitalist representation that, powerful though it was, left other forms of representation intact. In fact its very dominance implied the existence of alternative forms of representation such as survived within the working class as well as in literary circles and among the avant-garde. In *Ulysses*, written between 1914 and 1922, Gerty MacDowell's spectacular narrative takes up only a fraction of the novel as a whole; by 1967 Guy Debord believed that there was no room left for anything else. In that year of political hyperbole Debord declared that the spectacle had become a kind of semiotic perpetual-motion machine. This was "the moment when the commodity has attained the *total occupation* of social life," the moment when "not only is the relation to the commodity visible but it is all one sees: the world one sees is its world." Back at the turn of the century, Debord concedes, it may still have been possible for representation to exist outside the stratum of spectacle. But now the commodity had done away with any alternatives for representation. Outside of commodity culture, the possibility of representation has disappeared. In the period of the first great peace, from 1814 to 1914, bourgeois society had devoted its resources to inventing and refining spectacle—but "only locally at some points." In the period of the second great peace, from 1945 to the present, that society has now perfected the semiotics of spectacle—so much so that spectacle became and has remained the sum total of what it means to live under a late capitalist regime.[8]

This is a dark view of the world as an irreparably damaged social space. Like many social theorists, Debord cannot resist overextending his analysis and driving it to logical and doctrinaire conclusions. The reality of a society completely saturated by spectacle—a kind of reality now called "hyperreal"—is remote. All the most vivid accounts of a fully spectacular society remain complete fictions, like the dystopia of Aldous Huxley's *Brave New World* (1922) or the totalized nightmares of social theorists like Debord, Theodor Adorno, or Jean Baudrillard. Though spectacle is commodity culture at its most powerful, Debord's proclamation of a "society of the spectacle" may be a bit premature. It is worth remembering, with Michel Foucault, that in actual fact "our society is not one of spectacle, but of surveillance; under the surface of images, one invests bodies in depth; behind the great abstraction of exchange, there continues the meticulous, concrete training of useful forces; the circuits of communication are the supports of an accumulation and a centralization of knowledge; the play of signs defines the anchorages of power."[9] By itself spectacle would be at best a hazy ideological projection, an aurora borealis flickering at the horizon of actual social relations; as *advertising*, however, spectacle succeeded in becoming something more than a mere light show. As we have seen, advertised spectacle was not just a set of conventions governing the representation of things but a set of procedures regulating the presentation of self in everyday life. In the course of the late nineteenth century spectacle became an economy of small things completely embedded in the minutiae of everyday life. Advertising became what there was to know about the world; it became what passed for knowledge; it became, to use the modern term, information.[10]

The capitalist system of representation has not been fixed or foreordained by the nature of capitalism itself. The fact that it can remain stable for quite some time does not mean that it can cut itself off from the forces of history. The expansionist tendencies of capitalism guarantee that it will always continue to re-present itself as what Deleuze and Guattari call "neocapitalism."[11] In nineteenth- as in twentieth-century commodity culture, the one word that has traditionally taken precedence above all others has been "new." Sometimes, as when an old product gets repackaged and sold under another name, new and different merely means more of the same. At other times, the capitalist system of representation can change irremediably, adapting itself to new circumstances with lightning speed. In the 1950's Barthes noted how capitalist mythologies "can come into being, alter, disintegrate, disappear completely."[12] Recently Baudrillard has raised the possibility that capitalism has itself brought about "the *very abolition of the spectacular*," by which he means that current technologies have far surpassed the spectacular system of representation developed and perfected in the late nineteenth century.[13] Selling things has now become the domain of cybernetics, the modern science concerned with analyzing the flow of information in electronic, mechanical, and biological systems. In a world in which electronic pulses, blips on a television screen, and patented genetic structures count as quantifiable commodities, the days of spectacle may well be numbered. In the years to come it may turn out that the semiotics of spectacle played a transitional role in capitalist mythology, combining as they did for a time the imagery of what Foucault calls "the monarchical, ritual exercise of sovereignty" with that of "the hierarchical, permanent exercise of disciplinary power."[14] For now it makes sense to consider spectacle as one element among many in modern commodity culture, one historically circumscribed strain of representation synthesized powerfully in the nineteenth century, one manifestation of what Martin Jay has called the many "scopic regimes of modernity."[15] No one description better sums up the disparate matrix of modern spectacle than the beginning of Thomas Pynchon's *Gravity's Rainbow* (1973), in which the central symbol of the new cybernetic society, the rocket, destroys what we have seen to have been the most powerful symbol of the nineteenth century: "the glass will fall—soon—it will be a spectacle: the fall of a crystal palace. But coming in total blackout, without one glint of light, only great invisible crashing."[16]

Under these darkening conditions, surrounded by missile silos, haunted by the screaming that threatens to come across the sky at any minute, it is perhaps easy to be nostalgic for the serenely confident world of late-Victorian commodity culture. To us Victorian advertising looks like a cottage industry, and in a fit of nostalgia we have made Victorian advertisements into "Victoriana," the sort of kitsch that can be found in bins at antique stores or on bathroom wallpaper. Lost in a longing for the good old days when the hard sell was still soft, we may choose to make the past look primitive. The purpose of this book, rather, has been to bring this world closer to ours, to see in it the history of the present. What placed advertising at the dead center of the modern world was its early recognition that the commodity, far from being a trivial thing, had a world-historical role to play in a global industrial economy. Late-Victorian advertisers carried commodity culture into the central core of industrial society and imagined bringing it to the periphery. Modern advertisers continued the work they had begun, bringing the constructions of Victorian commodity culture into new and hegemonic formations. The semiotics of Victorian commodity culture persist, often as unexamined details of everyday life: on the shelves of modern supermarkets the Campbell's soup can continues to display the small gold medallion won at a turn-of-the-century commodity exhibition. Commodity culture is now over one hundred years old, and the cycles of spectacle that Victorian advertisers fashioned for us show no sign of abating soon. The world in which they lived and from which they drew their inspiration has passed beyond the horizon of living memory. The world they created is all around us.

Reference Matter

Notes

The following abbreviations are used in the notes:

G   *The Graphic*
GSN   *The Graphic Stanley Number* (Apr. 30, 1890)
ILN   *The Illustrated London News*

Introduction

1. See "Of the Natural and Market Price of Commodities," in Adam Smith, *The Wealth of Nations* (Harmondsworth: Penguin, 1982), 157–66. When Marx says that it is possible to think of commodities as trivial things, one of the things he has in mind is the scant attention that Smith and other classical economists had paid to the status of individual articles. What distinguished early- from late-Victorian representations of things, however, was not the fact that they articulated commodities individually (advertising had done that for several hundred years), but rather the astonishing variety of resources they mobilized to mark off and aggrandize various separate objects. Marx's statement that "a commodity appears at first sight an extremely obvious, trivial thing" is at the beginning of the commodity fetishism chapter of *Capital, Volume One* (New York: Vintage Books, 1977), 163.

2. In the 1820's David Ricardo was one of the first to base exchange on a theory of labor rather than on a theory of circulation. This shift in bourgeois political economy led to a search for more anthropomorphic renditions of the commodity's role in a market economy; people now wanted to place commodities in the context of labor, which is necessarily a social context. As we shall see, the Great Exhibition was a social enclosure designed expressly to confer the panache of labor on the circulation of commodities. In the eighteenth century the central question of political economy had been, as Michel Foucault points out, "how . . . can prices characterize things?" In the nineteenth century this question became, how can social relations characterize things? In a sense the

Great Exhibition and the commodity fetishism chapter of *Capital* offered remarkably similar answers to this question, both proceeding from the assumption that, in Foucault's words, "value had ceased to become a sign; it had become a product." Whereas the classical economists were interested in the *wealth* of nations, especially the sign system of money, Victorian political economy took as its starting point the *produce* of nations, what the *Official Catalogue of the Great Exhibition* called "The Works of Industry of All Nations." This book is a study of how the product, far from resisting representation, became a sign system in its own right. For a description of the problem of representing commodities as it appeared to eighteenth- and nineteenth-century political economy, see Michel Foucault, *The Order of Things: An Archaeology of the Human Sciences* (New York: Vintage, 1973), 166–214, 250–302.

3. Horace Greeley, "The Crystal Palace and Its Lessons: A Lecture" (private copy, Harvard College Library, 1852), 7.

4. The classic account of the flaneur as a prototype of a modern consumer is Walter Benjamin, *Charles Baudelaire: A Lyric Poet in the Era of High Capitalism* (London: Verso, 1983).

5. For a full view of Althusser's theory of practical ideology, see *For Marx* (London: Verso, 1979), 252; and *Lenin and Philosophy* (New York: Monthly Review Press, 1971), 155. The theory will be discussed at greater length in Chapter 5.

6. Diana and Geoffrey Hindley follow the various editions of the *Advertiser's Guardian* in *Advertising in Victorian England: 1850–1914* (London: Wayland, 1972), 28ff.

7. Henry Sampson, *A History of Advertising from the Earliest Times* (London: Chatto and Windus, 1874).

8. For Marx's basic position on the economic and intellectual hegemony of the dominant class, see *Manifesto of the Communist Party* in *The Marx-Engels Reader*, ed. Robert C. Tucker (New York: Norton, 1978), 473–500.

9. See the "Io, Saturnalia!" chapter, which details a working-class visit to the Crystal Palace; George Gissing, *The Nether World* (Brighton: The Harvester Press, 1982), 104–13. Like so much Victorian criticism of mass culture, Gissing's invocation of the Roman Saturnalia is out of synch with the experiences of consumption it purports to describe. Patrick Brantlinger traces the persistence of the old Roman topos of mass culture as social decay in *Bread and Circuses: Theories of Mass Culture as Social Decay* (Ithaca, N.Y.: Cornell University Press, 1983).

10. "Advertising Prehistory" is the title of the first chapter of Stephen Fox's *The Mirror Makers* (New York: Vintage, 1983). In the 1940's Theodor Adorno voiced his suspicion that the cultural forms of consumerism preceded the consumer economy by many years: "Reading popular novels a hundred years old like those of Cooper, one finds

in rudimentary form the whole pattern of Hollywood. The stagnation of the culture industry is probably not the result of monopolization, but was a property of so-called entertainment from the first" (*Minima Moralia: Reflections from Damaged Life* [London: Verso, 1984], 147). More recently, Jennifer Wicke has pointed out that "the institutional formation of modern advertising did not begin to be discernible until the mid-1800s" (*Advertising Fictions: Literature, Advertisement, Social Reading* [New York: Columbia University Press, 1988], 1). For an overview of how people came to be "dazzled by goods" in late-nineteenth-century America, see Michael Schudson, "Historical Roots of Consumer Culture," in *Advertising, the Uneasy Persuasion: Its Dubious Impact on American Society* (New York: Basic Books, 1984), 147–77.

11. William Leiss, Stephen Kline, and Sut Jhally, *Social Communication in Advertising: Persons, Products, and Images of Well-Being* (New York: Methuen, 1986).

12. Jean Baudrillard, "Requiem for the Media," in *For a Critique of the Political Economy of the Sign* (St. Louis: Telos, 1981), 164.

13. "The concrete is concrete because it is the concentration of many determinations, hence unity of the diverse. It appears in the process of thinking, therefore, as a process of concentration, as a result, not as a point of departure" ("The Method of Political Economy," *Foundations [Grundrisse] of the Critique of Political Economy*, in *Marx-Engels Reader*, 237).

14. "Avaunt this vile abuse of pictured page! / Must eyes be all in all, the tongue and ear / Nothing?" (William Wordsworth, "Illustrated Books and Newspapers," in *Complete Poems* [Oxford: Oxford University Press, 1965], 383).

15. Facts and figures about the nineteenth-century advertising industry are hard to come by, and given their source, even harder to trust. Working mostly from the memoirs of advertisers, W. Hamish Fraser juggles the available information in a chapter on advertising in *The Coming of the Mass Market, 1850–1914* (Hamden, Conn.: Archon Books, 1981), 134–46. Raymond Williams does somewhat better in "Advertising: The Magic System," in *Problems in Materialism and Culture* (London: Verso, 1980), 170–95. The only reliable information to be found in nineteenth-century advertising handbooks deals with three subjects: the price per inch of advertising copy in daily and weekly papers, whether a given paper will accept blocks of print, and whether it will accept illustrations. See, for example, the tables and charts in Thomas Smith, *Successful Advertising: Its Secrets Explained* (London: Smith's Advertising Agency, 1886), 167–244.

16. "Manchester is unique in the systematic way in which the working classes have been barred from the main streets. Nowhere else has such care been taken to avoid offending the tender susceptibilities of the eyes and nerves of the middle classes. Yet Manchester is the very

town in which building has taken place in a haphazard manner with little or no interference from the authorities" (Friedrich Engels, *The Condition of the Working Class in England* [Stanford, Calif.: Stanford University Press, 1968], 56). Engels's observation serves to remind us that although human agency produces ideologies, it often acts in accordance with them. For a further exploration of the ideological role of urban design within capitalist development, see Manfredo Tafuri, *Architecture and Utopia* (Cambridge, Mass.: MIT Press, 1976). For an example of how easy it is to attribute human agency to urban design, see Asa Briggs, *Victorian Cities* (Harmondsworth: Penguin, 1968).

17. Baudrillard gets very angry with Marx for using anthropocentric language to describe commodities, but he does not fare much better. One striking example: "We can observe that objects are never offered for consumption in an absolute disarray. In certain cases they can mimic disorder to better seduce" (*Consumer Society*, in Mark Poster, ed., *Jean Baudrillard: Selected Writings* [Stanford, Calif.: Stanford University Press, 1988], 31). For Baudrillard's assault on Marx's use of the fetishism metaphor, see "Fetishism and Ideology: The Semiological Reduction," in *Critique*, 88–101.

18. Jean Baudrillard, "Toward a Critique of the Political Economy of the Sign," in *Critique*, 146. My account of the linguistic problems Darwin confronted follows Gillian Beer, *Darwin's Plots: Evolutionary Narrative in Darwin, George Eliot and Nineteenth-Century Fiction* (London: Ark Paperbacks, 1985), 49–103. Incidentally, Baudrillard has Darwin clearly in mind as he begins his masterly account of the system of objects: "Peut-on classer l'immense végétation des objets comme une flore ou une faune, avec ses espèces tropicales, glaciaires, ses mutations brusques, ses espèces en voie de disparition?" (*Le système des objets* [Paris: Gallimard, 1968], 7).

19. E. S. Turner describes the American influence in *The Shocking History of Advertising!* (New York: Dutton, 1953), 128–49, 169–86. See also Wicke, *Advertising Fictions*, 54–119.

20. Michel Foucault, "What Is an Author?" in Donald F. Bouchard, ed., *Language, Counter-Memory, Practice: Selected Essays and Interviews* (Ithaca, N.Y.: Cornell University Press, 1977), 137. Recent research has shown the content of advertisements cannot be reduced to a set of institutional procedures and strictures. Michael Schudson cautions that advertising agencies do not deliberately create a commodity culture and that their attempts to manipulate it often misfire; see *Advertising, The Uneasy Persuasion*, 3–89. Rather than trying to trace commodity culture back to the boardrooms of advertising agencies, my concern has been to analyse advertising at the point at which it enters cultural discourse at large, taking on significance through contact with a great variety of cultural materials.

21. Karl Marx, "The Fetishism of the Commodity and Its Secret," *Capital, Volume One*, 163.

22. Roland Barthes, *Mythologies* (New York: Hill and Wang, 1972), 120.

23. Guy Debord, *Society of the Spectacle* (Detroit: Black and Red, 1977), 6, 37. For an overview of Situationist thought (probably the only one there is), see the special issue of *Yale French Studies* devoted to "Everyday Life" (no. 73, 1987), particularly Edward Ball, "The Great Sideshow of the Situationist International," 21–37. To date, the best application of Situationist thought to nineteenth-century culture is T. J. Clark, *The Painting of Modern Life: Paris in the Art of Manet and His Followers* (Princeton, N.J.: Princeton University Press, 1984). Greil Marcus reconstructs the tangled genealogy of the Situationist International in *Lipstick Traces: A Secret History of the Twentieth Century* (Cambridge, Mass.: Harvard University Press, 1989). More recently, see the essays in *'On the Passage of a Few People Through a Rather Brief Moment in Time': The Situationist International, 1957–72* (Cambridge, Mass.: MIT Press, 1989).

24. Georg Lukács, *History and Class Consciousness: Studies in Marxist Dialectics* (Cambridge, Mass.: MIT Press, 1971), 83.

25. Mark Poster's assessment of Baudrillard in his introduction to *Selected Writings* is absolutely right: "he totalizes his insights, refusing to qualify or delimit his claims" (*Selected Writings*, 7). My use of Baudrillard throughout this book is highly selective, as will be clear. Primarily I am indebted to him for highlighting the many ways in which advertising contributes to the formation of a sign system of commodities. His statement that "if we consume the product as product, we consume its meaning through advertising" is one of the grounding assumptions of this book (*Selected Writings*, 10).

26. Two recent books offer clear examples of the false antithesis between production and consumption that has so far limited the analytical power of commodity aesthetics. Rachel Bowlby, in *Just Looking: Consumer Culture in Dreiser, Gissing and Zola* (New York: Methuen, 1985), regards commodities almost exclusively as objects directed at consumers. And Norman Feltes, in *Modes of Production of Victorian Novels* (Chicago: University of Chicago Press, 1986), regards them equally exclusively as objects issuing from producers. In a recent review essay Catherine Gallagher calls attention with great insight to the unfortunate way in which the two studies share no common ground; see her review in *Criticism* 29, no. 2 (1987): 233–42. Gallagher's essay echoes the program of commodity aesthetics first advanced by W. F. Haug in 1971: "to derive the phenomena of commodity aesthetics from their economic basis and to develop and present them within their systematic connections" (*Critique of Commodity Aesthetics: Appearance, Sexuality and Advertising in Capitalist Society* [Minneapolis: University of Minnesota Press,

1986], 8). See also Haug, *Commodity Aesthetics, Ideology and Culture* (New York: International General, 1987).

Debord's concept of spectacle is useful because it goes beyond the chicken-and-egg question of whether to privilege production or consumption. The first thesis of *Society of the Spectacle* lays out a different approach to their relationship: "In societies where modern conditions of production prevail, all of life presents itself as an immense accumulation of *spectacles*. Everything that was lived has moved away into a representation" (1). Debord's representations are, of course, of commodities, but he sees the production and consumption of those commodities as complementary parts of a *commodity culture* in which the dominant system of representation is what he calls "spectacle."

Properly speaking, commodity culture must be distinguished from what has been called "consumer culture." In addition to placing the emphasis far too strongly on consumption, the term "consumer culture" makes it sound like there is something uniquely modern about consumption. But it must be remembered that all human cultures are consumer cultures. Cultures have always produced things, distributed them, and used them up. What distinguishes industrialized market societies from earlier societies is the fact that they produce vast quantities of commodities and vast quantities of discourse about commodities. Far from being directed exclusively at consumers, this discourse about commodities can be found far and wide in the cultures of market societies—sometimes in the most unexpected places. Thus it makes more sense to speak of a "commodity culture" that consists purely and simply of discourse about the production, distribution, and consumption of commodities. As we shall see, the discourse of commodity culture serves a variety of social functions, only one of which involves the figuration of a consuming subject.

27. Karl Marx, *Grundrisse: Foundations of the Critique of Political Economy* (New York: Vintage, 1973), 90.

28. Henri Lefebvre, *Everyday Life in the Modern World* (New York: Harper and Row, 1971), 108.

29. Marx, *Grundrisse*, 89.

One

1. The basic text of the Great Exhibition is the labyrinthine *Official Descriptive and Illustrated Catalogue* (London: Spicer Brothers, Wholesale Stationers; W. Clowes and Sons, Printers, 1851). I have culled much of my narrative from this invaluable document. All specific references to this four-volume work, hereafter cited as *Catalogue*, will appear in the text. To a lesser extent I have also relied on three more recent works: Christopher Hobhouse, *1851 and the Crystal Palace* (London: John Murray, 1951); Yvonne Ffrench, *The Great Exhibition: 1851* (London: Harvill, 1950); and Folke Kihlstedt, "The Crystal Palace," *Scientific*

American, Oct. 1984, 132–43. For a general sense of how the Crystal Palace fit into the London landscape, consult William Gaspey, *Tallis's Illustrated London; in Commemoration of the Great Exhibition of All Nations in 1851* (London: London Printing and Publishing Company, 1851), in two volumes. The anthropological background to the Exhibition is the centerpiece of George W. Stocking's *Victorian Anthropology* (New York: Free Press, 1987). The four-volume *Catalogue* was often edited down to size; the most popular short versions were the one-volume *Official Catalogue* (London: Spicer and Clowes, 1851), and Richard Hunt's two-volume *Hunt's Hand-Book to the Official Catalogues* (London: Spicer and Clowes, 1851). The general orientation of this chapter to this wealth of material can best be summed up in a sentence found in a three-page essay by Walter Benjamin called "Grandville or the World Exhibitions": "The world exhibitions erected the universe of commodities" (*Charles Baudelaire: A Lyric Poet in the Era of High Capitalism* [London: Verso, 1983], 166).

2. On previous exhibitions see Richard Altick, *The Shows of London* (Cambridge, Mass.: Harvard University Press, 1978), and the "Introduction" to the *Catalogue*, 1:1–4, which surveys exhibitions that took place in 1756–57, 1798, 1801, 1802, 1806, 1819, 1829, 1844, and 1849.

3. Thomas Carlyle, *Past and Present* (New York: New York University Press, 1965), 144.

4. Henry Mayhew, *London Labour and the London Poor*, ed. Victor Neuburg (Harmondsworth: Penguin, 1985), 16. The complete four-volume edition is also available in a modern reprint (New York: Dover, 1968). Subsequent citations from the Penguin edition appear in the text.

5. Two of the three volumes of Braudel's masterly *Civilization and Capitalism, 15th–18th Century* deal at length with development of markets in Early Modern and Enlightenment Europe: see *The Structures of Everyday Life: The Limits of the Possible* (New York: Harper and Row, 1981), 436–563; and especially *The Wheels of Commerce* (New York: Harper and Row, 1982).

6. William Smith, *Advertise: How? When? Where?* (London: Routledge, Warne, and Routledge, 1863), 7. Subsequent citations appear in the text.

7. See [Abraham Hayward], "The Advertising System," *Edinburgh Review* 77 (Feb. 1843): 1–43; Carlyle, *Past and Present*, 144.

8. E. A. Moriarty, "Official Catalogue of the Great Exhibition," *Edinburgh Review* 94 (Oct. 1851): 574.

9. Walter Benjamin calls attention to the bourgeois fascination with casing in *Charles Baudelaire*, 46: "The bourgeoisie cheerfully takes the impression of a host of objects. For slippers and pocket watches, thermometers and egg-cups, cutlery and umbrellas it tries to get covers and cases. It prefers velvet and plush covers which preserve the impression of every touch. For the Markat style, the style of the end of the Second Empire, a dwelling becomes a kind of casing."

10. John Ruskin, "The Nature of Gothic," in *The Genius of John Ruskin*, ed. John Rosenberg (London: Routledge & Kegan Paul, 1979), 187. For Ruskin's mixed review of the Exhibition, see "The Opening of the Crystal Palace Considered in Some of Its Relations to the Prospects of Art," in *Ruskin's Works* (New York: John Lovell, 1875), 1–16.

11. For a searching analysis of the plates from Diderot's *Encyclopedia*, see Roland Barthes, "The Plates of the *Encyclopedia*," in *New Critical Essays* (New York: Hill and Wang, 1980), 23–39.

12. "The Great Exhibition and the Little One," *Household Words* 67 (1851): 356–60.

13. Quoted in J. W. Burrow, "The Sense of the Past," in Laurence Lerner, ed., *The Victorians* (New York: Holmes and Meier, 1978), 121.

14. Horace Greeley, "The Crystal Palace and Its Lessons: A Lecture" (private copy, Harvard College Library, 1852), 11. Subsequent citations appear in the text.

15. Charles Darwin, *The Origin of Species* (Harmondsworth: Penguin, 1968), 444, 71, 443.

16. Ffrench, *Great Exhibition*, 52.

17. Barry Supple, "Material Development: The Condition of England 1830–1860," in Lerner, *The Victorians*, 56.

18. "The Exhibition.—The Crystal Palace," *The Economist*, May 10, 1851: 5, 29. Subsequent citations appear in the text.

19. Moriarty, "Official Catalogue," 586.

20. *ILN*, May 3, 1851: 364.

21. Baudrillard anatomizes this "phenomenology of consumption" in two groundbreaking books, both of which have assisted me immeasurably in fashioning my analysis of the Exhibition and its contents. See *Le système des objets* (Paris: Gallimard, 1968), and *La société de consommation: ses mythes, ses structures* (Paris: Gallimard, 1970). In particular I draw on the latter's first chapter, "La liturgie formelle de l'objet," 17–56.

22. In the *Grundrisse* Marx stresses that in a great many ways, production creates consumption, and consumption production. His dictum is worth bearing in mind as we analyze how the Great Exhibition produced consumption: "Production creates the material, as external object, for consumption; consumption creates the need, as internal object, as aim, for production. Without production no consumption; without consumption no production." Production and consumption can no more be separated from one another than can the paired bodily functions of ingestion and excretion. See *Grundrisse: Foundations of the Critique of Political Economy* (New York: Vintage, 1973), 93.

23. John Ruskin, "Of Truth of Space," from *Modern Painters*, in *The Genius of John Ruskin*, 26–27.

24. Quoted in Hobhouse, *1851*, 175.

25. For a detailed account of the rise of the Parisian department store, see Michael B. Miller, *The Bon Marché: Bourgeois Culture and the De-*

partment Store, 1869–1920 (Princeton, N.J.: Princeton University Press, 1981).

26. Roland Barthes, *Mythologies* (New York: Hill and Wang, 1972), 90.

27. *ILN*, June 14, 1851: 570.

28. Hobhouse, *1851*, 130.

29. *ILN*, June 14, 1851: 570.

30. Rev. Robert Willis, "Machines and Tools for Working in Metal, Wood, and Other Materials," in *Lectures on the Results of the Great Exhibition of 1851* (London: G. Barclay, 1851), 295.

31. Oscar Wilde, "The Preface," *The Picture of Dorian Gray* (Harmondsworth: Penguin, 1985), 22. Baudrillard calls attention to the importance of the gadget in consumer society in *La société de consommation*, 33.

32. Jean Seznec, *Flaubert à l'Exposition de 1851* (Oxford: Clarendon Press, 1951), 16–17.

33. Benjamin, *Charles Baudelaire*, 55.

34. For a thorough survey of the impact of utilitarian political economy on literary representation, see Patrick Brantlinger, *The Spirit of Reform: British Literature and Politics, 1832–1867* (Cambridge, Mass.: Harvard University Press, 1977), 35–59.

35. Henry Mayhew and George Cruikshank, *1851: or, The Adventures of Mr. and Mrs. Sandboys, Their Son and Daughter, Who Came Up to London to Enjoy Themselves and See the Great Exhibition* (New York: Stringer and Townsend, 1851), 17. Subsequent citations appear in the text.

36. *ILN*, May 31, 1851: 501.

37. Benjamin studies the commercialization of the crowd in some detail. See *Charles Baudelaire*, 62ff.

38. "Helix" [W. B. Adams], "The Industrial Exhibition of 1851," *Westminster Review* (1850): 97.

39. Rosalind H. Williams, *Dream Worlds: Mass Consumption in Late Nineteenth-Century France* (Berkeley: University of California Press, 1982), 59.

40. *ILN*, June 14, 1851: 569.

41. "Helix," "Industrial Exhibition," 97.

42. Ruskin, "The Advent Collect," *Genius of John Ruskin*, 405.

43. "Helix," "Industrial Exhibition," 89.

44. Charles Dickens, *Bleak House* (New York: Norton, 1977), 123.

45. Mayhew compiled statistical evidence from marriage registers to show "the intensity of ignorance" (i.e., illiteracy) in England. The percentage of illiterates varied between 25 and 50 percent. It was probably much higher among London street people, though the exact figure would be difficult to ascertain. In his vast archive Mayhew gives examples of both; see *London Labour* (Dover edition), 4:459–65.

46. In a multifaceted exploration of the materiality of narrative,

Susan Stewart explores the still life as "a configuration of consumable objects"; see *On Longing: Narratives of the Miniature, the Gigantic, the Souvenir, the Collection* (Baltimore, Md.: Johns Hopkins University Press, 1984), 29ff.

47. By One Who Thinks Aloud [James Dawson Burn], *The Language of the Walls: And A Voice from the Shop Windows. Or, The Mirror of Commercial Roguery* (Manchester: Abel Heywood, 1855), 2, 11, 4, 2. For an extended account of the basic concerns of nineteenth-century philology, see Michel Foucault, *The Order of Things: An Archaeology of the Human Sciences* (New York: Vintage, 1973), 250–302.

48. Carlyle, *Past and Present*, 144. Friedrich Engels relates just how unconvincing this gigantism could be: "They [opponents of the Corn Laws] have actually had the effrontery to parade two models of loaves of bread through the streets. The big loaf bore the legend 'American 8d. loaf. Wages 4s. a day.' The much smaller loaf bore the words: 'English 8d. loaf. Wages 2s. a day.' But the English workers are not taken in by propaganda of this sort" (*The Condition of the Working Class in England* [Stanford, Calif.: Stanford University Press, 1968], 317). As unsuccessful as commodity gigantism often was, it was an attempt to distinguish objects from their immediate surroundings by making them, as Dickens saw in *Martin Chuzzlewit*, "disproportionate." Dickens summons up the nature of this appeal in a brief passage: "After the first glance, there were slight features in the midst of this crowd of objects, which sprang from the mass without any reason, as it were, and took hold of the attention whether the spectator would or no" (*Martin Chuzzlewit* [Harmondsworth: Penguin, 1968], 188).

49. Defoe remarks the prevalence of these cordials in *A Journal of a Plague Year* (Penguin: Harmondsworth, 1966), 50. Edmund Gosse reminisces about streetsellers in *Father and Son* (Harmondsworth: Penguin, 1970), 57ff. A comprehensive listing of Pepys's jottings can be found under "Entertainments" in the index to *The Diary of Samuel Pepys* (Berkeley: University of California Press, 1983), 11:98.

50. See Mayhew, *London Labour* (Dover edition), 4:17.

51. Claude Lévi-Strauss, *The Savage Mind* (Chicago: University of Chicago Press, 1966), 17.

52. Ibid.

53. Dickens, *Martin Chuzzlewit*, 210.

54. Samuel Johnson, "Idler 40," *The Works of Samuel Johnson* (New Haven, Conn.: Yale University Press, 1980), 126–27. The advertiser William Smith echoes Johnson's idea when he remarks that advertisers themselves often believed that "all that is possible has been done already" (*Advertise*, 62).

55. "Advertisements," *Quarterly Review* 97 (June and Sept. 1855): 222.

56. The term "master fiction" is Clifford Geertz's. It appears in "Centers, Kings, and Charisma: Reflections on the Symbolics of Power," in *Local Knowledge: Further Essays in Interpretive Anthropology* (New York: Basic Books, 1983), 146.

57. Much of the following discussion of the Victorian taste for spectacle rests on a recent book by Michael R. Booth, *Victorian Spectacular Theatre, 1850–1910* (London: Routledge & Kegan Paul, 1981). In addition to containing much useful material on early exhibitions, Altick's *Shows of London* also surveys the forms of spectacle peculiar to the early Victorian theater. For a sense of how spectacle fits into cultural production at large, see Eric Hobsbawm, *The Age of Capital, 1848–1875* (New York: Meridian, 1984), and *The Age of Empire, 1875–1914* (New York: Pantheon, 1987).

58. "The origins of melodrama can be accurately located within the context of the French Revolution and its aftermath. This is the epistemological moment which it illustrates and to which it contributes: the moment that symbolically, and really, marks the final liquidation of the traditional Sacred and its representative institutions (Church and Monarch), the shattering of the myth of Christendom, the dissolution of an organic and hierarchically cohesive society, and the invalidation of the literary forms—tragedy, comedy of manners—that depended on such a society" (Peter Brooks, *The Melodramatic Imagination: Balzac, Henry James, Melodrama, and the Mode of Excess* [New Haven, Conn.: Yale University Press, 1976], 14–15).

59. Walter Scott, Review of Jane Austen's *Emma, Quarterly Review* (1815), quoted in Janet Todd, *Sensibility: An Introduction* (London: Methuen, 1986), 145.

60. On the fate of the operatic high style in the nineteenth and twentieth centuries, see Herbert Lindenberger, *Opera: The Extravagant Art* (Ithaca, N.Y.: Cornell University Press, 1984).

61. Reproduced (Fig. 24) and analyzed in Chapter 3.

62. See Catherine Gallagher, *The Industrial Reformation of English Fiction: Social Discourse and Narrative Form, 1832–1867* (Chicago: University of Chicago Press, 1985). For Georg Lukács's classic explication of the "antinomies of bourgeois thought," see *History and Class Consciousness: Studies in Marxist Dialectics* (Cambridge, Mass.: MIT Press, 1971), 110–49.

63. Booth, *Victorian Spectacular Theatre*, 4.

64. Ibid., 7.

65. Guy Debord, *Society of the Spectacle* (Detroit: Black and Red, 1977), 1.

66. Barthes explores the eighteenth-century origins of what he calls an "autonomous iconography of the object" in "The Plates of the Encyclopedia," 23ff. Another of Barthes's essays brings his analysis up to date; see "Objective Literature: Alain Robbe-Grillet," in *Two Novels by*

Robbe-Grillet: Jealousy and In the Labyrinth (New York: Grove Press, 1965). The seventeenth- and eighteenth-century origins of the iconographic commodity are the subject of Chandra Mukerji's *From Graven Images: Patterns of Modern Materialism* (New York: Columbia University Press, 1983). On the ritual character of commodities, see Arjun Appadurai, ed., *The Social Life of Things: Commodities in Cultural Perspective* (Cambridge, Eng.: Cambridge University Press, 1986), and W. J. T. Mitchell, *Iconology: Image, Text, Ideology* (Chicago: University of Chicago Press, 1986), 160–208. Since the use of commemoration becomes much more pronounced during Victoria's Jubilee, I cite materials relating to it in Chapter 2. The fashioning of a democratic ideology for consumption is explored in three very different, but equally valuable, books: Neil McKendrick, John Brewer, and J. H. Plumb, *The Birth of a Consumer Society: The Commercialization of Eighteenth-Century England* (Bloomington: Indiana University Press, 1982); Theodor W. Adorno and Max Horkheimer, *Dialectic of Enlightenment* (New York: Continuum, 1982); and W. F. Haug, *Critique of Commodity Aesthetics: Appearance, Sexuality, and Advertising in Capitalist Society* (Minneapolis: University of Minnesota Press, 1986). The fashioning of a docile subject for consumerism comes under scrutiny in Erich Fromm's account of the "marketing character" in *Man for Himself: An Inquiry into the Psychology of Ethics* (New York: Holt, Rinehart, and Winston, 1947). Also useful for understanding capitalist subjectivity are the essays in Richard Wrightman Fox and T. J. Jackson Lears, eds., *The Culture of Consumption: Critical Essays in American History, 1880–1980* (New York: Pantheon Books, 1983). On the myth of the abundant society, see Colin Campbell, *The Romantic Ethic and the Spirit of Modern Consumerism* (Oxford: Basil Blackwell, 1987); W. Hamish Fraser, *The Coming of the Mass Market, 1850–1914* (Hamden, Conn.: Archon Books, 1981); and William Leiss, *The Limits to Satisfaction: An Essay on the Problem of Needs and Commodities* (Toronto: University of Toronto Press, 1976). For a look at the language of the commodity, see Judith Williamson, *Decoding Advertisements: Ideology and Meaning in Advertising* (London: Marion Boyars, 1978); Herbert Marcuse, *One Dimensional Man* (London: Sphere Books, 1968), 77–102; Roland Barthes, "The Rhetoric of the Image," in *Image/Music/Text* (New York: Hill and Wang, 1977), 32–51; and Richard Ohmann, "Doublespeak and Ideology in Ads: A Kit for Teachers," in Donald Lazere, ed., *American Media and Mass Culture: Left Perspectives* (Berkeley: University of California Press, 1987), 106–15. Apart from the suggestive but unsystematic analysis of Debord in *Society of the Spectacle*, amplified by Henri Lefebvre in *Everyday Life in the Modern World* (New York: Harper and Row, 1971), the closest we have to a cogent account of how the whole system of spectacle works are the structuralist inquiries of Barthes's *Mythologies* (1957) and Baudrillard's *La société de consommation* (1970). For an anatomy of the functioning of dominant discourses under capitalism, see Richard Terdiman, *Discourse/Counter-Discourse: The Theory and Practice of Symbolic Resistance in Nineteenth-Century France* (Ithaca, N.Y.: Cornell University Press, 1985).

67. C. B. MacPherson traces the philosophical development of bourgeois individualism in *The Political Theory of Possessive Individualism* (Oxford: Oxford University Press, 1965).

68. On the cultic status of certain commodities, see Hobhouse, *1851*, 93ff.

69. Debord, *Society of the Spectacle*, 66.

70. *Westminster Quarterly Review* (1850): 90.

71. William Whewell, "The General Bearing of the Great Exhibition on the Progress of Art and Science," in *Lectures on the Results of the Great Exhibition of 1851* (London: G. Barclay, 1852), 14.

72. Jonathan Swift, *Gulliver's Travels* (Boston: Houghton Mifflin, 1960), 150.

73. "The Catalogue's Account of Itself," *Household Words* 74 (1851): 519. Subsequent citations appear in the text.

74. Francis Galton, *Natural Inheritance* (New York: Macmillan, 1894), 18. For an illuminating treatment of the statistical subject, see also Mark Seltzer, "Statistical Persons," *Diacritics*, Fall 1987, 82–98.

75. Adam Smith, *The Wealth of Nations, Books I–III* (Harmondsworth: Penguin, 1982), 438. Subsequent citations appear in the text.

76. For analyses that seek to localize the operation of the commodity by examining patterns of distribution in the Eastern Solomon Islands, in prehistoric and medieval Europe, in northeast Africa, in revolutionary France, and in turn-of-the-century India, see Appadurai, ed., *The Social Life of Things*.

77. Karl Marx, "The Fetishism of Commodities and the Secret Thereof," in *The Marx-Engels Reader*, ed. Robert C. Tucker (New York: Norton, 1978), 320–21. This chapter is one of the densest in *Capital*, and it has inspired dozens of interpretations. Three of the most inspired are Jean Baudrillard, "Fetishism and Ideology: The Semiological Reduction," in *For a Critique of the Political Economy of the Sign* (St. Louis: Telos Press, 1981), 88–101; G. A. Cohen, "Fetishism," in *Karl Marx's Theory of History: A Defence* (Princeton, N.J.: Princeton University Press, 1978), 115–33; and W. J. T. Mitchell, "The Rhetoric of Iconoclasm: Marxism, Ideology, and Fetishism," in *Iconology*.

78. Anthony Trollope, *The Struggles of Brown, Jones, and Robinson* (New York: Arno Press, 1981), 231, 51.

79. For a detailed analysis of the sensation form see Winifred Hughes, *The Maniac in the Cellar* (Princeton, N.J.: Princeton University Press, 1981), and Brooks, *The Melodramatic Imagination*. For an advertiser's definition of "sensation advertising," see Smith, *Advertise*, 107ff.

80. Writing about the 1862 Exhibition, the advertiser William Smith remarks that "though none could help admiring the wonders brought together at the Great Exhibition of 1862, still many nuisances were met with which ought to have been avoided in the 19th century." By this he means that too much labor was on display during the Exhibition. Invariably, advertisers like their labor fetishized; as Smith says, "the interior mysteries of preparing food are amongst those into which it will not do to *examine too curiously*" (*Advertise*, 76–77).

81. "Official Catalogues of the Industrial Exhibition," *Westminster Quarterly Review* (1851): 359. Among examples of the nostalgia for the soft sell is *Tom Brown's School Days* (1857), where the narrator wails: "Oh young England! Young England! You who are born into these racing railroad times, when there's a Great Exhibition, or some monster sight, every year; and you can get over a couple of thousand miles of ground for three pound ten, in a five weeks' holiday; why don't you know more of your own birthplaces?" (Thomas Hughes, *Tom Brown's School Days* [Harmondsworth: Puffin Books, 1971], 16). More famous is George Eliot's lament on the passing of "Old Leisure": "Leisure is gone—gone where the spinning-wheels are gone, and the pack-horses, and the slow waggons, and the pedlars who brought bargains to the door on sunny afternoons. Ingenious philosophers tell you, perhaps, that the great work of the steam-engine is to create leisure for mankind. Do not believe them: it only creates a vacuum for eager thought to rush in. Even idleness is eager now—eager for amusement: prone to excursion trains, art-museums, periodical literature, and exciting novels: prone even to scientific theorizing, and cursory peeps through microscopes. Old Leisure was quite a different personage: he read only one newspaper, innocent of leaders, and was free from that periodicity of sensations which we call post-time" (*Adam Bede* [Harmondsworth: Penguin Books, 1980], 557).

82. For an account of the various exhibitions that punctuated the late nineteenth century, see Williams, *Dream Worlds*, 58–66.

Two

1. Benjamin Disraeli, *Tancred, or the New Crusade* (London: Longmans, Green, 1900), 341.

2. Thomas Smith, *Successful Advertising: Its Secrets Explained* (London: Smith's Advertising Agency, 1886), 117.

3. Jacob Larwood [pseud. for Herman Diederik Johan von Scherihaven] and John Camden Hotten, *The History of Signboards from the Earliest Time to the Present Day*, 11th ed. (London: Chatto and Windus, 1900), 149.

4. *ILN*, June 25, 1887: 707.

5. Quoted in David Cannadine, "The Context, Performance, and Meaning of Ritual: The British Monarchy and the 'Invention of Tradi-

tion,' c. 1820–1977," in *The Invention of Tradition*, ed. Eric Hobsbawm and Terence Ranger (Cambridge, Eng.: Cambridge University Press, 1983), 118.

6. Walter Bagehot, "The Monarchy and the People," *The Economist*, July 22, 1871; reprinted in Norman St. John-Stevas, ed., *The Collected Works of Walter Bagehot* (London: The Economist, 1974), 5:432.

7. *ILN*, Jan. 30, 1886: 119.

8. *Punch*, June 18, 1887: 294 (the dandified British lion appears in the same issue, 295); *Times*, June 20, 1887: 6. For an examination of the many snafus of the Jubilee, see Jeffrey L. Lant, *Insubstantial Pageant: Ceremony and Confusion at Queen Victoria's Court* (New York: Taplinger, 1980).

9. Quoted in Caroline Chapman and Paul Raben, eds., *Debrett's Queen Victoria's Jubilees, 1887 & 1897* (London: Debrett's Peerage, 1977), 1.

10. The *Times* called special attention to the fact that "the music will be rendered by 300 selected voices from the best choirs" (*Times*, June 14, 1887: 10). For the Jubilee preparations of the clergy, see Cannadine, "Context," 131–32. A typical order of procession appears in *ILN*, June 25, 1887: 707.

11. These, along with other examples of Jubilee eavesdropping, can be found in Chapman and Raben, *Victoria's Jubilees*, 12, 17.

12. George Gissing, *In the Year of Jubilee* (New York: Dover, 1982), 46.

13. S. N. Eisenstadt, ed., *Max Weber on Charisma and Institution Building* (Chicago: University of Chicago Press, 1968), 48.

14. Clifford Geertz, "Centers, Kings, and Charisma: Reflections on the Symbolics of Power," in *Local Knowledge: Further Essays in Interpretive Anthropology* (New York: Basic Books, 1983), 122. See also Eisenstadt's introduction to *Weber on Charisma*, ix–lxi; Edward Shils, "Charisma, Order, and Status," *American Sociological Review*, 30 (1965): 199–213.

15. For the Children's Jubilee see *ILN*, June 25, 1887: 710–11, 724–25. For an account of an "entertainment to six thousand poor" in Edinburgh's Waverley Market see *ILN*, July 2, 1887: 24. For the "Monster Free Gala" in Peel Park, Bradford, see *ILN*, July 2, 1887: 20.

16. Eisenstadt, *Weber on Charisma*, 22–27.

17. Thomas Carlyle, *On Heroes, Hero-Worship, and the Heroic in History* (1840), quoted in Elisabeth Darby and Nicola Smith, *The Cult of the Prince Consort* (New Haven, Conn.: Yale University Press, 1983), 1. An earlier compendium of stories detailing Victoria's passion for Albert encomiums is Clare Jerrold, *The Widowhood of Queen Victoria* (London: Eveleigh Nash, 1916).

18. An 1861 bestseller (over 100,000 copies sold) was Reverend William Brank's *Heaven Our Home*, which Victoria and Albert read together early in the year. Branks believed that heaven would be a sort of family reunion in an "eternal home of love" in which friends could hold

conversations in the "language of heaven." Quoted in Darby and Smith, *Cult of the Prince Consort*, 4.

19. Walter Bagehot, "The Thanksgiving," *The Economist*, Feb. 24, 1872; reprinted in *Collected Works*, 5:439. Bagehot's various articles in defense of the monarchy appear in this same volume, 411–49. Following Cannadine, we must regard Bagehot's pronouncements to a certain extent as prescriptive and predictive rather than descriptive; Victoria took on the semblance of inherent charisma only during and after her two Jubilees (see "Context," 107).

20. Ernst Kantorowicz, *The King's Two Bodies: A Study in Mediaeval Political Theology* (Princeton, N.J.: Princeton University Press, 1957), 5. Though the fiction of the king's two bodies was more or less legally defunct by the beginning of the eighteenth century, its general outline can be discerned in William Blackstone's *Commentaries*, first published in 1765. Blackstone, however, thinks that the monarch has *three* bodies: not just a material body (what used to be called "the body natural") and an immaterial body (what used to be called "the body politic") but a *financial* body as well. He writes, "These substantive or direct prerogatives [of the monarchy] may be divided into three kinds: being such as regard, first, the king's royal *character*; secondly, his royal *authority*; and, lastly, his royal *income*" (*Commentaries on the Laws of England* [Portland: Thomas B. Wait, 1807], 1:240). This tripartite construction of embodied royal power persisted at least until the 1870's, when Walter Bagehot could still feel compelled to write article after article detailing "The Cost of Public Dignity," "The Income of the Prince of Wales," and the expenses incurred by the upkeep of "The Residence of the Queen" (*Collected Works*, vol. 5). After the Jubilee these kinds of expenditures were approved without hesitation; the monarch had ceased to have a financial body. Accordingly, a recent history of cartoons about the monarchy finds that lampoons about the Court's expenses largely disappeared after the 1887 Jubilee; see Michael Wynn Jones, *A Cartoon History of the Monarchy* (London: Macmillan, 1978).

21. "Sir Charles Dilke on the Civil List," *The Economist*, Jan. 10, 1874; reprinted in *Collected Works*, 5:414. There was one exception to Bagehot's rule; as Ian Gilmour notes, "since Queen Victoria, monarchs have been important, politically, only during a crisis. Victoria was a useful conciliator between the Houses in 1869 over Irish Disestablishment and in 1884 over Reform and Redistribution" (*The Body Politic* [London: Hutchinson, 1969], 316).

22. [Abraham Hayward], "The Advertising System," *Edinburgh Review* 77 (Feb. 1843): 6.

23. By One Who Thinks Aloud [James Dawson Burn], *The Language of the Walls: And A Voice from the Shop Windows. Or, The Mirror of Commercial Roguery* (Manchester: Abel Heywood, 1855), 36–38. For an analysis

of the social space of celebrity in the late nineteenth century, see Philip Fisher, "Appearing and Disappearing in Public: Social Space in Late-Nineteenth-Century Literature and Culture," in Sacvan Bercovitch, ed., *Reconstructing American Literary History* (Cambridge, Mass.: Harvard University Press, 1986), 155–88.

24. The two historians are Richard Altick, *The Shows of London* (Cambridge, Mass.: Harvard University Press, 1978), 217, 334, 433; and Robert Opie, *Rule Britannia: Trading on the British Image* (Harmondsworth: Penguin Books, 1985), 9, 43–49. For a history of the objects produced to commemorate Victoria's life between 1817 and 1861, see John May, *Victoria Remembered: A Royal History 1817–1861, Entirely Illustrated with Commemoratives* (London: Heinemann, 1983). Victoria's aura also extended to the Prince Consort, who in life and death inspired the makers of linens, bookmarks, and statues; see Darby and Smith, *Cult of the Prince Consort*, 85–105.

25. [Hayward], "The Advertising System," 35.

26. Many agencies then existed, but they were not responsible for the unified imagery of the Jubilee. See Diana Hindley and Geoffrey Hindley, "A New Professionalism: The Agencies Develop," in *Advertising in Victorian England: 1850–1914* (London: Wayland, 1972), 27–41. See also W. Hamish Fraser, *The Coming of the Mass Market, 1850–1914* (Hamden, Conn.: Archon Books, 1981), 134–46.

27. Gissing, *In the Year of Jubilee*, 57, 58, 68.

28. T. Smith, *Successful Advertising*, 34.

29. See, for example, the Christmas 1886 sales advertised in the *ILN*, Dec. 4, 1886: 610, 614, 619; Dec. 11, 1886: 639, 647. Rachel Bowlby studies the impact of department stores on late-Victorian culture in *Just Looking: Consumer Culture in Dreiser, Gissing and Zola* (New York: Methuen, 1985).

30. Quoted in Hindley and Hindley, *Advertising in Victorian England*, 28.

31. Advertising agencies were largely responsible for moving early-twentieth-century advertising away from the excesses of late-Victorian kitsch. Though kitsch aestheticized commodities, it did not attempt to systematically coordinate them with the styles approved by the established institutions of art. The classic text on the reaction against kitsch in early-twentieth-century advertising is Walter Shaw Sparrow, *Advertising and British Art: An Introduction to a Vast Subject* (London: John Lane, 1924).

32. For an extensive catalogue of the modern manifestations of touristic kitsch, see Dean MacCannell, *The Tourist: A New Theory of the Leisure Class* (New York: Schocken Books, 1976).

33. This analysis of kitsch draws on Susan Stewart's definition of kitsch in *On Longing: Narratives of the Miniature, the Gigantic, the Sou-*

venir, the Collection (Baltimore, Md.: Johns Hopkins University Press, 1984), 166–69. Stewart calls particular attention to the etymology of "kitsch." For a sense of what happens to kitsch (as well as other outmoded artifacts) after its moment of glory, see Michael Thompson, "Stevengraphs—Yesterday's Kitsch," in *Rubbish Theory: The Creation and Destruction of Value* (Oxford: Oxford University Press, 1979), 13–33. In choosing to follow the trajectory of a piece of nineteenth-century kitsch, Thompson also locates the origin of kitsch in late-nineteenth-century commodity culture. Here it is worth recalling that in its final years, the Crystal Palace became something of a haven for kitsch, perhaps even becoming a kitsch object in its own right.

34. Stewart, *On Longing*, 167.

35. This discussion of the historicity of kitsch draws extensively on Matei Calinescu's groundbreaking work, *Five Faces of Modernity: Modernism, Avant-Garde, Decadence, Kitsch, Postmodernism* (Durham, N.C.: Duke University Press, 1987), 236, 240–48.

36. Roger Fry, *Vision and Design*, quoted in Calinescu, *Five Faces*, 251. The manifestoes of the various schools of early-twentieth-century art almost always denounce Victorian kitsch. Henry van de Velde's 1903 "Programme" proclaims that "Religious, arbitrary, sentimental flights of fancy are parasitic plants." Adolf Loos's 1908 "Ornament and Crime" underscores the point that "the evolution of culture is synonymous with the removal of ornament from utilitarian objects." Frank Lloyd Wright's 1910 "Organic Architecture" calls for "one great thing instead of a quarrelling collection of little things." For these and other similar statements, see Ulrich Conrads, ed., *Programs and Manifestoes on 20th-Century Architecture* (Cambridge, Mass.: MIT Press, 1975), 13, 20, 25. For a survey of the "bibelots" that became the basis for our modern idea of kitsch, see Remy G. Saisselin, *The Bourgeois and the Bibelot* (New Brunswick, N.J.: Rutgers University Press, 1984). The best overall encyclopedia to Victorian material culture is Asa Briggs, *Victorian Things* (Chicago: University of Chicago Press, 1989).

37. "The thing was wonderfully made and contrived, excellent craftsmanship of the Victorian order. But somehow it was monstrous. Some Chatterley must even have felt it, for the thing had never been used" (D. H. Lawrence, *Lady Chatterley's Lover* [New York: Bantam, 1968], 159).

38. The advertisements for the Jubilee balloon and the Jubilee game appear in *Times*, June 14, 1887: 10; the charm bracelet in *ILN*, Apr. 23, 1887: 477; the Jubilee brooch in *ILN*, Feb. 26, 1887: 242; the onyx portraits in *G*, Mar. 12, 1887: 271; the offer to convert anything into "Jubileeana" in *Times*, June 14, 1887: 10. The publishing industry advertised its own Jubilee offerings in *Athenaeum*, June 18, 1887: 810–23; June 25, 1887: 843–48. Grocers like W. Tonks of Scarborough often presented their customers with souvenir photographs of the Queen, suitably

stamped with the name of the proprietor. Tonks's card is reproduced in Colin Ford and Brian Harrison, eds., *A Hundred Years Ago: Britain in the 1880's in Words and Photographs* (Cambridge, Mass.: Harvard University Press, 1983), 31. The Continental Novelty Company offered souvenir photographs in *ILN*, Dec. 11, 1886: 656; Dec. 18, 1886: 688.

39. The unveiling of the last Jubilee monument, a bronze equestrian statue of Prince Albert at Windsor, actually took place on May 12, 1890, over three years after the January meeting at which the Countess of Strafford proposed presenting the Queen with a Jubilee gift from the women of England. For the projected design of various monuments see *ILN*, June 11, 1887: 650; July 23, 1887: 93; for the unveilings see *ILN*, May 25, 1889: 663; May 17, 1890: 609.

40. Stewart makes this point about souvenirs in *On Longing*, 136.

41. A great variety of commemoratives have been reproduced in May, *Victoria Remembered*. Further examples can be found in Chapman and Raben, *Victoria's Jubilees*.

42. For information on Victorian funerary practice, see James Stevens Curl, *The Victorian Celebration of Death* (London: David and Charles, 1972).

43. Lytton Strachey, *Queen Victoria* (Harmondsworth: Penguin, 1971), 206.

44. *Times*, Oct. 12, 1863: 8.

45. *ILN*, Jan. 29, 1887: 125.

46. Anthony Trollope, *The Struggles of Brown, Jones, and Robinson* (London: Smith, Elder, 1870), 138–50. For a detailed consideration of the changing role of women as consumers in late-Victorian England see Bowlby, *Just Looking*, 18–34.

47. Walter Bagehot, *The English Constitution* (1867), in *Collected Works*, 5:229.

48. Quoted in Donald Koch's introduction to *Mary Jane Holmes, 'Tempest and Sunshine' and Maria Susanna Cummins, 'The Lamplighter'* (New York: Odyssey Press, 1968), vii. Victoria's reference to "peace and security" appears in a May 26, 1862 letter; see Hector Bolitho, ed., *Further Letters of Queen Victoria* (London: Thornton Butterworth, 1938), 127.

49. Koch, ed., *The Lamplighter*, 43.

50. Karl Marx, *Capital, Volume One* (New York: Vintage Books, 1977), 165.

51. Before the Jubilee, advertisers such as Louis Velveteen and Carter's Little Liver Pills only occasionally used illustrations, relying for the most part on copy and bold type (see, for example, *ILN*, July 17, 1886: 79; July 29, 1887: 133). After the Jubilee advertisers took to commemorating various anniversaries of their own: Keen's Mustard conveniently extended the Jubilee by celebrating the anniversary of its product (*ILN*, Apr. 2, 1892: 438).

52. *ILN*, Nov. 24, 1888: 624.

53. Marx, *Capital, Volume One*, 138.

54. Henri Lefebvre, *Everyday Life in the Modern World* (New York: Harper and Row, 1971), 110–27. Eric Hobsbawm discusses the yen for anniversaries in "The Centenarian Revolution," in *The Age of Empire, 1875–1914* (New York: Pantheon, 1987), 13–33.

55. Edward Shils, "Center and Periphery," in *Center and Periphery: Essays in Macrosociology* (Chicago: University of Chicago Press, 1975), 9.

56. The best description of how these "consumption communities" operated in the nineteenth century is Daniel Boorstin, *The Americans: The Democratic Experience* (New York: Vintage, 1974), 89–164.

57. See Walter Dill Scott, *The Psychology of Advertising* (Boston: Small, Maynard, 1902), v.

58. Strachey, *Queen Victoria*, 202, 231–32.

59. Carl A. Naether, *Advertising to Women* (New York: Prentice-Hall, 1928). At the turn of the century many books offered up Victoria as a model for Victorian women; one unequivocal example is Marie Corelli, *The Passing of a Great Queen: A Tribute to the Noble Life of Victoria Regina* (New York: Dodd, Mead, 1901).

60. [A Member of the Royal Household], *The Private Life of the Queen* (New York: D. Appleton, 1897), 264.

61. For a remarkable inventory of these catalogues, see ibid., 120.

62. Strachey's wonderful description of Victoria's archive of objects appears in *Queen Victoria*, 232. Stewart analyzes the hermetic quality of the collection in *On Longing*, 151–66.

63. Figs. 7 and 8 in Chapter 1 give a good idea of what a mid-Victorian hoarding looked like. For photographs and engravings of others, see Hindley and Hindley, *Advertising in Victorian England*, 130–38; Ford and Harrison, *A Hundred Years Ago*, 87.

64. Thomas Carlyle, *Past and Present* (New York: New York University Press, 1965), 209.

65. Guy Debord, *Society of the Spectacle* (Detroit: Black and Red, 1977), 3, 12.

66. Walter Bagehot, "The New Title of the Queen," *The Economist*, Mar. 18, 1876; reprinted in *Collected Works*, 5:447–49.

67. William Stead, Jr., *The Art of Advertising: Its Theory and Practice Fully Described* (London: T. B. Browne, Ltd., 1899), 12–14.

68. Debord, *Society of the Spectacle*, 42, 62; Kantorowicz, *The King's Two Bodies*, 5.

69. Debord, *Society of the Spectacle*, 36, 66; see also 34, 40, 41.

70. Jean Baudrillard, "Toward a Critique of the Political Economy of the Sign," in *For a Critique of the Political Economy of the Sign* (St. Louis: Telos, 1981), 146.

71. Marx, "The Fetishism of the Commodity and Its Secret," in *Capital, Volume One*, 163–64.

72. For these imaginings, see Henry Sampson, *A History of Advertising from the Earliest Times* (London: Chatto and Windus, 1874), 597–616. For an unrealized scheme that involved pinning little slips of paper on consumers, see "A New System of Personal Advertising," in [Burn], *The Language of the Walls*, 383–402.

73. Gissing, *In the Year of Jubilee*, 67.

74. See Sampson, *History*, 2. Though Sampson's interpretation of all history in the light of advertising appeared in 1874, it did not become a staple item in the discourse of advertisers until the 1880's. Thomas Smith's 1886 *Successful Advertising* goes so far as to include an illustration of Romans posting bills. Many early-twentieth-century historians of advertising have taken these accounts at their word; see the opening chapters of Frank Presbrey, *The History and Development of Advertising* (New York: Doran, 1929).

75. *Athenaeum*, Jan. 15, 1887: 93.

Three

1. On the Victorian invention the standard of living, see Eric Hobsbawm, "Standards of Living," in *Industry and Empire* (Harmondsworth: Penguin, 1968) and *The Age of Capital, 1848–1875* (New York: Meridian, 1984); W. Hamish Fraser, *The Coming of the Mass Market, 1850–1914* (Hamden, Conn.: Archon Books, 1981); Barry Supple, "Material Development: The Condition of England 1830–1860," in Laurence Lerner, ed., *The Victorians* (New York: Holmes and Meier, 1978).

2. See Hobsbawm, *Age of Capital*, 3–47.

3. Karl Marx, *The German Ideology* (New York: International Publishers, 1981), 41. See also Wolfgang Mommsen, *Theories of Imperialism* (Chicago: University of Chicago Press, 1980), 146–47. Mommsen observes that "one thing at least can be said with certainty at the present time, namely that there is no foundation in the old thesis, originally accepted by bourgeois as well as Marxist writers, that expansionist opportunities are necessary to the preservation of capitalism. . . . Imperialism was primarily the consequence of the overflowing energy of European societies in the economic, military and political fields: it was not a necessity inherent in their socio-economic system."

4. See J. R. Seeley, *The Expansion of England* (Chicago: University of Chicago Press, 1970; orig. pub. 1883).

5. Henry Stanley, *In Darkest Africa, or the Quest, Rescue, and Retreat of Emin Governor of Equatoria* (New York: Charles Scribner's Sons, 1890), 9. Subsequent citations appear in the text.

6. David Livingstone articulates his missionary program in *Missionary Travels and Researches in South Africa* (New York: Harper and Brothers, 1858), 1–54.

7. Karl Marx, *Theories of Surplus Value* and *Grundrisse*, quoted in

G. A. Cohen, *Karl Marx's Theory of History: A Defence* (Princeton, N.J.: Princeton University Press, 1978), 124–25.

8. For Stanley's view of his carriers, see *Darkest Africa*, 160, 244; for the trial and execution scenes, 212–13, 244. Because the slave trade had been going on for three centuries, most Africans had at least an inkling that articles of Western manufacture were highly valued. Articles like rifles thus had both evident use value and rudimentary exchange value. Stanley, however, did his best to mystify exchange value by conferring immense mystery on his possession of Western goods. He makes a fetish of property by imposing capital punishment on his carriers (by the 1890's capital punishment for theft was inconceivable in Britain), and at several points in his narrative he makes it clear he wants Africans to regard his property with superstition.

9. Awakened one night by howls and horn blowing, Stanley records the following (*Darkest Africa*, 112):

> The first Speaker said, "Hey, strangers, where are you going?"
> The Parasite echoes, "Where are you going?"
> SPEAKER. This country has no welcome for you.
> PARASITE. No welcome for you.
> SPEAKER. All men will be against you.
> PARASITE. Against you.
> SPEAKER. And you will be surely slain.
> PARASITE. Surely slain.
> SPEAKER. Ah-ah-ah-ah-aah.
> PARASITE. Ah-aah.
> SPEAKER. Ooh-ooh-ooh-ooh-ooooh.
> PARASITE. Ooh-ooh-ooooooh.

Rather than meditating on the scene as an ominous manifestation of Africa's dark interior, Stanley thinks it offers his troops a little comic relief. Stanley is decidedly not haunted, not "wondering and secretly appalled," as Conrad's Marlow had been, by the otherness of the African people; see Joseph Conrad, *Heart of Darkness* (New York: Norton, 1971), 36. To the contrary, he treats the scene as light entertainment, and not without reason, for it is a polished performance culled from literary sources. He derives the speaker and his parasite from the Elizabethan convention of the fool and his half-wit zany; with their volleying stichomythic dialogue, this prattling pair could have stepped directly into the forest of equatorial Africa after an engagement in Shakespeare's Forest of Arden.

10. For these nervous tics, see H. Rider Haggard, *She: A History of Adventure* (Harmondsworth: Penguin, 1982), 31, 55–56; and Samuel White Baker, *The Albert Nyanza, Great Basin of the Nile and Explorations of the Nile Sources* (London: Macmillan, 1866).

11. Karl Marx, "The Fetishism of Commodities and the Secret

Thereof," in *The Marx-Engels Reader*, ed. Robert C. Tucker (New York: Norton, 1978), 320. For Stanley's use of nouns, see *Darkest Africa*, 46–47; his abridgment of syntax bears a remarkable resemblance to the commodity language of the Great Exhibition noted in Chapter 1.

12. Thomas Fowell Buxton, *The Slave Trade in Africa* (London, 1840), 306, 342.

13. For the story of the East Africa Company, see Ronald Robinson, John Gallagher, and Alice Denny, *Africa and the Victorians: The Climax of Imperialism in the Dark Continent* (New York: St. Martin's Press, 1961), 307–11.

14. A series of lectures given from 1895 to 1898 at the South Place Institute in Finsbury provides a short account of what one lecturer called "Natives Under British Rule." For these lectures, see *British Africa* (London: Kegan Paul, Trench, Truber & Co., 1901). A more detailed look at what colonized peoples suffered at the hands of Europeans can be found in Claude Lévi-Strauss, *Tristes Tropiques* (New York: Washington Square Press, 1977). For a third-world perspective, see Frantz Fanon, *The Wretched of the Earth* (New York: Grove, 1968). The problem of the economic structure of African capitalism in the nineteenth century has been addressed by a number of recent works: see Peter Duignan and L. H. Gann, eds., *Colonialism in Africa, 1870–1960*, Vol. 4, *The Economics of Capitalism* (Cambridge, Eng.: Cambridge University Press, 1975); John Iliffe, *The Emergence of African Capitalism* (Minneapolis: University of Minnesota Press, 1983); John Sender and Sheila Smith, *The Development of Capitalism in Africa* (London: Methuen, 1986).

15. Karl Marx, "The Fetishism of the Commodity and Its Secret," in *Capital, Volume One* (New York: Vintage, 1977), 163–77.

16. See Arthur Helps, ed., *The Speeches of the Prince Consort* (London: William Pickering, 1862). See also Asa Briggs, "The Crystal Palace and the Men of 1851," in *Victorian People* (Chicago: University of Chicago Press, 1972), 15–51. As noted in Chapter 2, after his death the Prince Consort became something of an icon in material culture; see Elisabeth Darby and Nicola Smith, *The Cult of the Prince Consort* (New Haven, Conn.: Yale University Press, 1983).

17. The imperial importance of commodities was recognized widely before the era of the new imperialism. A passage from Harriet Martineau's *Dawn Island* (1845) lays particular emphasis on the commodity's role: "The exchanges of food and foreign goods were carried on with more order than is usual on the first occasion of a newly-discovered people being one of the parties; and when even the most fortunate sellers found that, much as they gained, there were many other desirable things which they could not have till they could offer commodities less perishable and more valuable than food, it was not difficult to bring them to a purpose of preparation for a better traffic, if the Europeans would promise to come again" (quoted and analyzed in Patrick Brantlinger,

Rule of Darkness: British Literature and Imperialism, 1830–1914 [Ithaca, N.Y.: Cornell University Press, 1988], 30–32).

18. Quoted in J. A. Hobson, *The Psychology of Jingoism* (London: Grant Richards, 1901), 4; subsequent citations appear in the text. In addition to commenting on the great stress the song places "upon the money bags," Hobson calls attention to "the affected modesty of the opening disclaimer, the rapid transition to a tone of bullying braggadocio," and "the unconscious humor of an assumption that it is our national duty to defeat the Turk" (4).

19. A variety of treaties, agreements, and ententes contributed to maintaining what was known as "the concert of Europe." For accounts of the balance of power in late-nineteenth-century Europe see Eric Hobsbawm, *The Age of Empire, 1875–1914* (New York: Pantheon, 1987), and Richard Shannon, *The Crisis of Imperialism* (London: Paladin, 1974). For an account of how the "excess of capitalist production over the demands of the home market" led to imperialism, see J. A. Hobson, *Imperialism: A Study* (London: George Allen and Unwin, 1902). Hobson was the first to undertake a large study of the economics of imperialism, and much of his work has stood the test of time remarkably well.

20. It is important not to take Hobson's attack on the music hall at face value. For an exact sense of the conditions the music hall created, as well as a clear definition of exactly who the "jingoes" were, see Gareth Stedman Jones, "Working Class Culture and Working Class Politics in London, 1870–1900: Notes on the Remaking of the Working Class," *Journal of Social History* 7, 4 (1974): 460–508. See also Peter Bailey, ed., *Music Hall: The Business of Pleasure* (Philadelphia: Open University Press, 1986).

21. See, for example, Adam Smith, *An Inquiry into the Nature and Causes of the Wealth of Nations* (London: T. Nelson and Sons, 1884), 115–35, 173–83; David Ricardo, *Works*, ed. Piero Straffa (Cambridge, Eng.: Cambridge University Press, 1955), 1:133–38; and Andrew Ure, *The Philosophy of Manufactures; or, An Exposition of the Scientific, Moral, and Commercial Economy of Great Britain* (London: C. Knight, 1835).

22. There are very few studies of jingo kitsch and very few places where one can go to look at them. Far and away the best work has been done by John MacKenzie, *Propaganda and Empire: The Manipulation of British Public Opinion, 1880–1960* (Manchester: Manchester University Press, 1984); see especially 15–38, "The Vehicles of Imperial Propaganda," a chapter on which I have relied extensively in writing my account of jingo material culture. For photographs of these articles, see Robert Opie, *Rule Britannia: Trading on the British Image* (Harmondsworth: Penguin, 1985); and Colin Ford and Brian Harrison, eds., *A Hundred Years Ago: Britain in the 1880's in Words and Photographs* (Cambridge, Mass.: Harvard University Press, 1983).

23. Richard Whiteing, *No. 5 John Street* (London: Thomas Nelson and Sons, 1902), 59. Subsequent citations appear in the text. James Morris has a real appreciation for the variety of forms Victorian allegory took; his "Pax Britannica" trilogy contains hundreds of examples. See *Heaven's Command: An Imperial Progress* (New York: Harcourt Brace Jovanovich, 1973); *Pax Britannica: The Climax of an Empire* (New York: Harcourt Brace Jovanovich, 1968); and *Farewell the Trumpets: An Imperial Retreat* (New York: Harcourt Brace Jovanovich, 1978). For a recent study that touches on the social construction of Victorian allegory, see Richard Altick, *Paintings from Books: Art and Literature in Britain, 1760–1900* (Columbia: Ohio State University Press, 1987).

24. Frank Hird, *H. M. Stanley: The Authorized Life* (London: Stanley Paul, 1935), 278–85. A number of endorsements appear soon after his return in *GSN*, Apr. 30, 1890. Later endorsements of soap, pipes, and tents appear in the *ILN*, Aug. 8, 1891: 195; *G*, Dec. 5, 1891: 681; *ILN*, Aug. 25, 1894: 258; *ILN*, May 4, 1895: 567. The review of *In Darkest Africa* is quoted in M. E. Chamberlain, *The Scramble for Africa* (London: Longman, 1974), 28. Shaw's letter to Ellen Terry can be found in Christopher St. John, ed., *Ellen Terry and Bernard Shaw: A Correspondence* (London: Constable and Co., 1931), 247–48. William Morris coined the term "jingo jubilee"; for an account of Morris's reaction to jingoism, see E. P. Thompson, *William Morris: Romantic to Revolutionary* (New York: Pantheon, 1955), 479–82.

25. Victor Turner, *The Ritual Process: Structure and Anti-Structure* (Ithaca, N.Y.: Cornell University Press, 1969), 97.

26. *GSN*: 6, 10, 13, 15, 18–19, 22, 23.

27. Two remarkable studies—one philological, the other semiotic—have been written about the sun topos in advertising. See Leo Spitzer, "American Advertising Explained as Popular Art," in Alban K. Forcione, Herbert Lindenberger, and Madeline Sutherland, eds., *Leo Spitzer: Representative Essays* (Stanford, Calif.: Stanford University Press, 1988), 327–56; and Jean Baudrillard, "Fetishism and Ideology: The Semiological Reduction," in *For a Critique of the Political Economy of the Sign* (St. Louis: Telos, 1981), 88–101.

28. Turner, *Ritual Process*, 95.

29. Rosa Luxemburg, *The Accumulation of Capital* (New Haven, Conn.: Yale University Press, 1951); quoted in Hannah Arendt, *Imperialism* (New York: Harcourt, Brace & World, 1968), 28.

30. For a history of the "darkest Africa" image, see Patrick Brantlinger, "Victorians and Africans: The Genealogy of the Myth of the Dark Continent," in *Critical Inquiry* 12 (Autumn 1985): 166–203.

31. William Cornwallis Harris, *The Wild Sports of Southern Africa* (Cape Town: C. Struik, 1963), 19.

32. *How I Found Livingstone: Travels, Adventures, and Discoveries in*

Central Africa; Including Four Months' Residence with Dr. Livingstone (London: Sampson Low, Marston, Low & Searle, 1873); *My Kalulu, Prince, King, and Slave: A Story of Central Africa* (London: Sampson Low, Marston, Low & Searle, 1873); *Coomassie and Magdala: The Story of Two British Campaigns in Central Africa* (London: Sampson Low, Marston, Low & Searle, 1874); *Through the Dark Continent; Or, The Sources of the Nile Around the Great Lakes of Equatorial Africa and Down the Livingstone River to the Atlantic Ocean* (London: Sampson Low, Marston, Searle & Rivington, 1878); *The Congo and the Founding of the Free State: A Story of Work and Exploration* (London: Sampson Low, Marston, Searle & Rivington, 1885).

33. See Leonard de Vries, *Victorian Advertisements* (Philadelphia: Lippincott, 1968), 12, 30, 42, 44, 75, 81, 108, 111, 124, 127; Opie, "The British Abroad," in *Rule Britannia*, 102–9.

34. Mayhew admits that the sandwich-board men were among the lowest of the low. A bankrupt draper told him, "I have tried to get work at carrying placard boards, but I can't. My clothes are now too bad for me to do anything else" (from Henry Mayhew, *London Labour and the London Poor*, quoted in T. R. Nevett, *Advertising in Britain: A History* [London: Heinemann, 1982], 57). The "H. E. L. Y. ' S." sandwich-board men wend their crooked way through Joyce's *Ulysses*, making one of their more prominent appearances in the "Wandering Rocks" chapter; see *Ulysses* (New York: Vintage, 1961), 187.

35. In 1863 William Smith put the problem bluntly: "The present style of sandwich-men is not up to the standard of the age. It is not to be expected, out of the small remuneration they receive, that these men should create a great sensation in the way of personal appearance, by parading the streets in evening dress; still an improvement might be made in their style. For instance, let the advertisers supply the men with a good strong suit of clothes, hat, and boots, and all complete, and a neat board" (*Advertise: How? When? Where?* [London: Routledge, Warne, and Routledge, 1863], 136–37). Smith's high hopes were not realized. By the turn of the century sandwich-board men were considered such a beggar's opera that London banished them from its streets, and this antiquated form of advertising was relegated to the colonies; see Clarence Moran, *The Business of Advertising* (London: Methuen, 1905), 47.

36. At times English advertisers appear to view the colonial world as their personal fiefdom. An ad for Stone's Ginger Wine shows a white man on horseback supervising the work of several black laborers; G, Sept. 3, 1892: 300. Ads for Lipton Tea show Ceylon carved up into tea plantations; G, Feb. 27, 1892: 289; G, Jan. 20, 1894: 81; ILN, Sept. 14, 1895: 346. One advertiser, Clark's Night Lights, went so far as to deface the pyramids by showing them illuminated by slogans pushing their product; ILN, Aug. 10, 1895: 189.

37. For an account of the fluctuating English interest in central Af-

rica, see Robinson, Gallagher, and Denny, *Africa and the Victorians*, 307ff. See also Alan Cairns, *Prelude to Imperialism: British Reactions to Central African Society, 1840–1890* (London: Routledge & Kegan Paul, 1965).

38. J. A. Hobson, *Gold, Prices and Wages* (London: Methuen, 1913), vii.

39. John Maynard Keynes, *A Tract on Monetary Reform* (1923), quoted in Marcello de Cecco, *Money and Empire: The International Gold Standard, 1890–1914* (Oxford: Basil Blackwell, 1974).

40. Arthur Conan Doyle, *The Great Boer War* (London: Smith, Elder and Co., 1900), 30.

41. Ibid., 29.

42. Rudyard Kipling, "The Captive," in *A Sahib's War and Other Stories* (Harmondsworth: Penguin, 1971), 32. Subsequent citations appear in the text.

43. Though Zigler does not refer to particular passages in the classical economists (he can hardly be expected to have read them), his arguments often run parallel to theirs. See Thomas Hobbes, "Of the First and Second Natural Laws, and of Contracts," in *Leviathan* (New York: Collier, 1962), 108–12; John Locke, "Of Property," in *Two Treatises of Government* (New York: Hafner, 1947), 133–46; Adam Smith, "Of the Division of Labour," in *The Wealth of Nations* (Harmondsworth: Penguin, 1982), 2–6.

44. Marx, *German Ideology*, 79.

45. Marx, "Fetishism," in *Marx-Engels Reader*, 321.

46. Marx, *German Ideology*, 78. For an account of the limitations to Marx's theory of nationalism, see Benedict Anderson, *Imagined Communities: Reflections on the Origin and Spread of Nationalism* (London: Verso, 1983), 11–16.

47. G. A. Henty, *With Roberts to Pretoria: A Tale of the South African War* (New York: Charles Scribner's Sons, 1901), 6.

48. Ibid., 376.

49. Conrad, *Heart of Darkness*, 36.

50. The "welcome comrade" ad appears in *G*, Feb. 3, 1900: 178; Captain Kettle first enlists for Tortoise-Shell cigarettes in *G*, Apr. 21, 1900: 597; he wards off enemy fire in *G*, Oct. 27, 1900: 633.

51. The "joyful voice" ad appears in *G*, June 23, 1900: 930; "the charge," *G*, Dec. 1, 1900: 827; the enamel cans, *G*, Mar. 17, 1900: 389; the artillery battery, *G*, Feb. 3, 1900: 180. A reproduction of the Bovril map can be found in Diana Hindley and Geoffrey Hindley, eds., *Advertising in Victorian England, 1850–1914* (London: Wayland, 1972), plate 3.9.

52. Sydney Brooks, "England and the Transvaal," in *Briton and Boer: Both Sides of the South Africa Question* (New York: Harper and Brothers, 1900), 63.

53. Arendt, *Imperialism*, 74.

54. Thorstein Veblen's classic argument appears in his chapter on "Conspicuous Consumption," in *The Theory of the Leisure Class* (Harmondsworth: Penguin, 1979), 68–101.

55. I base my account of this pamphlet on large segments of it quoted in William Stead, Jr., "Colonial Advertising," in *The Art of Advertising: Its Theory and Practice Fully Described* (London: T. B. Browne, 1899), 85–86.

56. Veblen, *Theory of the Leisure Class*, 44, 50, 116.

57. Buxton, *Slave Trade in Africa*, 6.

58. Raoul Vaneigem, *The Revolution of Everyday Life* (London: Aldgate Press, 1983), 50.

59. Rabindranath Tagore, *The Home and the World* (Harmondsworth: Penguin, 1985), 26. For an incisive account of the Swadeshi movement and its effects, see Arjun Appadurai, ed., *The Social Life of Things: Commodities in Cultural Perspective* (Cambridge, Eng.: Cambridge University Press, 1986).

60. Tagore, *Home and World*, 26.

61. Marx, "Fetishism," in *Marx-Engels Reader*, 319.

62. For the dates and exact contents of each of these exhibitions, see "The Imperial Exhibitions," in MacKenzie, *Propaganda and Empire*, 96–120.

63. William Booth says that Stanley's "presentation of life as it exists in the vast African forest" seemed to him to be "only too vivid a picture of many parts of our own land." At several points he blames the capitalists, whom he calls "the ivory raiders who brutally traffic in the unfortunate denizens of the forest glades," and who thus, to continue the analogy, "flourish on the weakness of the poor" (*In Darkest England, and the Way Out* [London: International Headquarters of the Salvation Army, 1890], 11–12). J. A. Hobson was also aware that the emphasis on external markets had diverted attention from the massive internal extension of the market. He astutely comments, "The absorption of so large a proportion of public interest, energy, blood, and money in seeking to procure colonial possessions and foreign markets would seem to indicate that Great Britain obtained her chief livelihood by external trade. Now this was not the case. Large as was our foreign and colonial trade in volume and value, essential as was much of it to our national well-being, nevertheless it furnished a small proportion of the total industry of the nation" (*Imperialism*, 28).

64. Stead, *The Art of Advertising*, 25.

Four

1. Guy Debord, *Society of the Spectacle* (Detroit: Black and Red, 1977), 12, 20.

2. Much of the first volume of Henry Mayhew's *London Labour and the London Poor* (1861–62) is taken up with descriptions of itinerant vendors of various sorts. For a representative selection see *London Labour and the London Poor,* ed. Victor Neuburg (Harmondsworth: Penguin, 1985), 5–189. Thomas Hardy's description of Physician Vilbert in *Jude the Obscure* captures the lives of these itinerant quacks, who were dying out at the end of the nineteenth century: "Vilbert was an itinerant quack-doctor, well known to the rustic population, and absolutely unknown to anybody else, as he, indeed, took care to be, to avoid inconvenient investigations. Cottagers formed his only patients, and his Wessex-wide repute was among them alone. His position was humbler and his field more obscure than those of the quacks with capital and an organized system of advertising. He was, in fact, a survival" (*Jude the Obscure* [New York: Norton, 1978], 23).

3. There were provisions of other acts that dealt with patent medicines; I list only the ones explicitly intended to regulate the trade. For a complete list see *Reports from Committees: Patent Medicines* (session 10 Feb. 1914–18 Sept. 1914), vol. 9. Also listed as *Report from the Select Committee on Patent Medicines, Together with the Proceedings of the Committee, Minutes of Evidence, and Appendices* (London: Wyman and Sons, 1914). Hereafter referred to as the *Report.*

4. The speaker is "Mr. Lynch," a member of Parliament who participated in hearings on the quack-trade held between February and September of 1914 (*Report,* 178; subsequent citations appear in the text).

5. British Medical Association, *Secret Remedies: What They Cost and What They Contain* (London: British Medical Association, 1909), 182. (A companion volume appeared a few years later, called *More Secret Remedies: What They Cost and What They Contain* [London: British Medical Association, 1912].)

The moment *Secret Remedies* came out, Beecham's Pills ran a huge spread in *The Graphic* proclaiming that "THE LORDS AND THE COMMONS AGREE ABOUT BEECHAM'S PILLS." The small print elaborates: "It is perfectly reliable although it is a 'Secret Remedy,' it has been tried by the Public for upwards of sixty years, and in spite of all opposition, and in the face of calumny prompted by jealousy caused by success, the voice of the people is practically unanimous in favor of BEECHAM'S PILLS." *G,* Dec. 4, 1909: 741.

6. Sydney Hillier, *Popular Drugs: Their Use and Abuse* (London: T. Werner Laurie, 1910), 37. In 1911 the *British Medical Journal* devoted a special issue to "Quackery and the Medical Profession." Before the nineteenth century, most quacks called themselves doctors, and most doctors adhered to taxonomies that differed little from those upheld by quacks. In publishing a series of articles on the history of quackery, including "Cancer, Credulity, and Quackery," "Quackery and Female Complaints," "Quackery in the Past," and "Some Notable Quacks,"

the *Journal* was actually undertaking to insert a chapter in the history of the medical profession. See *British Medical Journal*, May 27, 1911: 1218–92. Over the years the quacks kept pace with new developments in the medical profession; Michel Foucault's account of the replacement of a unitary model for the formation of the medical body by the empirical gaze of the physician applies equally well to the various pronouncements of quacks. The development of what I will later term "the therapeutic commodity" presupposes the pedagogical and technical reorganization of medicine charted by Foucault in *The Birth of the Clinic: An Archaeology of Medical Perception* (New York: Vintage, 1975).

7. Friedrich Engels, *The Condition of the Working Class in England* (Stanford, Calif.: Stanford University Press, 1968), 118. Engels also notes that "by means of advertisements, posters, and other publicity stunts they recruit their clients from the poorer classes" (118). Because the working class formed the great majority of people in mid-Victorian Britain, Engels is right to point to working people as the prime targets of patent medicine advertising. The appeal of quackery, however, transcended class boundaries, for the middle-class people who profited from the sale of remedies often felt compelled to believe in them. George Eliot relates how "Felix [Holt] was heir to nothing better than a quack medicine," called "Holt's Cathartic Lozenges and Holt's Restorative Elixir." When Felix confesses that he feels ashamed of the family business, a friend gives him this little lecture: "I know they have been well reported of, and many wise persons have tried remedies providentially discovered by those who are not regular physicians, and have found a blessing in the use of them" (*Felix Holt, The Radical* [Harmondsworth: Penguin, 1972], 130, 141).

8. "Advertisements," *Quarterly Review* 97 (June and Sept. 1855): 212.

9. This clause from the Stamp Acts is quoted in *Secret Remedies*, 182.

10. Quoted in *Secret Remedies*, 175.

11. *ILN*, Jan. 5, 1907: 39. For the claims made by the makers of "Bile Beans," see *Secret Remedies*, 77; *More Secret Remedies*, 96.

12. Joseph Conrad, *The Secret Agent* (Harmondsworth: Penguin, 1963), 52 (orig. pub. 1907). Conrad speaks of "the air of moral nihilism common to keepers of gambling hells and disorderly houses; to private detectives and inquiry agents; to drink sellers and, I should say, to the sellers of invigorating electric belts and to the inventors of patent medicines."

13. *Secret Remedies*, 183. This book juggled a few statistics as best it could, but there were no reliable figures. Like today's Mafia, the patent medicine brethren were scrupulous about not keeping records. For an account of how adept advertisers were at infiltrating the press, see Terry Nevett, "Advertising and Editorial Integrity in the Nineteenth Century," in Michael Harris and Alan Lee, eds., *The Press in English So-*

ciety from the Seventeenth to the Nineteenth Centuries (New York: Acton Society Trust, 1986), 149–67.

14. For summaries of these various acts, see *Report*, v–vi.

15. The evidence for this pharmaceutical intertextuality is contained in *Report*, 368, 594–95, 677. A concise turn-of-the-century guide to the mammoth *Pharmacopoeia* is Peter Wyatt Squire, *Squire's Companion to the Latest Edition of the British Pharmacopoeia* (London: J. & A. Churchill, 1908). For a sense of how patent medicines were used therapeutically by doctors, see Charles D. F. Phillips, *Materia Medica, Pharmacology, and Therapeutics: Inorganic Substances* (London: J. & A. Churchill, 1894), which classifies remedies under the names of the diseases they claimed to cure.

16. See *Report*, 630.

17. See *Report*, 120–55, 343.

18. Quoted in Noel Parry and José Parry, *The Rise of the Medical Profession: A Study of Collective Social Mobility* (London: Croom Helm, 1976), 131.

19. George Bernard Shaw, *The Doctor's Dilemma, with Preface on Doctors* (New York: Brentano's, 1909), 27–28, 32, 14, lxxii.

20. Much of what follows rests on conclusions reached by Ivan Illich in *Medical Nemesis: The Expropriation of Health* (New York: Pantheon, 1976). Illich calls particular attention to the role that drugs play in advancing the medicalization of life. As he perceives, "the pharmaceutical invasion" does not really require doctors: "Doctors are not needed to *medicalize* a society's drugs. Even without too many hospitals and medical schools a culture can become the prey of a pharmaceutical invasion" (62).

21. H. G. Wells, *Tono-Bungay* (Lincoln: University of Nebraska Press, 1978), 124, 120.

22. See *Tono-Bungay*, 173, 182, 191.

23. Sidney Webb, "Introduction" to G. W. Goodall, *Advertising: A Study of a Modern Business Power* (London: Constable & Co., 1914), ix–xvii. Webb's description of future advertising sounds very Orwellian: "The advertising of the future, we may expect, will aim, in all cases, in so far as Collectivist organization prevails, at that which is believed to be some advantage to the community as a whole; it will not be swayed by any considerations of individual gain; it will be directed by persons acting only as the servants of the particular branches of public administration concerned; and it will be controlled not by private capitalists but by the representatives of the community" (xvii). Though Webb claimed to be arguing only for "the elimination from [advertising] of all motives of personal self-interest and private gain," his plan makes it clear that he wishes to abolish advertising altogether and replace it with some sort of propaganda agency. Webb was also a leading expo-

nent of the medicalization of life; his argument for "a unified medical service" was very influential. See his *The State and the Doctor* (London: Longmans, Green and Co., 1910).

24. See *Tono-Bungay*, 121–23.

25. *Secret Remedies*, 32–33.

26. Thomas Carlyle, *Past and Present* (New York: New York University Press, 1965), 230.

27. See Karl Marx, "The Fetishism of Commodities and the Secret Thereof," in *The Marx-Engels Reader*, ed. Robert C. Tucker (New York: Norton, 1978), 319–29.

28. *ILN*, Nov. 16, 1907: 739.

29. *More Secret Remedies*, 252–55.

30. *Tono-Bungay*, 175.

31. *ILN*, July 24, 1909: 145.

32. Illich, *Medical Nemesis*, 76–88.

33. A quack did not have to sell pills to be selling health "culture." Eugen Sandow made a killing by inventing what he called "physical culture," a course of lectures and calisthenics that claimed to cure almost everything. Sandow's followers did their best to distinguish his cure from others of its kind, but to little avail: "Mr. Sandow is not like the patent medicine people who profess to cure all and every illness that nature is heir to. He confines his attention principally to sufferers from constipation (and the country is simply overrun with this and its attendant ills), nervous disorders, indigestion, brain fag, loss of vigor, and insomnia." See Eugen Sandow, *Health from Physical Culture* (New York: Sandow's Correspondence Instruction, 1908), 10ff.

34. *G*, May 23, 1908: 725.

35. Louis Althusser, "Ideology and Ideological State Apparatuses (Notes Towards an Investigation)," in *Lenin and Philosophy and Other Essays* (New York: Monthly Review Press, 1971), 174. Turn-of-the-century patent medicine comes very close to confirming Althusser's account of the constitution of human subjectivity as an ideological process. In patent medicine, too, the consuming subject cannot be understood apart from its having been addressed by the representatives of capitalist medicine.

36. The problem of pain occupies Illich in *Medical Nemesis*, 133–54. See also Elaine Scarry, *The Body in Pain: The Making and Unmaking of the World* (New York: Oxford University Press, 1985).

37. See Jean Baudrillard, "Toward a Critique of the Political Economy of the Sign," in *For a Critique of the Political Economy of the Sign* (St. Louis: Telos, 1981), 143–63.

38. On the relationship between consumption and therapy, see T. J. Jackson Lears, "From Salvation to Self-Realization: Advertising and the Therapeutic Roots of the Consumer Culture, 1880–1930," in Richard

Wrightman Fox and T. J. Jackson Lears, eds., *The Culture of Consumption: Critical Essays in American History, 1880–1980* (New York: Pantheon, 1983), 3–38.

39. Carlyle, *Past and Present*, 205.

40. *G*, Apr. 21, 1906: 505; *ILN*, May 9, 1908: 681.

41. *G*, Nov. 10, 1906: 618.

42. *ILN*, Jan. 23, 1909: 140.

43. For other Allcock ads, see *ILN*, Mar. 30, 1907: 503; *G*, Jan. 20, 1906: 87.

44. James Joyce, *Ulysses* (New York: Vintage, 1961), 151–83.

45. *G*, Feb. 3, 1907: 295. For Jacques Lacan's account of the mirror stage in the formation of the self, see *Ecrits* (New York: Norton, 1977), 30–113.

46. Here I join two recent critics in refusing to dismiss advertising as a specimen of what Marx called "false consciousness." Hans Magnus Enzensberger argues that "the attractive power of mass consumption is based not on the dictates of false needs, but on the falsification and exploitation of quite real and legitimate ones" ("Constituents of a Theory of the Media," in *The Consciousness Industry* [New York: Seabury, 1974], 110). Frederic Jameson develops the point: "Our proposition about the drawing power of the works of mass culture has implied that such works cannot manage anxieties about the social order unless they have first revived them and given them some rudimentary expression; we will now suggest that anxiety and hope are two faces of the same collective consciousness, so that the works of mass culture, even if their function lies in the legitimation of the existing order—or some worse one—cannot do their job without deflecting in the latter's service the deepest and most fundamental hopes and fantasies of the collectivity, to which they can therefore, no matter how distorted a fashion, be found to have given voice" ("Reification and Utopia in Mass Culture," *Social Text* 1 [Winter 1979]: 144).

47. On the pathology of material satisfaction in modern consumer societies, see William Leiss, *The Limits to Satisfaction: An Essay on the Problem of Needs and Commodities* (Toronto: University of Toronto Press, 1976).

48. Jacob Bell, "Chemical and Pharmaceutical Processes and Products," in *Lectures on the Results of the Great Exhibition of 1851* (London: G. Barclay, 1852), 140. As Bell's title implies, drugs intended for human consumption were by no means his major concern. Problems occasioned by the widespread use of drugs did occupy the attention of his contemporaries, however. In a series of articles entitled "The Narcotics We Indulge In," *Blackwood's Edinburgh Magazine* (74, 458 [Dec. 1853]: 678–95) called attention to the relation of dependency in which drugs place consumers. At times *Blackwood's* could be describing an incipient

consumerism: "the practice once begun, creates a craving, as the other practices do, and becomes a *necessity of life*" (688). See also *Blackwood's* 74, 454 (Aug. 1853): 9–139; 74, 457 (Nov. 1853): 605–28.

49. Hillier, *Popular Drugs*, 148–79. The fact that drugs and placebos were often spoken of in the same breath indicates that the line dividing drug abuse from placebo abuse was thin and shifting. Today the rhetoric of placebo abuse survives in the domain of cheap body-care commodities such as baby food, toothpaste, shampoo, skin lotion, and soap.

Five

1. The gendering of nineteenth-century Christianity is the subject of Ann Douglas, *The Feminization of American Culture* (New York: Avon, 1978). The analogy to women and their ministers offers an apt parallel, for as Douglas shows, they became a ready audience for advertising.

2. John Byers, "Quackery—With Special Reference to Female Complaints," *British Medical Journal*, May 27, 1911: 1240–41.

3. Leo Lowenthal, *Literature, Popular Culture, and Society* (Palo Alto, Calif.: Pacific Books, 1968).

4. Sigmund Freud, "The Sexual Aberrations," in *Three Essays on the Theory of Sexuality* (New York: Basic Books, 1962), 19–21; also *The Interpretation of Dreams* (New York: Avon, 1965), 313.

5. James Joyce, *Ulysses* (New York: Vintage, 1961). Although Gerty does not remain confined to "Nausicaa," her appearances elsewhere in the novel nowhere approach the variety and vivacity of the forms in which Stephen and Bloom appear. In "Wandering Rocks" Gerty catches sight of the viceregal procession but laments characteristically that she "couldn't see what Her Excellency had on" (253); an interpolation in "Cyclops" that mimics the idiom of graffiti reveals only that "Gerty MacDowell loves the boy [Reggy Wylie] that has the bicycle" (333); sentimental idiom intact—"with all my worldly goods I thee and thou" (442)—she limps into Bloom's consciousness in "Circe" to reproach him for his voyeurism; in "Ithaca" Gerty comes to mind when Bloom reflects that he can still make a good impression on the opposite sex (722). Subsequent citations appear in the text.

6. Maria Susanna Cummins, *The Lamplighter* (New York: Odyssey, 1968), 433. A 1904 survey of a Lancashire community showed that Cummins's novel was nearly as popular as the Bible or *Pilgrim's Progress*; see John Garrett Leigh, "What Do the Masses Read?," *Economic Review* 14 (1904): 166–77.

7. Frequently Gerty's narrative misquotes or distorts an idiom so as to suggest a materialist adaptation of language. Gerty, we have seen, consistently turns human attributes into things. Among many examples of this reification we find: "And Gerty, wrapt in thought, scarce saw or heard her companions . . ." (354). The cliché just missed by the narrative is "rapt in thought." Joyce marshals the archaic form of the

past participle, "wrapt" (instead of "wrapped," the common spelling in Joyce's time), to point to the near miss. The result is a word that makes material sense—meaning "covered or packaged"—in addition to making common sense as a probable cliché.

8. Richard Ellmann, ed., *Selected Letters of James Joyce* (New York: Viking, 1975), 246.

9. Quoted in Susan Sontag, "On Style," in *Against Interpretation* (New York: Delta, 1966), 17.

10. See Karl Marx, "The Fetishism of Commodities and the Secret Thereof," in *The Marx-Engels Reader*, ed. Robert C. Tucker (New York: Norton, 1978), 319–29.

11. Gerty undeniably approaches a state of what Lukács was the first to call "reification." His first and fullest definition remains "The Phenomenon of Reification," in *History and Class Consciousness: Studies in Marxist Dialectics* (Cambridge, Mass.: MIT Press, 1971), 83–110.

12. Cummins, *The Lamplighter*, 306.

13. Ibid., 307–8.

14. Ibid., 303.

15. Karl Marx, "Private Property and Communism" (1844), in *Writings of the Young Marx on Philosophy and Society*, ed. Loyd D. Easton and Kurt H. Guddat (Garden City, N.Y.: Doubleday, 1967), 308.

16. W. Livingston Larned, "The Product in Heroic Size," in *Illustration in Advertising* (New York: McGraw-Hill, 1925), 124.

17. The "Ithaca" chapter waggishly raises the issue of truth in advertising when, despite the common sight of the firm's sandwich-board men in Dublin, it reports the wrong street address for Wisdom Hely's (see *Ulysses*, 720).

18. Walter Benjamin, "The Work of Art in the Age of Mechanical Reproduction," in *Illuminations* (New York: Schocken, 1969), 217–53.

19. Roland Barthes, *The Fashion System* (New York: Hill and Wang, 1983), xi, 272.

20. Advertisements for Beetham's Larola abound during and after 1904. See *G*, Sept. 17, 1904: 378. See also *ILN*, Feb. 9, 1907: 243; July 18, 1908: 72; Aug. 15, 1908: 250. To keep Gerty on her toes the company altered its slogan slightly from time to time, adding and deleting such qualities as "COOLING," "REFRESHING," "SOOTHING," and "Delightful."

21. Quoted in Don Gifford and Robert J. Seidman, *Notes for Joyce: An Annotation of James Joyce's 'Ulysses'* (New York: Dutton, 1974), 67.

22. Historians have long been fascinated by the prominent role seaside resorts played in nineteenth-century life. For a thorough treatment of the subject see James Walvin, *Beside the Seaside: A Social History of the Popular Seaside Holiday* (London: Allen Lane, 1978).

23. Eric Hobsbawm makes this observation in *The Age of Empire, 1875–1914* (New York: Pantheon, 1987), 205.

24. Quoted in Walvin, *Beside the Seaside*, 70.

25. See *The Poster* 3.13 (August 1899): 281. A number of advertisements that appeared between 1870 and 1900 and depicted women at the seashore have been collected in Leonard de Vries, *Victorian Advertisements* (Philadelphia: Lippincott, 1968), 35, 49, 56, 71, 115, 116; and in Diana Hindley and Geoffrey Hindley, *Advertising in Victorian England: 1850–1914* (London: Wayland, 1972), plate 6.7. A turn-of-the-century trade publication for English advertisers, *The Poster*, also contains many examples of the seaside girl. See *The Poster: An Illustrated Monthly Chronicle* 2.11 (May 1899): 191; 2.12 (June–July 1899): 251; 3.13 (Aug. 1899): 281; 3.15 (Sept. 1899): 42; 3.18 (Jan. 1900): 199; 4.20 (Sept. 1900): cover illustration. Hundreds of typical examples exist. Among the most representative are those for the *Graphic*, in *The Graphic Summer Number*, July 8, 1899: 33; for Ogden, *G*, July 21, 1900: 108; Plantol, *ILN*, Dec. 19, 1903: 963; Players, *G*, Nov. 19, 1904: 680; Kaloderma, *G*, Feb. 10, 1906: 195; Beecham's, *ILN*, Sept. 18, 1908: 417; Zotos and Bovril, *G*, Dec. 12, 1908: 753. Beecham's Pills used the phrase "that Tired Feeling" in *G*, Dec. 31, 1904: iii.

26. For another example of a typical Beetham's advertisement of the 1890's, see Hindley and Hindley, *Advertising in Victorian England*, plate 6.8. The advertising campaign for Beetham's "Glyc'rine & Cucumber" evidently used an early version of the same slogan that later achieved such success in marketing Beetham's Larola: "ENTIRELY REMOVES and PREVENTS all SUNBURN, TAN, REDNESS, ROUGHNESS . . . A little applied daily after washing will keep the SKIN SOFT and BLOOMING all the Year Round." With Joyce's love of tacit correspondences in mind, it comes as no surprise that an advertisement for one of Gerty's favorite products promises to restore the Bloom to her face.

27. James Joyce, *A Portrait of the Artist as a Young Man* (New York: Vintage, 1968), 171.

28. Louis Althusser, *For Marx* (London: Verso, 1979), 252.

29. Louis Althusser, *Lenin and Philosophy* (New York: Monthly Review Press, 1971), 155.

30. Jacques Derrida, "Structure, Sign, and Play in the Discourse of the Human Sciences," in *The Structuralist Controversy* (Baltimore, Md.: Johns Hopkins University Press, 1972), 253.

31. Roland Barthes, *Mythologies* (New York: Hill and Wang, 1972), 140.

32. William Smith, *Advertise: How? When? Where?* (London: Routledge, Warne, and Routledge, 1863), 45.

33. See Sigmund Freud, "Infantile Sexuality" and "The Transformations of Puberty" in *Three Essays*, 39–96.

34. G. Stanley Hall, *Adolescence: Its Psychology and Its Relations to Physiology, Anthropology, Sociology, Sex, Crime, Religion and Education* (New York: D. Appleton and Company, 1904), 1:ix, xii, xv; 2:39.

35. Ibid., 1:xiv, xv.

36. Carl A. Naether, *Advertising to Women* (New York: Prentice Hall, 1928), 80.

37. Hall, *Adolescence*, 1:385.

38. For a hard look at the ways in which modern youth subcultures resist the dominant forms of capitalist representation, see Michael Brake, *Comparative Youth Culture: The Sociology of Youth Cultures in America, Britain and Canada* (London: Routledge & Kegan Paul, 1985) and Dick Hebdige, *Subculture: The Meaning of Style* (London: Methuen, 1979).

39. Rosalind Coward develops this idea in *Female Desires: How They Are Sought, Bought and Packaged* (New York: Grove Press, 1985), 79.

40. Naether, *Advertising for Women*, xiv.

41. *ILN*, May 26, 1906: 780.

Conclusion

1. Quoted in Richard Shannon, *The Crisis of Imperialism* (London: Paladin, 1974), 206.

2. Thomas Russell, *Commercial Advertising: Six Lectures at the London School of Economics and Political Science* (London: G. P. Putnam's Sons, 1919), 47.

3. See Cate Haste, *Keep the Home Fires Burning: Propaganda in the First World War* (London: Allen Lane, 1977), and Harold D. Lasswell, *Propaganda Technique in the World War* (New York: Knopf, 1927). Advertising historian E. S. Turner gets his facts all wrong when he asserts that propaganda invented modern advertising; see *The Shocking History of Advertising!* (New York: Dutton, 1953), 251ff.

4. *Printer's Ink* (1905), quoted in W. F. Haug, *Critique of Commodity Aesthetics: Appearance, Sexuality, and Advertising in Capitalist Society* (Minneapolis: University of Minnesota Press, 1986), 24–25.

5. Roland Barthes, *The Fashion System* (New York: Hill and Wang, 1983), 246–48. Though most patent medicine has died out, the pharmaceutical industry still effectively exploits the mythology of the therapeutic commodity the quacks developed. Modern commercials for all sorts of drugs continue to proclaim the miracle-working properties of pills.

6. A few crucial components of this print revolution were the invention of Applegarth's vertical rotary-action press (1846), the Hoe horizontal press (1846), the Walter reel-fed rotary press (1846), stereotyping (1850's), and Hattersley's composing machine (1850's). A. E. Musson has shown how these technologies came together in the 1880's and 1890's; see "Newspaper Printing in the Industrial Revolution," *Economic History Review* 10–11 (1957–59): 424–26. See also Ellic Howe, "News Compositors' Methods of Working, 1868–1894," chap. 18 in *The*

London Compositor (London: The Bibliographic Society, 1947); Alan J. Lee, *The Origins of the Popular Press in England, 1855–1914* (London: Croom Helm, 1976), 54–63.

7. See Paul Theroux, *The Great Railway Bazaar* (Boston: Houghton Mifflin, 1975).

8. Guy Debord, *Society of the Spectacle* (Detroit: Black and Red, 1977), 42, 39.

9. Michel Foucault, *Discipline and Punish: The Birth of the Prison* (New York: Vintage, 1979), 217.

10. This avenue of research has been pursued by a number of recent studies examining the social role things play in human information systems. See Arjun Appadurai, ed., *The Social Life of Things: Commodities in Cultural Perspective* (Cambridge, Eng.: Cambridge University Press, 1986); Mary Douglas and Baron Isherwood, *The World of Goods: Toward an Anthropology of Consumption* (New York: Norton, 1979); Jean-Francois Lyotard, *The Postmodern Condition: A Report on Knowledge* (Minneapolis: University of Minnesota Press, 1984).

11. "There is no universal capitalism, there is no capitalism in itself; capitalism is at the crossroads of all kinds of formations, it is neo-capitalism by nature." Gilles Deleuze and Felix Guattari, *A Thousand Plateaus* (Minneapolis: University of Minnesota Press, 1987), 20.

12. Roland Barthes, *Mythologies* (New York: Hill and Wang, 1972), 120.

13. Jean Baudrillard, *Simulations* (New York: Semiotext(e), 1983), 54. In a vague way Baudrillard locates the origins of the capitalist system of representation in the nineteenth century: "All through the 19th and 20th centuries political and economic practice merge increasingly into the same type of discourse. Propaganda and advertising fuse in the same marketing and merchandising of objects and ideologies" (*Simulations*, 125). Jonathan Crary follows out the implications of Baudrillard's remarks in "Eclipse of the Spectacle," in *Art After Modernism: Rethinking Representation* (Boston: Godine, 1984), 283–94. Debord, however, believes that the system of spectacle has continued to reinforce itself; see *Commentaires sur la société du spectacle* (Paris: Editions Gérard Lébovici, 1988), 12.

14. Foucault, *Discipline and Punish*, 217.

15. Martin Jay, "Scopic Regimes of Modernity," in Hal Foster, ed., *Vision and Visuality* (Seattle: Bay Press, 1988), 3–23.

16. Thomas Pynchon, *Gravity's Rainbow* (New York: Viking Penguin, 1987), 3. As Hal Foster has shown, contemporary art keeps returning to the image of the shattered crystal palaces and other monuments of the nineteenth century; see "Contemporary Art and Spectacle," in *Recodings: Art, Spectacle, Cultural Politics* (Seattle: Bay Press, 1985), 78–97.

Index

Library of Congress Cataloging-in-Publication Data

Richards, Thomas
    The commodity culture of Victorian England : ad-
vertising and spectacle, 1851–1914 / Thomas
Richards.
        p.   cm.
    ISBN 0-8047-1652-8 (alk. paper)
    ISBN 0-8047-1901-2 (pbk.)
    1. Capitalism—Great Britain—History.   2. Com-
mercial products—Great Britain—History.   3. Advertising—Great Britain—History.   4. Great
Exhibition (1851 : London, England)   I. Title.
HC255.R53   1990
659.1'0941—dc20   89-37035
                                                           CIP